Lore of Light

volume 2

Lives of the Prophets and Messengers According to Traditional Islamic Sources

Hajjah Amina Adil

INSTITUTE FOR SPIRITUAL AND CULTURAL ADVANCEMENT

Library of Congress Publication Control Number: TBD
ISBN: 978-1-930409-62-0

Originally published as *Lore of Light.*

Library of Congress Cataloging-in-Publication Data Forthcoming.

Published and Distributed by:
Institute for Spiritual and Cultural Advancement

17195 Silver Parkway, #401
Fenton, MI 48430 USA
Tel: (888) 278-6624
Fax:(810) 815-0518
Email: staff@naqshbandi.org
Web: http://www.naqshbandi.org
Shop for other titles online at:
http://www.isn1.net

Second Edition: November 2009
ISBN:978-1-930409-62-0

Author, the late Hajjah Amina Adil Shaykh Muhammad with her daughter Hajjah Naziha.

contents

Dhu 'l-Kifl عليه السلام

The fourteenth prophet was named Bishr which means "a messenger who carries joyful news." His epithet was Dhu 'l-Kifl, which literally means "possessor of, or giving, a double requital or portion" and there are two stories concerning this appellation. According to one, he was called Dhu 'l-Kifl because he wore his hair parted in the middle. According to the second, he was called this because he could be relied on to carry out his mission with justice and without ever giving vent to anger. Also, in Syria, there is a mountain chain stretching to the river Euphrates which is called Bishr, most probably in honor of this prophet.

Bishr was the son of Ayyūb عليه السلام and his wife Raḥmah, who was descended from Yūsuf عليه السلام. Bishr was born after Ayyūb عليه السلام had triumphed over the temptations of Shayṭān and been given back twice as much as he had lost. Ayyūb عليه السلام was seventy four years old when his son, Bishr, was born in the village of Besniye, which lies between Rām and Shām in Syria. He was tall of stature and very handsome. He wore his hair parted in the middle. Ayyūb's eldest son was known as Heymel. On his deathbed Ayyūb عليه السلام called both sons to him and blessed them. He told them that Bishr would succeed him in prophethood, whilst Heymel would govern the land.

Although Ayyūb عليه السلام had been dead for five years, his people had not forgotten him. Their hearts remained steadfast and filled with the love of God. They remembered, yet, the trials of Ayyūb عليه السلام. On the crest of the hill where the idol temple had once stood of old, a new mosque was erected and people came from all the surrounding villages to worship there. The prophet Ayyūb عليه السلام had bequeathed all of his newly gained possessions to them and they worked together, sharing their profits in a brotherly fashion, paying taxes to the Assyrian overlords and experiencing no trouble.

Heymel, their chief, was a strong and courageous man. He looked after his father's heritage well, though he was only twenty five years old. Bishr, his younger brother, was five years his junior, and he already preached to the people even though he had not yet received his first revelation of prophethood. He exhorted them to remain on the straight path and commit neither crime nor injustice. Everyone was hopeful of the day when Bishr's prophethood would be revealed, for he was well loved by all on account of his innate wisdom and pleasant countenance. He spoke kindly to everyone and never showed his anger. People recognized in him the signs of an extraordinary man and set their hopes upon him. When their prophet, Ayyūb ﷺ, was dying some people had grown confused and asked, "How is it possible that Ayyūb ﷺ, who is a prophet, can die and leave us?" It was Bishr, his son, who answered them and allayed their doubts. He reminded them that before Ayyūb ﷺ, a great number of prophets had come and gone and that prophets were but human beings and mortal like themselves.

Bishr was very particular about his personal appearance, washing and dressing himself with care and wearing his hair rather long, parted neatly in the middle. This is how he came to be called Dhu 'l-Kifl ﷺ and in time his first name, Bishr, was nearly forgotten.

People would ask him, "Are you pleased with your father's prayer for you to become a prophet after him, if it be the Lord's Command?"

Dhu 'l-Kifl ﷺ would answer, "I do not think much about this matter but if the Almighty should arrange the matter, He alone knows with how much joy I shall receive His Command, for there is no greater honor for man than to be a messenger of God. There is also no more exacting task and no burden heavier upon a man's shoulders than the responsibility of a prophet."

One day his mother, Raḥmah, said to him, "Even though your brother is king in this land, people have given your name to a mountain chain that stretches towards the river Euphrates for the love they have for you and to remember your original name."

Bishr answered, "Oh my mother, I expected no such honor during my lifetime and I shall pray with all my strength that my people might always hold such love in their hearts for the servants of the Lord Almighty; that their hearts might never harden and freeze. When the heart of man is frozen, his whole life becomes as a sheet of ice upon which he may easily slip and slide into the ditch of corruption and when he falls he draws everything down with him."

His mother was frightened by these words for she remembered only too well, how evil times had been in the past and she implored him to pray to Allah that Shayṭān might not lead them astray once again and that their beautiful country might not be destroyed by the ruses of the Evil One.

Now, there lived a king to the north, who watched the people of Ayyūb ﷺ prospering once again with growing envy. The king's favorite soothsayer, his most trusted advisor, watched him gradually fall into despondency. He understood well what was bothering him. This man taught one of the slave girls a certain song which she was to sing to the king and it had the desired effect on him.

The king awoke from his depressive mood, jumped up and cried, "What are we waiting for, watching those who are our tributaries growing richer and richer? Best we fall upon them while they are yet unaware before they grow too strong for us to handle! They must have countless treasures hoarded up in those unassuming villages. Was there not a rain of golden locusts in the time of their father, Ayyūb ﷺ? No one knows where they came from or where they went to. They are not a numerous people. We can easily overpower them and bring their goods into our possession!" He spoke to his commander-in-chief who was also his son-in-law. The son-in-law, being a man of honor, opposed this wicked plan. The king, therefore, had him executed and appointed a new man in his place who would do his will.

He spoke to this man in private because he wished no one to betray his plans. However, there was a man picking apples from a tree in the palace gardens that day who overheard all that was spoken. He rushed out through a secret passage and conveyed his message to a trusted friend. This man came to Dhu 'l-Kifl ﷺ whilst he was praying in the mosque. He told him all that he had heard of the secret plot. At once, Dhu 'l-Kifl ﷺ rushed out to inform his brother Heymel. He found him working in the fields, for although he was the chief of the village he went to work along with his men with a bag slung over his shoulder as the peasants and shepherds carry. Dhu 'l-Kifl ﷺ informed his brother of the intended attack and of the path the invaders were expected to take. He told them they planned to come through the valley of Karasakiz and along the winding river (the Nahr 'Awaj, as it is still called in Syria today). Heymel ordered his men to go out into the mountains as if they were cutting wood, and they armed themselves under this pretext with axes, hatchets, spears and swords and took to the woods.

It so happened that this very same day, the Assyrian tax collectors were expected in the village to assess their fields and livestock. Dhu 'l-Kifl ﷺ went out to meet them as they approached the outskirts of the village.

They asked him, "Where is the headman of the village who is always seen with his donkey bags?"

Dhu 'l-Kifl ﷺ answered and explained to them that today he had come in his brother's stead for they were expecting an enemy attack.

"Oh", said the chief officer, "a good opportunity for me to observe a battle for once without being involved in it. But tell me one thing, Dhu 'l-Kifl. When your men die in battle, it has been observed that they fight bravely until they fall and do not hesitate or swerve for a moment. How do you achieve such steadfastness?"

"It is on account of our moral education and religious training," answered Dhu 'l-Kifl ﷵ.

"Indeed," said the soldier, "we have heard about the moral excellence of your people; in your country there is no bloodshed, no theft, no drinking or debauchery. There is neither immorality nor willful injury amongst you. No man infringes upon his neighbor's rights or honor. Even if a man leaves his door wide open, no one steals from his house. If a person takes even a bunch of grapes from his neighbor, he will either ask his permission, or pay him a fair price. No one speaks badly or slanders his neighbor and each man rejoices in extending hospitality and friendliness. Your people are a smiling and happy lot. What is the secret behind all this? I would like to know."

Dhu 'l-Kifl ﷵ answered the man, "I am sure you remember what conditions were like here twenty five years ago. You remember what happened to my father, Ayyūb ﷵ, and you know how my people suffered under oppression. They drove my poor father out, burned and pillaged all he possessed and forced him to live in a dung heap. But when that miracle occurred and the healing water sprang forth from the earth, all things changed for them, and faith entered their hearts anew. They began to observe the Commands of the Almighty and living in the light of their newly found faith everything changed for them. Their lives were transformed. Now they love each other like true brothers and sisters. It is as if they are in living in Paradise already."

"Oh don't start on about that subject again," said the soldier. "You know we don't believe in your unseen god and all that nonsense."

"Ah, but I did not offer to talk about it," said Dhu 'l-Kifl ﷵ. "It was you who asked me about our conditions, so I had to answer you truthfully. For Allah Almighty has obliged us to say what we know; it is He who had created us, given us life and it is He who recalls us at death. He has sent us here to serve Him and therefore, we should live and deal with each other in a brotherly way, worshipping Him alone. This worship is not confined to the mosque alone. Our worship is life itself, a reflection of the way we treat each other and give mutual support, knowing that in the end we shall return to Him. Our ultimate destination is the eternal homeland of all souls. It is this knowledge that makes our eyes and hearts shine with light. How different is the situation of a man who travels to a certain place, knowing that however much he enjoys being there, one day he will have to leave again. His enjoyment is always marred by the knowledge of that final parting..." And he spoke to him in this vein for a long time.

At last the soldier lost patience and cried, "Be quiet! Now I understand the source of all your knowledge. Your father, Ayyūb ﷺ, has taught you his magic, the same as has come to him from his forebears who used to fool simple people from times immemorial!"

"It is no magic," said Dhu 'l-Kifl ﷺ. "It is inspiration from the Almighty Lord and you as well as all other unbelievers have always been mistaken in this point. Prophets have come to all peoples throughout the ages, and over and over again they have been decried, persecuted and even killed. Most of their names have been forgotten, but we remember the stories of a number of them. They are told as fairytales from one generation to the next."

"Enough of this!" cried the soldier. "I understand from all this only that you are not going to confide in me and tell me either the secret of your magic, or where you have hidden your treasures."

Dhu 'l-Kifl ﷺ grew sad and said, "If you could only see inside my breast, you would understand that I am hiding nothing at all from you and that I am speaking the plain truth. I don't even know what treasures you speak of."

"I speak of the vast stores of gold and gems that everyone knows you have hidden away."

"How very mistaken you are," replied Dhu 'l-Kifl 🕮, "We have no such treasures; everything we own we use for our simple livelihood. I find it hard to keep from laughing in your face; if you only knew our true condition."

"Very well," said the commander. "But soon I will remind you of your words, Dhu 'l-Kifl!"

"You may remind me of anything I have said to you, I will never feel ashamed of my words, for I have spoken nothing but the truth. I, for my part, understand now why you have come to us. It is not to survey our lands and to assess our livestock. It is to dig for a treasure which does not exist. Let me tell you once more for the last time, our treasure is found in the hearts of the believers. We have had no time to amass a fortune and to bury it in the earth; we do our work ourselves and don't employ slaves and servants; we live a simple life, give to the poor, pay our taxes and expend in the way of goodness. The treasure we carry is within our breasts and within the breasts of all true believers. It is valuable both in this world and in the world to come. If only you knew how valuable a treasure it is, you would cease your quest for mere stones! The name we give to this treasure is Jannah. Jannah means Paradise and is the reward of all who truly believe. If only you knew the worth of that great spiritual treasure you would not waste your time in trivial pursuits..."

Meanwhile, the army of that other king was stealthily approaching. As the soldiers neared the village they saw no one in the fields, nor on the roads. They mistrusted the silence and feared that they might run into a trap. They kept up their courage, however, by imagining all the spoils and pleasures they would gain from this campaign, how the markets of Shām would be filled with goods, the slaves they would carry off and how they would rebuild the great temple of idols on Mount Zeno and a new palace for their king which would outshine all the royal palaces of the surrounding kingdoms in its splendor. There were also women accompanying the army, who incited the soldiery with their songs, provoking them with lascivious thoughts and promises of the pleasures awaiting their victorious heroes.

Heymel and his men watched their approach from their hidden positions on the heights overlooking the narrow gorge through which this army had to pass. His men were all armed but they had strict orders not to shoot. Heymel intended to make a peaceful settlement once the men were trapped in the gorge and realized their position. "I wish no bloodshed," Heymel had told his men, "for our Lord has not created us so that we should kill each other. We shall resort to force only if we are attacked."

All proceeded according to plan. When the enemy soldiers grew aware of the trap they had walked into they were quite ready to give themselves up without a fight. Their commander exhorted them to useless deeds of bravery. His call was in vain for the soldiers reasoned, "What is the difference whether we work for you as slaves or for our captors. Death is surely no better than what we already know." So they all ascended the steep slopes and surrendered. Their commander last of all. They were all bound and led before Heymel who said to them, "We intend you no harm. We know you are forced to act under orders. We will not make you our slaves, for it is not our custom. If there is any man amongst you who will adopt our religion and way of life, we will treat him as our brother and he shall be free. As for the rest, they will be led off to the markets of Shām and sold there in the slave bazaar."

Then, Dhu 'l-Kifl ﷺ stepped forth and addressed them. He explained to them about their faith and way of life. None of the soldiers was willing to accept it, however. They all preferred slavery to the service of the unseen God. Finally, Heymel agreed with Dhu 'l-Kifl ﷺ that it would be better to hand over the prisoners to the Assyrian tax-collectors than to sell them for dubious profit. This was done, to the delight of the Assyrians.

Now there was one man amongst the prisoners who begged to speak privately with Dhu 'l-Kifl 🕮 as he had things of great interest to tell him and he hoped to be rewarded for this. Dhu 'l-Kifl 🕮 listened to him.

He said, "I have come to know a great many things in my time, as I have traveled widely in the world. For example, I can tell whether an unborn child will be male or female."

"This is not true knowledge," interrupted Dhu 'l-Kifl 🕮, "It is an art used by those who perform abortions."

"Maybe," continued the man, "but it is useful all the same. As a young man I was taken captive and came to Egypt where I spent eight years. It was there I learned this skill: One would take a handful of wheat and a handful of barley. The seeds were planted and watered with the urine of a pregnant woman. If the wheat sprouted first, the child was sure to be a girl. Later this knowledge earned me a lot of money. After I was free again, I traveled across the great streams into Asia Minor and came to a place called Jennatabad. There, I met a tribe that was ruled only by women. These women are in all ways as men. They are taught from earliest childhood how to run and to ride, to carry arms and to fight and they grew up in freedom. As young girls, they cauterize their right breast so that it will not impede their use of weapons. This tradition is very old among them."

"As for the perpetuation of their tribe, this is how I came to be useful to them. Once a year they have a ceremony and the women are free to roam and consort with men as they wish. If the resulting child is a girl, they let her live, if it is a boy, they either give him to the father or else they kill him. But many of the women cannot bear to be separated from their sons once they are born; they either choose to stay with the father or else they grieve bitterly over the loss of their children. Their tribe is always threatened with extinction because of this. By being able to tell in advance whether the child would be a boy or a girl I did them a great service. At the same time I did my duty to my king, for these warrior women used to attack and raid our caravans as they passed through their territory and inflicted heavy losses on our commerce. I managed to appease them by sharing this wisdom with them, and their attacks ceased."

Dhu 'l-Kifl ā became very interested in traveling to those lands but the man said, "If you wish to travel, take my advice and go to another place. These women are different from any other women on Earth. They are the sworn enemies of all men. If you go to visit them, they will surely burn you, kill you or even eat you up, so great is their hatred of men. I will tell you of other places I have seen on my journeys." He told Dhu 'l-Kifl عليه السلام about the lands he had seen; Jennatabad and the great mountain on which the Ark of Nūḥ عليه السلام had landed. Dhu 'l-Kifl عليه السلام remembered the stories his father had told him when he was young. But he knew that he was not free to travel and that his place was with his people for the moment. He released the man who had told him these tales who returned to the palace of the enemy king.

This king was disheartened by the failure of his campaign and he took counsel with his advisors and soothsayers. Their chief, Turāth, was a very wicked and power hungry man who was capable of long-term planning.

He spoke thus to his king, "Oh my king, you will never defeat these people who believe in the One God by force of arms. They stand firm together and do not betray one another. Their high moral code protects them and they will face any enemy bravely. They never lie, their conduct is impeccable and they know no fear. We must seek a different means in order to defeat them."

"And how should we do this, oh Turāth?" asked the king. "I am reminded of a rock. Just think how a little drop of water falling upon it gently, steadily, year after year, gradually melts it away, where as brute force achieves nothing. In this way we should proceed against those people. It is the only chance we have of vanquishing them. This will be our task: to implant in them all manners of bad character. We will bring to them drink and gambling, the lust for women, dishonesty and cheating, and you will see that within a space of ten years perhaps their virtuous ways will be eradicated. They will have become every bit as bad as the people of Ayyūb 樂 before them and in that way we can destroy them. However, this plan of ours must remain a secret. Leave it to me to select a few trusted men from among the soothsayers and priests and we will accomplish this task for you."

The king was a lazy man, he agreed and issued orders. Then he withdrew into his palace to enjoy the remaining years of his life in luxury, leaving the work of corruption to his servant Turāth.

Turāth wasted no time and gathered about him a small group of associates; seven of his most trusted apprentices. He explained the matter to them in terms of great urgency saying that if they took no measures against the town of Qudsīyya in time to come the whole land would be converted to the religion of the one God and, they, the priests of the idols, would became destitute and despised. He reminded them of the time of Ayyūb 樂, who had toppled their chief idol from the temple on the hill and made a laughing stock and a ridicule of them all.

Then he laid out his plan to them, "It is no use to march our armies against them. We must feed them the poison slowly, one gulp at a time. The young people must not know that it is poison they are being fed. They must believe it is medicine and a good thing. For the youth of a town resembles the center post of a tent: if rats and beavers slowly gnaw at it the tent will eventually collapse, burying beneath it all that are within. This must be our course of action. The first thing to do is this: We must try to prevent them from attending their rites of worship, for the more they pray the less likely they are to let go of their habits. The most effective means of distracting them is money. Money has tremendous power. When they come into town to trade with us, we must try to instill envy of the rich in the hearts of the poorer ones and greed and desire of more material possessions in the hearts of the wealthy. We must make them dissatisfied with their lot. If we succeed in estranging them from their prayers, their faith will weaken and the bonds between them will crack and loosen. Their hopes will be turned only towards material gain and profit and in that way, we will have won the first round."

Then, Turāth summed up for them the founding principles of the faith of Ayyūb: That there is One God who is neither born nor does He sire any other being but He is the Creator of all things. He is not a manmade invention but an unimaginable, unseen Entity. There is continuity of life beyond death and on a certain day known to Him alone, everyone will be called to account for his deeds and reward and punishment will be meted out in accordance with a man's actions. Those believing in these tenets fear their Lord and nothing else on Earth. They obey Him absolutely. They give *zakāt* (poor-due) on what they have lawfully earned, amass no excessive riches and tell no lies. They heed and respect the words of their elders and die happily in a battle which they know to be a holy war. They commit no adultery, do not drink or gamble, and preserve their health by observing strict cleanliness. They know not hate or envy, nor slanderous gossip among themselves and are always willing to help out those who are in a weaker position.

When he had finished explaining all this to the priests, one among their number could not hide his thoughts and he said, "All you have told us just now sounds very excellent. If all men were to act in such a way, no evil would remain on the face of the Earth and man would live in a paradise-like world."

The head priest Turāth turned on him and unleashed his anger, "O you ignorant one! You and I, we all are humans and many are our deeds! The order of the world is such that there are always two groups, no more: the dominant and the dominated, the rulers and the servants. What then about our position as priests? Sometimes we are in power, sometimes we are the dominated. The most important thing for us is to retain our power and influence in the order of Ayyūb ﷺ there is no room for us and we should have no authority."

He continued, "It is not a question of angering the idols, as we always say, for tell me truly, who of you actually believes in these things? Who believes that these statues we have fashioned have any power of their own?"

The young priests knew in their hearts that Turāth was speaking the truth and they all hung their heads and were silent.

Turāth smiled to himself and continued, "Your silence confirms my speech. Everything is just for show, a spectacle for the people, an excuse and an invention. Man thinks of nothing but his own advantage and profit. I speak to you openly now. Leave these silly idols, and never mind about their invisible God either. Look around and you will see that mankind comes into being all of his own accord and the person of sound mind is the only thing worth worshipping."

He continued, "If you follow my way, the whole world will soon be brought to worship us and we will be the supreme rulers. Myself, I have grown old but I am mindful of you who are young and designated to become my successors."

These and many similar words he spoke and they were sufficient to awaken the lust or power in the hearts of the young apprentices. When he was sure of their support for his evil designs, he laid before them the plan for action, "To begin with, it is enough if we work through the marketplace where they come to do their trading. There you and your helpmates will meet them and pass out the cups of poison, little by little. Sometimes you will talk to them of freedom, sometimes of gambling, drink and women. A drunk man will always drift towards women and a gambler will always seek to make up his losses, and he will have to lie to his parents and elders when he returns home without having even a profit and when nothing is left he will resort to stealing. In the end, he will not stop short of murder be it his own father, mother or brother and he will raid and plunder the passing caravans. In short, their conditions will change within a short while and nothing of their faith will remain."

The seven apprentices saw that their chief Turāth was right again.

"Now you know what your task is, but remember that it requires tact and delicacy. You must not frighten them away by being too blunt. In the beginning, great patience is required of you and your methods must be subtle."

So the spreaders of evil were sent out to do their work and they did it well. Within a space of five years, they had already worked a good deal of corruption and when they went to report to their chief Turāth , his envious heart was well satisfied.

These changes had also not escaped the notice of Dhu 'l-Kifl ﷺ and his brother Heymel, who were well aware that fewer and fewer people came to the mosque to attend worship there, whereas before, everyone, young and old, had concentrated there in order not to miss the blessings of prayer. Now only a few of the steadfast believers remained and most of them were old men and women. None of the young people bothered to come anymore. This was a bad sign to the brothers, for they knew that without the support of the younger generation the faith was doomed to die out. Dhu 'l-Kifl, himself, was about thirty years of age. One day, the brothers came together to discuss what could be done about this.

Dhu 'l-Kifl ﷺ said to Heymel, "I sense heavy clouds of darkness hanging over us. We must find out the cause and fight it. Our youth is becoming estranged from us."

His brother agreed and told him that he had already decided on the action he was going to take. "I know you will not like it but I have decided to deal harshly with those I find guilty of transgressing the law. I will not let this whole community of believers fall into the hands of Shayṭān, as our father Ādam ﷺ did aforetime. The rebellion must be quelled while it is still in its weak beginnings."

Dhu 'l-Kifl ﷺ was repelled by the idea of force and tried to dissuade his brother, "You may think that you are acting reasonably and correctly. You may believe that you can prevent the poison from spreading by cutting back the tree but by this, you will only help to increase the evil. If you cut the diseased branches the worms will spread all the faster in the remaining root-stock. That will never do. You must find the root cause of all this trouble and act against it."

"Oh, you are painting too black a picture, things are not as bad as all that," said Heymel.

"No," replied Dhu 'l-Kifl ﷺ, "I am wide awake and I see evil on the increase. More and more young people are doing what is forbidden with each new day. Soon you will see it gaining speed and spreading rapidly, even to our remotest villages. Your harshness dealing with the isolated evildoers will avail you nothing. You may vanquish an outward enemy with the sword but never an inward foe. It is happening in every household. The enemy is very close to us, poisoning their hearts."

"O brother," said Heymel, "how long is it since our mother has died?"

"It is not very long ago," replied Dhu 'l-Kifl ﷺ.

"Did not our mother will on her deathbed that you should get married and settle down?" retorted Heymel.

"I have not had the time to think of myself yet in these troubled times; I am too busy with care for the community," Dhu 'l-Kifl عليه السلام said.

"Well, I and all the people with me are waiting for these glad tidings, brother." With this, Heymel turned to leave.

Dhu 'l-Kifl عليه السلام stopped him and said, "It seems you give little weight to my words, brother, this is not a time for merrymaking."

But Heymel went off to look after his fields and left his brother deep in thought. By the time of the afternoon prayer, he had reached his decision. "My brother is right," he thought, "it will not do to simply remain here and wait. I must do something. I will go out and see for myself what is wrong and I will try to address those working against the will of the Lord with words of reason."

He set out on his way and before long he met the headman of a village who was very worried about the spread of mischief in his community. Dhu 'l-Kifl عليه السلام explained to him that he was out to find the root cause of the corruption and that he intended to confront those guilty of misconduct. The headman advised him to disguise himself and then to go about and mix with people. Then he should surely find out what was amiss. Dhu 'l-Kifl عليه السلام did so and wandered cross-country, passing through fields and gardens that had been fruitful and yielded plenty in the past. Now, he found them neglected and shriveled. He also saw that the flocks were decreasing in number, for many ewes had not given birth this year. These were signs to Dhu 'l-Kifl عليه السلام that the blessings over the land were drying up. He also noticed that the people he met, working in the fields, were all old men and women. There was no sign of the younger folk. Dhu 'l-Kifl عليه السلام spoke to one old woman of his acquaintance. She recognized him, dropped her tools and invited him into her house.

He said to her, "It is nearly nightfall, how is it you have not gone home yet?"

"My house is far from my fields," she explained, "and I have not yet finished the day's work in the field."

"Where then, are your sons and daughters-in-law?" asked Dhu 'l-Kifl ﷺ.

The old woman sighed and her eyes filled with tears. "Things are not as they used to be, Dhu 'l-Kifl. Your brother knows and I see that you understand. Is there nothing you can do about this? We have lost control over our sons and daughters. They have no more respect and they do not listen to us anymore." Then she gazed into the distance towards a slight hillock on which stood three great trees and she muttered almost inaudibly to herself, "There they go again."

"Who goes and where and what for?" asked Dhu 'l-Kifl in surprise.

"Who else but our sons and daughters? All the young people go there at night and revel and then spend the days asleep in our tents and houses."

"And what do they do there all night?"

"Oh, son of our prophet, what do the owls and jackals do at night? Our blessed country is falling into ruins and there is no one who might do anything about it. Even your brother Heymel is not as he used to be. He is busy with his affairs of government and thinks little of our needs and complaints."

Dhu 'l-Kifl ﷺ did not reply to this charge but asked, "There must have been a certain beginning, a first time for all these things. Can you tell me what happened?"

The old woman said, "That is easy to say. Last year I sent my son to the market along with our neighbor's son as usual, to buy and to sell. He used to stay out only for one night. This time he went again and stayed away for much longer than he used to and when he returned his condition was deplorable. All the light was gone from his face. His complexion was sallow and his knees were trembling. He hung his head when I asked him about his experiences and gave the impression of a guilty man. At first I thought he must be ill but he had no complaint. He had not brought home any proceeds from his sales, saying he had been attacked and robbed on the way. I believed him. He set out another time and again he returned empty handed. Slowly, I learned from my neighbors that their children were in a similar condition and we have now found out that there is a plot. There are certain forces in the capital working against us. They have begun to feed us poison in order to corrupt us and they are using our innocent children, turning them away from the straight path. They are succeeding. The tide has turned on us very quickly."

Dhu 'l-Kifl ﷺ was highly alarmed and said, "We have wasted a lot of time already, and the iron must be pounded while it is hot." But he was skeptical, still, of the idea of employing fire to fight fire even though the old woman had urged him to show a strong hand.

"Our children cannot be counted among the believers anymore," she said. "Go and see for yourself how evil has overtaken them."

Dhu 'l-Kifl ﷺ said, "As long as the riverbed has not become completely filled with mud, it may yet be possible to clean it with fresh running water, and restore the stream to its former purity."

"O, Dhu 'l-Kifl, you are still young and full of confidence. You have not seen what we old ones have seen and your love for your people is unbroken. How long will it be until you will succeed your father as a prophet?"

"Only Allah Almighty knows," answered Dhu 'l-Kifl ﷺ and thanking the woman for her hospitality, he went on his way.

Before it was yet dark, he met a young man who wished to speak to him urgently. He told Dhu 'l-Kifl ﷺ the full story of what was happening to the village youth through foreign influences, how they were being seduced to idol worship and all forms of immoral behavior on their trips into the city. He said it would not be long before there was be an uprising in the villages. The young men had long gambled away all they possessed and their new advisors had taught them that the goods of the rich were lawful for them just as they had made everything that was forbidden, lawful also. This was the fuel of the rebellion under the trees on the hilltop.

"But don't let them see you there," the young man entreated Dhu 'l-Kifl ﷺ, for they now know more restraint and I fear for your life."

"Never worry," said Dhu 'l-Kifl ﷺ and went on towards the fires burning upon the hill. He heard men speaking in loud voices and when he came to them he recognized the young men of the village and they knew him too. He gave them his greetings of peace and asked them what they were doing there at this hour. They were a little hesitant to answer and finally one retorted what he was doing there among them.

"I have come to see you," answered Dhu 'l-Kifl ﷺ and climbed atop a great rock.

"This is the son of our prophet," the boys whispered to one another, "and his father Ayyūb ﷺ prayed that prophethood might be passed on to him. Perhaps the time has now come and he is here to make this announcement to us."

There was a stranger amongst them who now stepped forth and spoke out, "I thought you were finally going to rid yourself of all this nonsense and become reasonable people but here you go again, babbling about prophets and prophecies and predictions and that invisible god. Were you not going to rid yourself of all those restrictions and those who impose them upon you? Were you not going to claim your birthright of freedom, and choose to do what you like? Why are you suddenly talking of prophets and wizards and the like?"

They said, "This man is the son of our prophet. We dare not act against him."

"You will run into trouble with the idols, for they will be wrathful. Have they not made everything lawful to you that these prophets forbade you? Did they not teach you that man is born with free will and the right to live as he pleases?"

Dhu 'l-Kifl ﷺ then took the word and said, "You are not from our people. You are a stranger amongst us."

"So what of it!" said the other. "I am of mankind and I have come to take my pleasure with these youths here and to free them from their prison in which you have trapped them; just like apes."

"And what do you claim that they are missing then?" challenged Dhu 'l-Kifl ﷺ.

"In your system everything enjoyable is forbidden. It is forbidden to drink, to play games, to have fun with the girls, to supplement one's own funds with those of one's neighbor. Everything you have made *ḥarām*. These boys are missing all the fun in life. They are just like trained monkeys, running on the leash by which you lead them; not like men of reason and free will," replied the stranger.

Now Dhu 'l-Kifl ﷺ had heard for himself the words of the insolent seducer and he trembled with rage. He prayed to the Lord for support and the power of self control. Then he turned in the direction of the Kaʿbah and spoke to the young men long and earnestly.

"In this direction," he said, pointing towards Mecca, "is the Kaʿbah, the first house of worship. He has sent prophets to mankind from the time of our father Ādam ﷺ onwards, to all nations, be they large or small. All prophets have called men to the same goal and man has always been ordered to do good, never evil. No one becomes a slave by doing good and honest work. Work, too, is a form of worship and it can be a pleasure. It behooves man not to worship what he has made with his own hands. The Creator is always above and beyond his own creation. All created beings are only signs of the greatness of the Lord and Him we must all obey."

But the stranger pursued the argument, "What sort of god is it who implants in man the taste for all sorts of enjoyments, then makes them forbidden to him?"

Dhu 'l-Kifl ⸎ answered him, "And what good has come out of all your teachings? What has become of these hopeful and prosperous young people? They do not sleep at night in order to squander away their possessions and to pursue their sordid enjoyment. In the day they have not the strength left to do their honest work. Their faces have become faded and aged before their time. They rise not before noon and are busy only at night to drown themselves in drink. Is this what you call enjoyment of life? Is not honest work a pleasure? And what is sweeter than the fruits of lawful gain? What is more tasteful, than to awake at daybreak as fresh as a budding rose and to thank the Lord with a prayerful heart for another day of His Creation?"

He continued, "Allah has sent us upon the Earth so that we might be His servants and vicegerents here. We belong to one nation, the family of man. It is a great degradation to believe only in this brief life in the present world. No real joy remains for a man who believes he has nothing to expect after death. Only his greed will be increased and he will seek to grab whatever he can on the face of the earth before he has to leave it. The source of light and happiness is the belief in the continuity of life and the eternity of the Lord."

"O my friends, this man is not of our people and his intentions towards you are not what you think. He is an emissary of a foreign power which seeks to destroy the happy life of contentment we have been leading and lay to waste our beautiful country, out of motives of envy and hatred. Be not deceived. For years they have been working towards this goal. We know of them and of their ulterior designs. They will tell you it is ridiculous to give poor-dues, they will make fun of you when you distribute your wealth in charity, they will prevent you from giving each other mutual help, they will tell you to hide away your money and hoard it in secret. They will tell you it is useless to go out and work, they will ridicule you for respecting your parents, they will make out that those appointed over you are tyrants and unjust rulers and that the respect and dignity they command is absurd. The peace and contentment you had of yore, what intoxicating cup can give it back to you, what night spent in illicit dissipation can return your peace of mind to you and what idolatrous rite can fill your heart as a single sincere moment of prayer to the Almighty can? Truly, what Allah has forbidden has been withheld from us for a good reason. It is for our own good that we are prevented from indulging in every low desire which only brings increased suffering upon man. It would only rob a man of his strength and of the power to enjoy what Allah has made lawful to him."

"Search your inner selves and don't think for a moment that there is no way back for you. Come over here, stand by my side and let us pray together and by the morning you will see that all this has passed like a fleeting nightmare. Your light will never be extinguished by the performance of holy deeds. This stranger and his confederates have spread among you with a clear aim in mind, to increase the appetite of your insatiable *nafs*. What have they not tempted you with: crazy and degraded pastimes, drunkenness and depravity, wasting your time with coarse jesting and general mischief, teaching you to lie, cheat and steal, shying away not even from murder and rebellion. They have bred in you greed, avarice and miserliness, dishonesty, ungratefulness and indifference towards a lofty spiritual goal and your state has become thoroughly miserable."

The stranger understood that his position was being undermined. He began to shout, "How long are you going to stand listening to this foolish prattle? The others are waiting for us. Everything is ready and prepared for our grand coup. You can't back out now; you will make fools of yourselves!"

Dhu 'l-Kifl ﷺ tried once more to warn them, "I am not talking to you of my own accord. There is a power backing me up and it is my holy duty to lead you back onto the straight way. I wish no harm to befall you and I am not acting out of self interest. It is my conscience prompting me to speak to you. Do not follow that man. It will be your undoing and one day you will be filled with regret. Turn back and repent now, for Allah will forgive you."

"Do you believe," he continues, "when you have taken over these lands which are not rightfully yours that you will be left in peace to enjoy what you have appropriated? Oh no! The neighboring kings are watching you as waiting lions and they will begin to roar as soon as they are sure of your weakness. Then, they will move against you and take everything out of your hands and you will be led from here in chains into slavery. They are not your friends and they know not mercy. One day, I fear, I will meet you again in the slave bazaar, but then it will be too late for regrets. You are deceiving only yourselves!"

But it was already too late for all of Dhu 'l-Kifl's admonitions. The poison was already streaming in their veins. Too many nights had they spent in drunkenness and they could no longer understand the important of Dhu 'l-Kifl's speech. They were annoyed by his words, to be sure, but the only remedy they could think of was drink. The stranger was well aware of this and from a hidden storage place he pulled out three wine skins and opened them, calling to the boys to come and strengthen themselves for the deed they were about to do. Dhu 'l-Kifl ﷺ watched them with mixed feelings of disgust and pity but he saw there was no more he could say to them. He had to worry about his own safety now.

For when the stranger saw that the wine had gone to their heads, he said to them, "O my friends, even if that miserable prophet of doom be the brother of your kind, now is the time to put an end to his ravings."

"Shall we kill him, then?" they asked, ready for anything in their intoxication.

"No," said the stranger, "let us just take him prisoner, for his brother Heymel will certainly pay considerable ransom to have such a valuable hostage released. In that way we are in a strong bargaining position and will have attained our ends without even having to fight for them."

A great cry of drunken enthusiasm arose and they all got up to seize Dhu 'l-Kifl ﷺ. However, he had disappeared. They searched for a long time among the rocks but could find no trace of him. They finally concluded that it must be another one of his 'magic tricks'.

Dhu 'l-Kifl ﷺ had anticipated their intentions and slipped away unnoticed and descended into the village. He noticed that no lights were burning and he found the people there already expecting an attack. He confirmed their fears and informed them of what they had to expect from their own children. Though it saddened their hearts to have to fight against their own flesh and blood, they prepared to defend themselves and the village headman took up the command.

Before long the rebellious mob stormed down upon the village, with loud and barbarous cries, and there ensured a fierce battle between fathers and sons. Even mothers were forced to fight against their own sons. There were many casualties, but the raid was not successful. Towards the morning an armed force sent by Heymel arrived and at the sight of the soldiers, the insurgents dispersed and hid in the hills. Heymel and his men pursued them but they returned with no prisoners. Dhu 'l-Kifl ﷺ was worried that he might have put them all to death but Heymel said, "We could not find any of them. They have all run over to the enemy lines."

A week or so passed. Then one day, a messenger came running into the village of Besniye and brought news that the Assyrians were going to war against the Egyptians. Now all the villages under

Heymel's leadership were beholden to the Assyrians and he was sure of their victory. But before long they beheld in the distance a long train of people, who turned out to be refugees from the more distant villages. They were so exhausted from their flight that they could hardly speak. When they finally told their story, there was a general outcry and people were dismayed. It appeared that their sons, seeing that their rebellion had been futile had run over to the enemy lines and betrayed their own people. They had directed them into the territories and shown them the ways into it that only they could know. The armies had fallen over their lands and ravaged and ransacked all they could lay hands on. The survivors had fled and were moving north to seek shelter in the city, before the enemy cut off the road. Dhu 'l-Kifl ﷺ and his brother took hurried counsel and decided that they, too, should take advantage of the darkness and lead the small band of believers into safety, rather than leaving them to fall into the hands-of the ruthless enemy. But Heymel hesitated for he was attached to his lands.

He argued with his brother, "Perhaps it is better we stay in our places. When they come upon us we can always pretend that we are on their side and worship their idols and they will leave us in peace. Then after they are gone we can live on as we are accustomed to living."

Dhu 'l-Kifl ﷺ was not pleased by these words. "I have always known that it would come to this one day. You are willing to sell out your faith and religion for the sake of maintaining your power and possessions. But it will not be as you expect, for once the filth of idolatry has entered a country, it cannot easily be dispelled. You will be very sorry in the end."

"It is easy for you who are free and unfettered to speak like this but I have a family and many responsibilities that bind me to this place. I can't just do as I please."

Dhu 'l-Kifl ﷺ resigned himself, "I leave it to you; you may count on the justice of the Egyptians, Hittites or Assyrians. It makes no difference to whom you lose your light. As for myself, I will head in the direction of the Ka'bah and whoever wishes may follow me there. Perhaps our destination is not as green and luscious as our homeland, but at least our faith will remain intact."

No more than forty people, mostly old men and women were prepared to follow Dhu 'l-Kifl ﷺ into exile and they swore by the light of their eyes not to stray from the way of truth as long as there was life in them. Dhu 'l-Kifl ﷺ took leave of his brother and led his band into the mosque to pray. He went and visited his mother's grave and prayed fervently to the Lord to give him guidance as to where he should lead his people. Then they set out under cover of the night and hid themselves in a dense wood for the enemy had come very close. Dhu 'l-Kifl ﷺ let his followers rest there, while he climbed atop a large rock to pray. He was not sure of what he should do.

His people preferred to go to the city where they would more easily be able to begin a new life but Dhu 'l-Kifl ﷺ feared that they would succumb to all the varied influences there and lose their purity of heart. On the other hand, he understood that the life of hardship he offered them in the harsh deserts around Mecca could not be very attractive to them. Thus, he debated with himself and his Lord and while he was in such meditations, he was overcome by a great drowsiness and his soul departed to the world of spirits. Towards the morning he saw a significant vision. His own difficult situation appeared to him and he felt its hopeless weight.

Suddenly, something gave way and he had the unexpected sensation of ease and breathed a lightness in the air which was as fragrant as a rose-garden in morning dew. He heard a voice calling him, "Oh Dhu 'l-Kifl, glad tidings to you The Lord of the Worlds has chosen you to be His prophet! Take your people and lead them to the city of Shām and the guidance of the Lord is with you." Dhu 'l-Kifl عليه السلام awoke full of wonder but at the same time he was doubtful as to whether it had not been a false vision inspired by the enemy of man, the accursed Shayṭān or even whether one of the people had whispered into his ear while he slept in order to make him take them to the city where they wanted to go. He saw them all fast asleep and he called upon his Lord in his heart to make him safe from error and falsehood. Then, the angel Jibrīl عليه السلام appeared to him and confirmed his calling. Dhu 'l-Kifl عليه السلام was filled with light and joy. Thus, the prayer of his father Ayyūb عليه السلام was granted and his son Dhu 'l-Kifl عليه السلام became his successor. Dhu 'l-Kifl عليه السلام is mentioned in the Qur'an:

وَإِسْمَٰعِيلَ وَإِدْرِيسَ وَذَا الْكِفْلِ ۖ كُلٌّ مِّنَ الصَّٰبِرِينَ

"And Ishmael, Idris, Dhu 'l-Kifl. Each was of the patient. And We admitted them into Our mercy. They were of the righteous." [1]

وَاذْكُرْ إِسْمَٰعِيلَ وَالْيَسَعَ وَذَا الْكِفْلِ ۖ وَكُلٌّ مِّنَ الْأَخْيَارِ

"And make mention Ishmael and Elisha and Dhu 'l-Kifl. All are of the chosen."[2]

Dhu 'l-Kifl عليه السلام arose and went to bathe in a nearby stream. Then, he awakened the believers and told them to perform their ablutions for it was the time to pray. They looked at him in surprise for his whole aspect had somehow changed. They prayed together and Dhu 'l-Kifl عليه السلام ordered them to gather fruits in the forest for their breakfast. This they did but even as they ate and prepared for the road ahead of them none could take his eyes off Dhu 'l-Kifl عليه السلام, the prophet.

At last, he rose to his feet, smiled at them and said, "O my brothers, I believe you are all sensing that a change has come over me and you

---

[1] Sūratu 'l-Anbīyā (The Prophets), 85-86.

[2] Sūrah Ṣād, 38,4.

are feeling the influence of the Divine Inspiration that has come to me this very night."

"Yes," they all agreed, "there is a light in your eyes and a power in your speech that we have not perceived before this time."

"It is true," said Dhu 'l-Kifl ﷺ, "for this morning the angel came to me and revealed to me my prophethood and from this day on all our steps will be guided by the Almighty. So take heart and rejoice with me. Allah has accepted your heart's desire and has commanded us to proceed towards Damascus."

All the believers fell down then and performed a prostration of thanks.

"Perhaps it will be a great trial for us to go there," continued Dhu 'l-Kifl ﷺ, "for we will encounter strange circumstances and all manner of unaccustomed things, both good and bad. Shām is a busy place and many different people come together there. Be not deceived by anything you may see there. The devil always accompanies us and the only road to escape from his wiles is prayer. Whenever you are distressed, remember to pray. That is the only way to repel his assaults."

"O prophet of Allah, you may depend on us," The believers said.

"O my brothers, that is what all people of all times have said to their prophets. They gave their word only to fall back on it later and demand miracles as proof or as an excuse not to carry out an order. They have always accused their prophets of sorcery and the like. There is no creature weaker than man and man is unjust and hasty. I already wonder what sort of miracle you will be demanding of me, for no prophet has come whose people did not make such a demand of him."

Hearing these words, the believers grew sad and said, "Have you so little trust in us, O Dhu 'l-Kifl? You have hardly begun with your mission and already you speak to us with bitterness. The light we perceive upon your face this day is enough proof for us. We will follow it, undaunted. Besides, is it not miracle enough to witness a man who survives without food and sleep, who only fasts and prays? This is a continuous miracle which we are witnessing and may Allah grant us patience."

They were about to set out on their journey when, they heard a whistle in the forest. When they answered, the headman of the village stepped out into the clearing. He said to them, "Your brother Heymel sends me to you to inform you that you might return to the village, for the danger is past. The enemy has passed us by and the Assyrians will leave us alone. We can continue to lead our lives and worship as we are used to. Come back with me, for who will lead us in prayer if not you?" Dhu 'l-Kifl ﵇ explained to the headman that he had become a prophet during the night and that the Lord's irrevocable order was for him to go to Shām. The believers stood and hung their heads, confused at this turn of events. "How do we know you speak the truth?" they asked of the headman. "How do we know we will not be harmed if we return?" The man reassured them over and over. The people were homesick already and yearned for the homes they had left.

"There is another thing I must tell you," said the headman. "If you come back with me, chances are that you may grow very rich all at once."

"How is that?" the people wished to know.

"Our overlords have promised to pay us for every object left from the time of Ayyūb ﵇. They will give us its weight in gold. Whatever is left from the time of his affliction: his rag, the straw on which he lay, the jug from which he drank, the dressings he applied to his wounds. For all this, they will pay us in gold."

In vain, Dhu 'l-Kifl ﷷ tried to counsel them against returning. The man's words seemed false to him and the last offer of gold sounded to him like a contemptuous jest with the simpleminded.

"Did I not hear you say to me a moment ago that you would follow me wherever I went, be it to the end of the world? If I threw myself into the river or off a cliff you would come after me. Allah has commanded me to go to Shām and there I shall go. Whoever comes with me let him come now and whoever returns, that is his will. But be warned, this message is a falsehood and you will find nothing in your return but charred ruins and only the dead are there to receive you..."

But no matter what he said to them, their hearts were bent on returning to their homes and they chose to believe the messenger. Their ways separated and Dhu-l Kifl ﷷ was left by himself on the road to Damascus.

One day, he stopped by the roadside in order to say his prayers when he heard a rustling sound near him in the bushes. A man emerged, muttering under his breath, "Nothing remains, no life, no soul, not stone upon stone, no trace of what used to be." Dhu 'l-Kifl looked up and recognized the man as a merchant from Qudsīyya who had left the village a long time ago to settle in Shām. Hearing of the enemy invasion, he had returned to the village to see what he could rescue of his belongings there. He had found the whole land burnt and devastated. The houses had been leveled to the ground and all the villagers killed or led off into slavery. Dhu 'l-Kifl ﷷ thought sadly of his group of believers and how they had been deceived and he wondered what fate they had met. Then he spoke to the man and told him that he had become a prophet and that the Lord had revealed for him to go to Shām.

"I don't really believe in all these things," said the man, "however, I like your looks and your manner and to tell you the truth, I am looking for a husband for my one and only daughter. I see you are a worthy person and would give her to you in marriage if you accompany me to Shām."

"But I am just as you see me here," said Dhu 'l-Kifl 좵. "I own nothing but the traveling cloak you see me in. I have nothing to my name and no skill wherewith to make a living to keep a wife and family."

The man said, "Then you may look after my sheep for five years."

"I know nothing about herding sheep," answered Dhu 'l-Kifl 좵.

"I will employ you as a shopkeeper," he said.

"About business I know even less," said Dhu 'l-Kifl 좵.

"Then you may work in my gardens and fields for me," said the man.

So Dhu 'l-Kifl 좵 agreed to look after the man's gardens for five years and receive the hand of his daughter with all her dowry in return.

As they stood talking, the sky suddenly darkened as if a dark rain cloud were passing overhead. But it was no cloud of rain. It was a swarm of locusts so dense that it obscured the sunlight. The locusts came from the direction of Qudsīyya and the men knew that not a green blade of grass remained standing once the locusts had passed over a place.

The man decried this as a further catastrophe to befall his homeland but Dhu 'l-Kifl 좵 said, "O my friend, the locusts are also a blessing to some people. For I have heard from my father Ayyūb 좵 that after having eaten their fill they fly towards the great desert and the poor Bedouins living there catch them and prize them highly as food. They collect and dry them and keep them stored for the meager years to come."

"Oh," said the merchant, "if that is so, then we are in luck, for each of these insects then, means money. Tell me, how do they eat them?"

"They roast them over a fire," answered Dhu 'l-Kifl 좵.

"Alright, we will try it and see if these things are really edible. They picked up a few locusts that had been blown against the rocks, made a small fire and roasted the insects. After having sampled them and having found them not too bad, he said to Dhu 'l-Kifl عليه السلام, "This will now be our deal since it was your idea: I give you fifty percent and that will make you a rich man. No need for you to be my gardener now. We will collect these insects now in great numbers and dry them. Then, we'll sell them to the Bedouins living in the desert. This way we will make a lot of money and you won't have to wait five years to marry my daughter. You can pay me back in time when our new enterprise has become established." Dhu 'l-Kifl عليه السلام agreed to all the man said. He had seen the signs of the Lord who had opened this way for him. Thus, camel-caravans were prepared and sent out loaded with dried locusts and sold to the Bedouins in the desert. Their profits were good, for there was no scarcity of locusts. Dhu 'l-Kifl عليه السلام received his share and was married to the merchant's daughter.

Ten years passed. Dhu 'l-Kifl عليه السلام had by now established himself and his family in an area around Damascus, He had sons, daughters and his own house. His gardens and fields bore fruit and he became prosperous. He was now forty years old.

One day, he looked out from his house and beheld a spectacle which touched his heart strangely. A procession of slaves was being led by their driver and they came to halt on the empty lot next to Dhu 'l-Kifl's house. Dhu 'l-Kifl عليه السلام had seen many slave caravans led by in his time but never had he seen any group of people more miserable than these. They were about twenty men and women and they were fair-skinned though their skin had been so burnt by the sun and wind that you could scarcely tell their color. They had barely rags to cover their nakedness and their backs were scarred horribly by the cruel lashes they had received as they were driven on mercilessly. They were so emaciated and weak that they could hardly walk, yet they were made to carry burdens upon their heads as they tottered along.

Their drivers yelled at them to keep singing, and though they scarcely had breath left in them they sang as they were ordered. Their songs were the songs of fire-worshippers. They praised the fire as a divinity and as the supreme Lord who creates and destroys.

When they were allowed to halt, they threw off their loads and fainted more than they lay down. Their drivers deliberated what to do with them and spoke among themselves, "Look at them. What shall we do with them? They are scarcely human anymore! We can't lead them into the city in this condition. We must send word to the owners to decide what shall be done with them. And it was true. Their nails had grown as long as claws. Their hair was tangled and matted and they had not washed for many months; worse than any animal ever kept in captivity.

The longer Dhu 'l-Kifl 🕮 watched, the more he felt moved to do something for these most wretched people but he could think of no good way to approach the matter. Whilst he was trying to make up his mind, the slave-driver came to him and demanded in no uncertain terms to be made his guest.

While he fed him, Dhu 'l-Kifl 🕮 asked the man about the unfortunates outside. "Well, what about them? They are the leftovers; we have sold the rest."

"What is to become of them? I don't know. It is up to their owners. Either we succeed in selling them off or else we lead them to the temple to be sacrificed to the sacred flames so that it might be counted in our favor by the gods."

Dhu 'l-Kifl 🕮 listened and said not a word. Later, when the man was leaving, he said to Dhu 'l-Kifl 🕮, "I have some place to go now. I will leave the slaves here in your care. They are bound hand and foot. They are too weak to flee."

When he was gone, Dhu 'l-Kifl 🕮 said to his wife, "Go and cook a soup for this miserable lot and we will feed them for the love of

God." When the soup was ready, Dhu 'l-Kifl ؑ took it down to them himself and gave them each a plate of hot broth and a loaf of bread. They looked at him in surprise and ate hungrily but there was also distrust and suspicion in their regard. They were not accustomed to kindness and even in this unexpected act of charity they suspected a hidden barb. Their captors tormented them day and night and had robbed their hearts of hope. They fed them no food at all but made them eat the flesh of their brothers who died along the way, thus degrading them even beyond the level of animals. They had become as wary as wild beasts and suspected nothing but a new form of cruelty.

Dhu 'l-Kifl ؑ withdrew and when it was night he stepped out onto his balcony to pray. "O Lord," he cried, "save these unfortunates, for are they not human beings and Your chosen servants?"

One of the slaves below was awake and watching and suddenly he cried out to his fellows, "It's he! I recognize him, I am sure!" The moon had hidden itself in a cloud but Dhu 'l-Kifl's form shone as if by a light of its own, clearly visible in the darkness of the night. All the others awoke and told him to quiet down, otherwise there would be more trouble for them. "No, I have recognized him," insisted the first one, "See how his hair is parted in the middle. There is no doubt! He is the one who gave us advice long ago, when he stood upon that hill and preached to us but, alas, we did not heed his words. Do you not remember how he said to us: 'Oh you who are ready to sell your fathers and mothers, one day you will know who is your enemy and I shall not be surprised to see you again one day led in chains through the slave markets of Damascus, nor should you be surprised, for you have been warned!' Ah, how true his words were, had we only known then!"

Dhu 'l-Kifl ؑ turned away from them and hid himself. He did not wish to humiliate them even further.

When the overseer returned from his errands, Dhu 'l-Kifl 过 made a bid to buy the remaining slaves off him. "Think again, my good man," said the slave-driver. "What use could these bags of skin and bones be to you? They are beyond restoration; you are buying only dead bodies." But Dhu 'l-Kifl 过 insisted and paid the price that was asked. Then he was handed the keys to the locks on their chains. The slave-drivers hastily made off, one saying to the other, "Quickly, let us leave, before that foolish man realizes what sort of rubbish he has purchased and wants his money back."

Dhu 'l-Kifl 过 released the slaves from their chains and revealed himself to them. Then he gave to each his freedom, saying, "As free men we are brothers." He settled them on his land, and each ploughed and tilled a corner of it and built huts for themselves. They married and had families and the Lord blessed them and showed them His forgiveness. In time, they founded a small new village on the outskirts of Damascus. Often they went about the slave-markets and found their own tribesmen who, like themselves, had been enslaved during the wars that had raged. They bought and freed them. All of them felt great shame and humiliation when they were brought before Dhu 'l-Kifl 过, the prophet whose warnings, they had not heeded in time. Dhu 'l-Kifl 过 showed them nothing but kindness and encouraged them to renew their faith and to repent sincerely. Allah forgave them and they became the best of Muslims.

Damascus was then a trade center and a town of lively commerce. Merchants from all over the world used to come there for business. The community of Dhu 'l-Kifl 过 became well known among them for their honesty and trustworthiness and word spread far and wide, so that many foreign merchants preferred to do business with them. They worked hard and their fields and gardens also prospered and they were blessed with health and good fortune.

As always, when the Lord has blessed one people more than another, they become envious and could not tolerate the well-being of the first. So it was, then, with the people of Shām. Dhu 'l-Kifl had not converted a single person among them to his faith and he had been all alone until he found his lost tribesmen and brought them to repentance. In Damascus, at that time, there were many different cults and sects. People worshipped the sun, the moon or the fire, and each group tried to convert the other by force. Dhu 'l-Kifl had tried to preach in Damascus, and people would listen to him as they would listen to any storyteller in the marketplace, for his speech was beautiful and spellbinding. However, they only shook their heads to his earnest appeals and soon went their ways, no one taking his message seriously.

Now, when the merchants of the town saw that Dhu 'l-Kifl's small community was flourishing, envy entered their hearts and they said, "This man is bad news. He and his freed slaves will soon take all our customers away from us. We must drive him out of town by some means." They knew that the Assyrian king was well disposed towards Dhu 'l-Kifl on account of his good reputation, but that the priests and soothsayers would like nothing better than to be rid of him, for they felt threatened by his purity and power. So the merchants turned to them. The priests went before the Assyrian king and spoke against Dhu 'l-Kifl saying, "He is the only person who does not worship any of our gods and idols," they said. "He is gathering a growing following of freed slaves. He is a foreigner, an alien, and we have understood his designs. He is preparing a base to take over power and to topple the throne. He is a danger to the state and should be dealt with immediately."

But the king was reluctant to act against Dhu 'l-Kifl because of the damage such a decree might do to the free trade of Damascus. He only sent word to Dhu 'l-Kifl suggesting to him that he should leave and settle in another town.

The envoys came and brought Dhu 'l-Kifl ﵇ this news and he talked to his opponents for a long time and tried to reason with them but was unable to melt their hearts of stone.

At last he said to them, "As it is your wish, I shall go. But know that I am a prophet, even if you do not believe in me. This is my final warning to you. The land from which a prophet is driven out will surely perish, it has always been so. This is the Lord's punishment and you will live to see it yet. You are driving me out of this thriving center of trade for fear of losing your gain to me, unwilling to share the bounties of the Lord in your hardheartedness. The punishment of the Lord may come from where you least expect it and when it happens and all your trade has come to a dead stop, then you will remember my words"

Dhu 'l-Kifl ﵇ had thought of leading his small following along with him but when he saw them content, peacefully enjoying their lives amidst their families and flourishing fields he had not the heart to uproot them once more and subject them to all the hardships and uncertainties of a vagrant life after all they had already suffered. So he gathered them all one last time and addressed them, "O my friends and brothers! O my very own family, I am leaving you and you must henceforth consider me as one who has died. I leave you the law of the Lord which you know, cling to it and live by it and do not revert to the evil ways of the people living around you, else you will fall into even greater misery than you have already known."

"You have known what it is to suffer and you have repented of your past wrongdoings. Beware of falling into the same trap again. Never give up your faith in Allah Almighty, no matter what the world may do to you. It is easy to slip down a slope which you have climbed with great difficulty, so be very careful and guard your steps. I leave it to you to choose a leader from among yourselves after I have gone and may you pursue the path of righteousness always."

They asked him, "And where are you going? What shall we do if they drive us away from this land? Where shall we find you?"

Dhu 'l-Kifl answered, "Allah's Earth is wide. Go and seek His bounties wherever you wish. As for my own path, I cannot say, for I am a prophet of the Lord and my coming and going rests only with Him. I would turn my face towards the Holy House of Allah, in Mecca, the first sanctuary of the Lord but I will go wherever I am commanded."

Dhu 'l-Kifl made ready to travel and took leave of his family as if he were never to see them again. His father-in-law accompanied him the first stretch of the way and said to him, "O my beloved son, will you not forsake this foolishness? You had found rest and peace in this rich land and have a family that loves you and makes you happy. Why do you want to go off now and tramp around in the wilderness? The road is full of dangers and unknown things. Why don't you make your peace with the priests and content yourself with worshipping what everybody else worships in this country? Is it really worth giving up all the good things in life for some invisible goal?" Dhu 'l-Kifl was saddened by the words of his old friend who had become dear as a father to him and he prayed for him, as he said in parting, "I ask of the Lord to send you guidance and understanding. Perhaps we shall meet again before our time is over."

Dhu 'l-Kifl set out for the south as the angel had revealed to him. When he reached the hills over looking Damascus, the sun was about to set. In the waning light the whole city was lit up as in a golden blaze and Dhu 'l-Kifl had a vision. The people in the city appeared to him to be running around just as little black ants, in the darkness of their ignorance. He perceived his small band of believers as bright specks among them but they were so very few. Then he saw hordes of big, black, poisonous ants falling upon them in great numbers and Dhu 'l-Kifl felt great distress. He rubbed his eyes and prayed fervently that Allah might not let the few believers fall prey to the misguided a second time. "Oh Lord, grant that I should come together with them once more in my life," he cried. Then, he made his way in the growing darkness through the hills and when he looked back again he saw nothing but the black rocks.

The angel had revealed to him that he must follow the way of all prophets and travel for there is great benefit in travel; it broadens one's scope and stretches the horizons of the mind. He traveled southwards along the coast. Dhu 'l-Kifl 쐸 had been traveling for a year already and reached the fruitful plains of Jericho. It was a blessed land but the inhabitants did not know whom to thank for the blessing. They were a wayward and rebellious folk. Dhu 'l-Kifl 쐸 spoke to them and counseled them to acknowledge the unity of Allah and to live in awe of Him. The people, however, just rolled their eyes and mimicked him as though he were a madman. Finally, they drove him off with sticks and stones and threatened him with death if he were to persist in bothering them.

Dhu 'l-Kifl 쐸 clothed himself in patience and went on. There were times however, when he was overcome by his human nature; his heart would burst from longing for his family and friends and he burned with the pangs of loneliness and separation. Quickly he would recall that he was never truly alone for when a man becomes immersed in the remembrance of his Lord, completely, with every cell of his body and every facet of his soul, how can he ever feel himself to be alone and a stranger? And how can he forget this, as long as he continues to be steadfast in his devotions and exercises of remembrance?

One day, he reached the outskirts of a lovely village at nightfall and considered spending the night there. As he regarded the beauty of the land he was overcome with feeling for all the goodness Allah Almighty has given to His servants and with which He has filled this wide world. Suddenly, he heard a coughing sound from somewhere in the rocks to his left. He looked about but couldn't see anyone. The coughing stopped and Dhu 'l-Kifl ﷺ heard an angry voice saying, "Can a worse bunch of miserly villagers be found anywhere in the whole world? I am lucky that I woke up quickly and saved myself from them." These words were followed by a burst of mad laughter and a snatch of song. Dhu 'l-Kifl ﷺ was intrigued by these words and wished to see the speaker. He looked again among the rocks and found a man sitting, facing the north. He looked up when he saw Dhu 'l-Kifl ﷺ and said to him, "O traveler, I can see that you are about to make the same mistake that I made. Whatever you do, don't let the beauty and bounty of this land deceive you and don't go down into the village, for you will perish there. Don't let yourself be bewitched by appearances and congratulate yourself on having met me! What is your name?"

"My name is Bishr but they call me Dhu 'l-Kifl," he replied."

"My name is Saha and I come from a village near the lake of Tut. Why are you headed north? What is your intention?"

"I am under orders," answered Dhu 'l-Kifl ﷺ.

"I am not a curious person, I will not ask you what your orders are, but I would like to know who has given you such orders, for surely he wishes for your speedy death!" said Saha.

"No, in that you are mistaken," said Dhu 'l-Kifl ﷺ.

"When they are stoning you down there, then you will think differently," said Saha." Look at me, Dhu 'l-Kifl, I used to be a big, fat man. After only three months of traveling, look what has become of me? For what does a hungry man do? He begins to live off himself!"

"You are speaking strangely," said Dhu 'l-Kifl. ﷺ

"Yes, and I would speak to you of stranger things yet, but I feel that you will not listen to my stories. Your mind is bent on going and mixing with those people who are of unrivalled meanness, deceitfulness and cruelty. Go your way then, and I will go mine."

As he turned to go, he heard the man laugh behind him a second time and it was a bitter, stinging laugh. Dhu 'l-Kifl 🕮 was undaunted. He was driven on by the voice of his conscience and felt responsibility for these people who had no guidance.

Dhu 'l-Kifl 🕮 descended and it was, indeed, as Saha had told him. He found himself among people even worse than those he had left behind. For when a man comes to worship Shayṭān what kind of evil will he not do? Anyone worthy of the name would blush from shame at the mere mention of the devil's name.

Dhu 'l-Kifl 🕮 had not yet reached the village when, he was stopped by men who claimed to be tax-collectors. They demanded from him a fee for entering the village and breathing its air. If he were unable to pay he would have to work off his debt. At first, Dhu 'l-Kifl 🕮 thought they must be joking, but he soon realized how serious they were, when they brought him to their headman.

"This man was found using and wearing out our road. He has no money and can only make up for our loss if he works for us for one week."

The headman had another cause to add to this, "While listening to you, I have wasted so much of my precious time. The fee for that is another three days work."

So within minutes of his stay in that village, Dhu 'l-Kifl had already incurred debts enough to enslave him for ten days. He was no fool and he quickly understood that it was their intention to force him to labor for them according to their arguments. He was, in effect, their prisoner for how can a man live without breathing the air or setting his foot upon the ground? He was taken to the slaves' quarters and during his stay there he witnessed the unhappy lot of many a caravan that passed through that place unawares. The headman would demand a high price from them as the rent of the air used up by men and beasts and they were made to pay him all their wares and trading goods. Then they had to sell themselves as slaves. This was a form of highway robbery, only under a different name.

The people of that place also behaved no better towards their own kith and kin and they even cheated the idols which they worshipped. When they sacrificed an animal, they would first supply themselves with meat and when they had eaten their fill, they took the bones and offered them to the idols.

Dhu 'l-Kifl ﷺ then took to preaching among his fellow slaves and he found an open ear there and converted many of them to his faith. The villagers soon found out about this and would have put him and his converts to death had not Dhu 'l-Kifl ﷺ been warned in time and aided by his loyal supporters, he managed to cut his chains and flee the area.

He traveled further to the north and reached Antakya, only to find the people there while at least not as bad as the ones he had just left yet their meanness remained beyond belief. They had posted guards not only around their fields and gardens to make sure no one took a single fruit from them but also in the surrounding shrub and wasteland. These men watched to ensure that not a single blade of grass or pebble was picked from the ground. In their orchards, the fruit was numbered on its branches. Not even the birds managed to eat of them. He witnessed a man beating his son so brutally for having eaten one olive too many that he lost an eye. They dug out wells in secret and hid their wealth in them forever. Rather than spend of their hidden treasures they preferred to lend money, and if they were unable to pay the interest on the loan they would sell themselves into slavery. Never would a man betray his secret hiding place—not even on the verge of death—and he would take his secret into the grave with him.

Dhu 'l-Kifl ﷺ spent long hours trying to explain to them how much better it was to enjoy the fruits of one's honest work rather than hoarding a useless treasure in a hole in the ground, but they were not willing to listen to him; it was an old custom, they said and it took the place of a religious observance. Dhu 'l-Kifl 🕮 lived among them for a year and a half and suffered their mistreatment but in the end he had to flee from them in order to save his life. It was the sixth spring since he had left Shām.

Now he turned inland and left the verdant coastline. He advanced into the arid deserts and the further he withdrew from the rich and lush country, the gladder his heart became. He sheltered in a cave and remained there in meditation for some time, purging his mind from the evil he had experienced. After a while, it all seemed to him as a bad dream. He thought of his family and the friends he had left behind in Shām. He missed them bitterly. Had he only had some news of them! But no revelation concerning them came to him. Most of all he feared that they might have forsaken the faith he had instilled in their hearts.

From there he was ordered to go on to the east. Eventually, he reached the heights overlooking the river Euphrates. The hills were rough and stony and though there was no wind, the air was not clear, being was as if full of soot. There were footmarks on the road and signs of flocks having passed that way, but for days Dhu 'l-Kifl 🕮 encountered not a living being. He was convinced that there were people living in that area, but all was mysteriously quiet in that region.

One day, at noon as he sat resting, two naked men appeared unexpectedly from behind a rock, seized him and dragged him down into a hole in the ground. They made him descend a flight of steps hewn into the rock and led him through a maze of corridors until they reached a spacious chamber. There sat an old man flanked and guarded by armed men. All as naked as on the day they were born.

Dhu 'l-Kifl's captors explained to the assembly how they had found him. "We were on watch and we observed this man in our area for four days. He was lingering in the hills, not continuing on his way, as if he were looking for something. We had the impression that he knew of our existence here, so we apprehended him and have brought him before you to be judged. One of the elders in the assembly spoke and said to their leader, "O our king! I recognize this man by his signs! He is none other than Bishr, the son of Ayyūb ﵇, the prophet who destroyed the idols in his time!"

The king sent out everyone from the room and remained alone with Dhu 'l-Kifl ﵇. He asked him to tell him his story and Dhu 'l-Kifl ﵇ did so, hiding nothing from the king. Then the king told him about his tribe. One day long ago, they had grown weary of all the senseless wars and violent crimes committed on the face of the Earth and had decided to dig themselves a new and better home in its belly. They had dug and hollowed out the insides of the hills with secret tunnels connecting them to freshwater supplies and a complicated system of air shafts. There were several hundred of them living in underground villages and they lived there peacefully off the proceeds of manufactured goods which they took to the city markets from time to time. So far, they had managed to keep their underground dwelling a complete secret and though people in the region knew of their existence, they believed them to be not human but a sort of demi-god or spirit of the hills.

"They have developed certain rituals concerning us, and we do our best to play along. These hills are holy to them and they come at certain times to perform pilgrim rites. Now I have certain relics that have come to me and on these days I show them to the crowd of worshippers, and they are filled with awe. I have with me the cloak of the prophet Nūḥ ﵇, the arrows of Idrīs ﵇, and I am always trying to add to the number of holy relics. This is my concern with you, Dhu 'l-Kifl. You, as the son of Ayyūb ﵇ will surely have something that belonged to your father? Give it to me."

Dhu 'l-Kifl ﵇ replied, "So you believe in the prophets and their mission to mankind?"

"What should I believe in?" answered the underground king. "I make use of these things; that is all."

Then he took Dhu 'l-Kifl عليه السلام on a tour throughout his subterranean realm, showing them all the amazing caverns they had hewn out of the rock patiently and though he was impressed, Dhu 'l-Kifl عليه السلام wished only to return to the open air above ground. He said to the king, "It is not right to go to your graves before you have died. Even if it is a risk to your lives, you must seek the Lord's bounties upon the face of the Earth and beneath His open skies; this type of spectral existence does not befit the sons of Ādam. You are as the living dead. What do you worship here, If not the Creator?"

"We do worship our creators," answered the king. "We worship the spirits of our ancestors who brought us into life. We revere them and we can do nothing without their permission."

This was Dhu 'l-Kifl's first encounter with a people who worshipped not gods or idols but human beings. He remained a long time with the king, disputing with him his set of beliefs. Then the king again asked Dhu 'l-Kifl عليه السلام for a relic that had belonged to his father Ayyūb عليه السلام.

"I have told you my story in full," said Dhu 'l-Kifl عليه السلام, "and you should realize that not a shred of cloth has come to me from my father. He has passed on to me the immaterial blessing of the prophethood."

"We shall speak of this again in the morning," said the king and bade him goodnight.

Dhu 'l-Kifl عليه السلام was taken to a room but he could find no sleep. So he took to strolling along the corridors. He made friends with one of the guards and persuaded him to open the lock for him so he could have a look at the starry skies and a breath of open air. When he beheld the familiar stars above, Dhu 'l-Kifl عليه السلام fell down in a prostration of thanks to the Almighty but made no attempt to flee, for he had given his word and he did not wish the sentry to be punished for his sake. As he stood gazing at the stars, there was suddenly a violent tremor and the earth shook. An avalanche of stones fell all around him. Sounds of terror and panic were heard below them as the underground structures collapsed, burying all the inhabitants of that subterranean city beneath them. Dhu 'l-Kifl ﷺ and the sentry scrambled to safety. After an hour, all was calm again. Below them, the silence of the grave echoed in the darkness.

Dhu 'l-Kifl ﷺ was full of compassion and said to the man, "What will you do now that you have lost your home and all your family?"

The man answered, "If you look at me closely in the daylight, you will see that I do not resemble this underground tribe. I am a stranger here and was caught by them one day as they caught you too. My home lies in the mountains to the north, about one month's journey away. It is a land covered by snow for eight months of the year, and I wish to return to the country of my birth."

Dhu 'l-Kifl ﷺ wished to know more about this country and the man talked about his home for a long time. He told him it was situated between Lake Van and the Caspian Sea, north of Igdir, on the banks of the river Araz. Its name was Jennatabad. Hearing this name for the second time, Dhu 'l-Kifl ﷺ grew excited for he recognized from the description that it must be the place Ādam ﷺ had passed through on his way from India and which he likened to Paradise for its unrivalled beauty. He knew also that it lay close to Mount Jūdī on which the Ark of Nūḥ ﷺ had come to rest and he felt a strong desire to visit these places.

He asked the man whether he would accept him as a traveling companion and lead him to his country. The man gladly agreed to take him along. Together they followed the course of the river Euphrates upstream for some weeks, until they reached the town of Bitlis. The people there listened to Dhu 'l-Kifl ﷺ and many of them accepted his call. Later, he continued on to Lake Van and traveled all around its shores. He saw the great mountain of Ararāt and at last came to the place called Jennatabād. From there, he wished to travel into the country that was ruled by women but he was told that he had come too late; their kingdom had already split up and they had disbanded into various small groups after the death of their last queen.

Dhu 'l-Kifl ﷺ returned once more to Bitlis and settled amongst the Muslims there. He sent messengers to Shām in order to learn what had become of his family and followers. He learned that his predictions had come true. After his departure, the Persians, Assyrians, Hittites and Egyptians had all become entangled in a struggle for power and all the trade of Damascus had ground to a halt. The commander of Shām had long ago sent out scouts in search of Dhul-l-Kifl ﷺ to ask him to return but a prophet never returns to a place he has been driven from. Dhu 'l-Kifl ﷺ sent word to the Muslims there that they should come to Bitlis and join him. It was reported that Dhu 'l-Kifl ﷺ was ordered by the Lord to return to Shām and that he rejoined his family and continued to live and preach there until he died.

According to another narration, while Dhu 'l-Kifl ﷺ was on his way to Shām, he passed through a place that had been devastated by the plague many years before that time. A certain group of people had fled from their villages then, leaving the dead and the dying behind in order to save their own skins. At a certain place they had encamped and there they were all found dead in the morning, whilst the sick people left behind in their village recovered. There was no one to bury the dead, so their bodies stayed in the place they had passed away and in time nothing remained of them but their white bones. Dhu 'l-Kifl ﷺ and his followers had to pass by this place on their way to Shām and he told them the story as he was informed of it by the revealing angel. The people were fearful of this place and the many bleached bones. They asked their prophet, "O prophet of Allah, show us a miracle: Make all those dead bodies come back to life and make these people believe in you and accept the message of Allah!"

Dhu 'l-Kifl ﷷ prayed and raised his hands in supplication. As they looked on, the dead bones began to stir by the Will of Allah and they clothed themselves in flesh and came back to life just as they had been aforetime. There were men, women and children. They all believed in Dhu 'l-Kifl ﷷ and became his followers, but there was a peculiar thing about them; for as long as they lived, their bodies had a heavy smell. As some people smell strongly of perspiration, these people's bodies smelt strongly of death even though they were alive and begot children.

There is a verse in the Qur'an which refers to this incident:

"Hast thou not regarded those who went forth from their habitations in their thousands fearful of death? God said to them, "Die!"

ثُمَّ أَحْيٰهُمْ ۚ إِنَّ اللّٰهَ لَذُو فَضْلٍ عَلَى النَّاسِ وَلٰكِنَّ أَكْثَرَ النَّاسِ لَا يَشْكُرُونَ

Then He gave them life. Truly God is bounteous to the people, but most of the people are not thankful. [3]

Dhu 'l-Kifl ﷷ continued to live and preach in the city of Shām until he was seventy-five years old. He had never been ill a single day of his life. Suddenly, his strength left him and he took to his bed, feeling death to be near. His family gathered around him and asked him to pray for his son, Abani, to succeed him as prophet as his own father Ayyūb ﷷ had prayed over him on his deathbed, but Dhu 'l-Kifl ﷷ said, "I will pray only for him who can promise that he will never give way to his anger, never stray from the path of guidance and rule with justice." No one had the courage to give this guarantee and they realized none of them could carry the immense burden Dhu 'l-Kifl ﷷ

[3] Sūratu 'l-Baqara (the Heifer), 2:2 43.

had borne as prophet. Thus, Dhu 'l-Kifl 鸞 passed away in his seventy-fifth year.

There are several traditions concerning his gravesite.

Some say it is in Shām, while other authorities maintain it is either in Bitlis or in his birthplace, the village of Besriye. There are a number of other places where he is commemorated as well. But the most probable site of his tomb is in Shām. There is a mosque and a cemetery of his name there today. I, myself, have seen him in a dream and our Grand Shaykh and Shaykh Nazim have confirmed that this is his true resting place. May Allah have Endless Mercy on his pure soul.

Shuʿayb عليه السلام

Shuʿayb عليه السلام (Jethro) was the son of Melka, the son of Yuzja, the son of Madīan and Madīan was of the sons of Ibrāhīm عليه السلام. His name means "one whose heart is enflamed with Divine Love." He is also known as the 'Khatīb-ul-Anbīyā', the Preacher of the prophets, because he was blessed with the ability to preach in a fashion that was so compelling. Shuʿayb عليه السلام was sent to the people of Madīan and of Aykah and he was the father-in-law of Mūsā. The Qur'an relates:

وَإِلَىٰ مَدْيَنَ أَخَاهُمْ شُعَيْبًا ۗ قَالَ يَٰقَوْمِ اعْبُدُوا اللَّهَ مَا لَكُم مِّنْ إِلَٰهٍ غَيْرُهُ ۖ قَدْ جَاءَتْكُم بَيِّنَةٌ
مِّن رَّبِّكُمْ ۖ فَأَوْفُوا الْكَيْلَ وَالْمِيزَانَ وَلَا تَبْخَسُوا النَّاسَ أَشْيَاءَهُمْ وَلَا تُفْسِدُوا فِى الْأَرْضِ
بَعْدَ إِصْلَٰحِهَا ۚ ذَٰلِكُمْ خَيْرٌ لَّكُمْ إِن كُنتُم مُّؤْمِنِينَ وَلَا تَقْعُدُوا بِكُلِّ صِرَٰطٍ تُوعِدُونَ
وَتَصُدُّونَ عَن سَبِيلِ اللَّهِ مَنْ ءَامَنَ بِهِ وَتَبْغُونَهَا عِوَجًا ۚ وَاذْكُرُوا إِذْ كُنتُمْ قَلِيلًا فَكَثَّرَكُمْ ۖ
وَانظُرُوا كَيْفَ كَانَ عَٰقِبَةُ الْمُفْسِدِينَ وَإِن كَانَ طَائِفَةٌ مِّنكُمْ ءَامَنُوا بِالَّذِى أُرْسِلْتُ بِهِ
وَطَائِفَةٌ لَّمْ يُؤْمِنُوا فَاصْبِرُوا حَتَّىٰ يَحْكُمَ اللَّهُ بَيْنَنَا ۚ وَهُوَ خَيْرُ الْحَٰكِمِينَ

"And to Madīan their brother Shuʿayb عليه السلام; he said, "Oh my people, serve God! You have no other god than He; there has now come to you a clear sign from your Lord. So fill up the measure and the balance and diminish not the goods of the people and do not spread corruption in the land, after it has been set right; that is better for you, if you are believers.

And do not sit in every path, threatening and barring from God's way those who believe in Him, desiring to make it crooked. And remember when you were few, and He multiplied you and behold,

how was the end of the workers of corruption. And if there is a
party of you who believe the Message I have been sent with and a
party who believe not, be patient till God shall judge between us;
He is the best of judges.'" [4]

Shu'ayb 🕊 lived and preached in Madīan until his people drove him out. He then gathered a group of followers, five hundred in number, and settled with them in the village of Aykah. Most of Shu'ayb's counsel to his people concerned their fraudulent business practices. He exhorted them to use correct weights and measures and not to lie, deceive or cheat. The people of this area were famed for their craftiness and highway robbery.

Shu'ayb 🕊 posted himself at a mountain-pass between the two towns and addressed all the passers-by. As he stood upon his rock, his staff in his hand, his beard reaching to his navel and his heart ablaze with Divine Love, people could not help but be impressed by this radiant figure. His words were strong and furious, and many people stopped and listened to him even against their will. Secretly, people would come from Madīan and gather in Shu'ayb's house to worship and to hear his preaching and Shu'ayb's following grew. But the earth has ears, and soon this secret meeting place became known and Shu'ayb 🕊 and his followers were driven out again. Shu'ayb 🕊 continued to preach at the pass until the Madīanites posted soldiers to prevent people from stopping there and listening to him. The soldiers were both godless and deaf, so they could not hear Shu'ayb's persuasive speech and be swayed by it.

Word of these threats to Shu'ayb's safety reached Milan, the chief of a Muslim tribe friendly to Shu'ayb 🕊, and he called for the prophet and said to him, "If you wish, we will migrate with you to another land, for I hear that the Madīanites are plotting against you."

---

[4] Sūratu 'l-'Arāf (the Heights),7:85-87.

Shuʿayb عليه السلام answered, "If I were to go anywhere it would be to the Kaʿbah but my Lord has commanded me to enter the cities of Madīan and Aykah and to preach openly there in spite of the opposition."

Milan was worried and asked, "What if they harm you?"

"Allah Almighty will protect me in the midst of all adversity and I must obey His Command. I am going alone and I fear that I am being sent to them to deliver the last warning before the Wrath of Allah comes upon them. I pray day and night that He may grant us more time, for it has been revealed to me that a terrible fate will befall them if they do not repent and mend their ways. As a shepherd herds his flocks, so a prophet looks over the herd of believers and takes care of them; but a day may come when a prophet is powerless over the lot of his nation as a shepherd may sometimes be helpless in the face of a fire or some other calamity that comes over his flock, and he stands by and looks on their destruction which he cannot avert. My heart burns for what I see coming upon the people of Madīan, for man is the crown of Allah's creation and it pains me beyond measure to see this perfection go to waste and be destroyed. Do not ask me, Milan, to reveal my vision to you, for this I may not do. It is too terrible to recollect, and I pray with all my might that it be Allah's Will to spare them and to make me the intercessor for my nation."

Milan watched him go down to Madīan and his heart was heavy, "Let us never forget the stories of the prophets of old," he said to his people," and the warnings they contain for us. For the Wrath of Allah may be unleashed upon us at any time and nothing will save us from it."

Shuʿayb عليه السلام entered Madīan just as the chiefs were gathered in conference, plotting to move against the Muslims and to drive them from their land. Shuʿayb عليه السلام stood up and spoke to them, reminding them of the unity of God and of the gratitude they owed to Him.

"Allah has granted you gifts He has given to no other idol-worshipping people: He has increased the years of your lives beyond the usual number and He has granted you health and wealth in abundance. Honor Him and show your thankfulness by dealing justly with your neighbors and partners in commerce. Do not use false weights when you are measuring and do not exchange truth for falsehood. If you do not mind my admonishment, the chastisement of the Lord will come upon you and woe unto you for there will be no escape!"

But the only answer he got was this, in the words of the Qur'an:

قَالَ الْمَلَأُ الَّذِينَ اسْتَكْبَرُوا مِن قَوْمِهِ لَنُخْرِجَنَّكَ يَٰشُعَيْبُ وَالَّذِينَ ءَامَنُوا مَعَكَ مِن قَرْيَتِنَا
أَوْ لَتَعُودُنَّ فِى مِلَّتِنَا ۚ قَالَ أَوَلَوْ كُنَّا كَٰرِهِينَ قَدِ افْتَرَيْنَا عَلَى اللَّهِ كَذِبًا إِنْ عُدْنَا فِى
مِلَّتِكُم بَعْدَ إِذْ نَجَّىٰنَا اللَّهُ مِنْهَا ۚ وَمَا يَكُونُ لَنَا أَن نَّعُودَ فِيهَا إِلَّا أَن يَشَاءَ اللَّهُ رَبُّنَا ۚ وَسِعَ
رَبُّنَا كُلَّ شَىْءٍ عِلْمًا ۚ عَلَى اللَّهِ تَوَكَّلْنَا ۚ رَبَّنَا افْتَحْ بَيْنَنَا وَبَيْنَ قَوْمِنَا بِالْحَقِّ وَأَنتَ خَيْرُ
الْفَٰتِحِينَ وَقَالَ الْمَلَأُ الَّذِينَ كَفَرُوا مِن قَوْمِهِ لَئِنِ اتَّبَعْتُمْ شُعَيْبًا إِنَّكُمْ إِذًا لَّخَٰسِرُونَ

"Said the Counsel of those of his people who waxed proud 'We will surely expel thee, O Shu'ayb, and those who believe with thee, from our city, unless you return to our creed.' He said, 'What, even though we detest it? We should have forged against God a lie if we returned into your creed, after God delivered us from it. It is not for us to return into it, unless God our Lord so will. Our Lord embraces all things in His knowledge. In God we have put our trust. Our Lord, give true deliverance between us and our people; Thou art the belt of deliverers." Said the Council of those of his

people who disbelieved, 'Now if you follow Shu'ayb, assuredly in that case you will be losers.'" [5]

With this answer they seized him and dragged him out of town, warning him not to show his face again if he valued his life at all. Shuʿayb ﷺ traveled throughout the surrounding villages and preached to whomever he encountered. At last, he came to a village of believers and rested there for a while. Again the believers implored him to leave this hostile land and to lead them out of danger but Shuʿayb ﷺ was driven by holy fire and he answered them, "Allah Almighty has charged me with this task and I may not turn from it unless it be His Command. As long as there is life, there is hope and He alone knows when a people is beyond reform. I intend now to descend into the town of Aykah, although it is already late in the day."

His people tried as they might to dissuade him, for they were fearful for their prophet. He was a stranger to that town and its inhabitants were known for their cruelty and hostility for which reason they are also called the Asḥābu 'r-Rass in the Holy Qur'an. But Shuʿayb ﷺ set out trusting in his Lord for protection and the believers prayed throughout that night for a good outcome. Shuʿayb ﷺ traveled through the night and at first light reached the town of Aykah. The women espied him first and quickly spread the word. "That crazy man from Madīan has arrived again. Come to the market-square, perhaps we'll have some fun."

Shuʿayb ﷺ stood atop a platform and with his staff and motioned for silence. "Tell us something new this time," someone cried. "We are tired of hearing the same thing over and over again."

Shuʿayb ﷺ spoke, "I have come to tell you what I have told you before but this time will be the last, for I am sent to warn you of the Wrath of Allah. If you do not repent and mend your stubborn ways,

---

[5] Sūratu 'l-ʿArāf (the Heights), 7:88-90.

nothing can save you from certain destruction." When he had finished speaking, people were brought up against him and accused him of being a liar and an impostor and challenged him:

قالوا إنما أنتَ مِنَ المُسَحَّرِينَ وَما أنتَ إلّا بَشَرٌ مِثلُنا وإن نَظُنُّكَ لِمنَ الكَذِبِينَ

فَأَسقِط عَلَينا كِسَفًا مِنَ السَّماءِ إن كُنتَ مِنَ الصَّدِقِينَ قالَ رَبّى أَعلَمُ بِما تَعمَلونَ

They said, "Thou art merely one of those that are bewitched; Thou art not but a mortal, like us. Indeed, we think that thou art one of the liars. Then drop down on us lumps from heaven, if thou art one of the truthful."

He said, "My Lord knows very well what you are doing."[6]

They insulted him and accused him of stealing their tune then they dragged him down from his place and threw stones at him and all the while Shuʿayb ﷺ was calling Allah to be his witness. As they were pushing and pulling him out of the gates, one man remarked in astonishment, "This madman is blind yet he addresses us as if he were seeing. He walks this road as if he sees it, never falling or stumbling or bumping into things yet he has been blind from birth." But Shuʿayb ﷺ was not born blind. He became blind three times during his life; each time he was completing another hundred years of age. He was blinded and then the Lord restored his eyesight again.

Shuʿayb ﷺ roamed the hills by night and received no further revelation. He climbed a mountain and looked sadly towards Aykah and muttered to himself, *"Lā ḥawla wa lā quwwata illa biLlāhi 'l-ʿalīyyi 'l-ʿaẓīm."*[7] These people have amassed so many riches and so great a fortune by unjust means - robbery, theft and fraud. All their wealth is unlawful. Their hearts have been poisoned by greed and miserliness

---

[6] Sūratu 'sh-Shuʿarā (the Poets), 26:185-188.

[7] Arabic: There is no might and no power except with Allah, the Most High, the Magnificent.

so that they have no understanding left." Then, he turned towards Madīan and saw a number of people in the distance. They approached and he recognized them as Milan's envoys and showed himself to them. They were out looking for him and when they met, they praised and thanked the Lord, and told him of what had happened after his departure from Madīan. The unbelievers had attacked their villages and robbed them and driven them out into the hills. There, they had sought refuge in caves and prayed only to be granted the company of their prophet for without him they knew not what to do.

Shuʿayb ﷺ went off by himself to meditate on the matter, and when he returned to them he looked very sad. He told them that revelation had come to him and that they should be patient. It was not yet the time for him to lead them to the Kaʿbah. They asked him the reason for his sorrow and in answer he pointed in the direction of Aykah and said "The Wrath of Allah is descending." Then he gathered the believers around him and led them in prayer.

Meanwhile, in Aykah the chastisement of Allah began. People had asked for fire to be sent down upon them from the skies and the Lord hears and sees. Suddenly, something happened to them so that they felt a great pain within their hearts and a burning as if fire had been dropped onto them. In their houses, on their fields, everyone was affected and began running around madly, not knowing how to escape. They crowded into the city, believing it to be cooler there but the heat within them and around them grew steadily and they found no relief. Strangely, it was only the people who were affected. None of the animals or flocks suffered. At last, they perceived a cloud in the sky, and they thought, "This cloud will surely bring us relief from this intolerable heat for a cloud in the desert is usually a good sign of rain, or at least a shade from the fiercely burning sun." People jumped about as if deranged on account of the extreme heat and they tried to hide themselves in wells and ditches which, they dug in hope of finding shelter. However, the earth itself had heated up and their wells were as furnaces and they burnt to death in them. Their last hope was the cloud overhead. They all ran to gather beneath it to find cooling shade. Finally, nobody remained outside of its shadow and whoever stretched out his hand beyond it quickly withdrew it again, for it seemed that everything was ablaze outside the shelter of that giant cloud. There they lay and relaxed for a while, expecting a refreshing rain to fall upon them. Some fell asleep, others began to sing songs in praise of their gods who had saved them, as they believed, from the scorching heat and Shuʿayb's sorcery.

Suddenly, the cloud burst. It was not water that rained upon them, however, but fire. Fire from the sky fell upon them and they perished there, each and every one, charred and blackened. Then the earth, itself, began to heave and rock, gently at first, then with increasing violence until the charred corpses were flung against the rocks and the bursting earth swallowed them up. All trace of them was lost. Nothing remained but the stench of burnt flesh which lingered in the air. All because of their chief and their denial of the true Owner of all the world. He took from them all He had given them and they had no power against Him who is the Giver and Taker of all things. This was the fate of the 'Companions of the Thicket' (Aykah), and it is mentioned in the Qur'an:

فَكَذَّبُوهُ فَأَخَذَهُمْ عَذَابُ يَوْمِ الظُّلَّةِ ۚ إِنَّهُ كَانَ عَذَابَ يَوْمٍ عَظِيمٍ

...then there seized them the chastisement of the Day of Shadow; assuredly it was the chastisement of a dreadful day[8]

انطَلِقُوا إِلَىٰ ظِلٍّ ذِى ثَلَٰثِ شُعَبٍ لَّا ظَلِيلٍ وَلَا يُغْنِى مِنَ اللَّهَبِ إِنَّهَا تَرْمِى بِشَرَرٍ كَالْقَصْرِ كَأَنَّهُ جِمَٰلَتٌ صُفْرٌ وَيْلٌ يَوْمَئِذٍ لِّلْمُكَذِّبِينَ

[8] Sūratu 'sh-Shuʿarā (the Poets), 26:189.

Depart to that you cried was lie! Depart to a triplemassing shadow unshading against the blazing flame that shoots sparks like dry faggots, sparks like to golden herds. Woe that day unto those who cry it lies![9]

The Muslims stood and watched this destruction and were struck speechless from horror and awe. Shuʿayb ﷺ said to them, "Let us turn away from this site of damnation, for it is not good to linger where the punishment of Allah has taken place; there is not a soul left alive and nothing for us to do here." They left and rejoined the encampment of their own people who received their prophet with great joy and relief. They were very moved when they heard of the events and they wept for those who had perished in godlessness. Then, they turned towards Madīan. When they had come within sight of the city, they perceived that the earth was trembling and rippling in waves like the sea, while the ground on which they stood remained firm. As they looked on, the city crumbled and fell. There arose a great tumult and shouts of terror were heard as the earth split open and everything was crushed and swallowed. Within the hour all was gone. The earth was flat and quiet once more and only a huge cloud of dust hung over the place where once the city of Madīan had stood:

فَأَخَذَتْهُمُ الرَّجْفَةُ فَأَصْبَحُوا فِى دَارِهِمْ جَٰثِمِينَ ٱلَّذِينَ كَذَّبُوا شُعَيْبًا كَأَن لَّمْ يَغْنَوْا فِيهَا ۚ
الَّذِينَ كَذَّبُوا شُعَيْبًا كَانُوا هُمُ الْخَٰسِرِينَ فَتَوَلَّىٰ عَنْهُمْ وَقَالَ يَٰقَوْمِ لَقَدْ أَبْلَغْتُكُمْ رِسَٰلَٰتِ
رَبِّى وَنَصَحْتُ لَكُمْ ۖ فَكَيْفَ ءَاسَىٰ عَلَىٰ قَوْمٍ كَٰفِرِينَ

So the earthquake seized them and morning found them in their habitation fallen prostrate.

[9] Sūratu 'n-Nāziʿat (Those sent forth), 79:30-34.

Those who cried lies to Shuʿayb ﷺ, as if never they dwelt there; those who cried lies to Shuʿayb ﷺ, they were the losers. So he turned his back on them and said, "O my people, I have delivered to you the Messages of my Lord, and advised you sincerely. How should I grieve for people of unbelievers?"[10]

وَلَمَّا جَاءَ أَمْرُنَا نَجَّيْنَا شُعَيْبًا وَالَّذِينَ ءَامَنُوا مَعَهُ بِرَحْمَةٍ مِّنَّا وَأَخَذَتِ الَّذِينَ ظَلَمُوا الصَّيْحَةُ فَأَصْبَحُوا فِي دِيَرِهِمْ جَثِمِينَ ۝ كَأَن لَّمْ يَغْنَوْا فِيهَا ۗ أَلَا بُعْدًا لِّمَدْيَنَ كَمَا بَعِدَتْ ثَمُودُ

And when Our command came, We delivered Shuʿayb ﷺ and those who believed with him by a mercy from Us and the evildoers were seized by the Cry, and morning found them in their habitations fallen prostrate as if they had never dwelt there; "So away with Madīan, even as Thamūd was done away!"([11]

The Muslims stood in silence watching the punishment descend upon Madīan and no one dared speak for a long time afterwards. In the morning, Shuʿayb ﷺ addressed his people and said, "Oh steadfast believers, the Lord orders us to leave this site of destruction and to pass on to the north. I will lead you through the desert of Tih, past the Lake of Lūṭ and the Dead Sea, through the land of Palestine as far as Shām. Make ready quickly, for we must leave this accursed place!"

The Muslims were ready to go wherever their prophet would lead them and they set out with no delay. Shuʿayb ﷺ walked on ahead of them but he turned to look back frequently. Why did he look back? Because the Lord had given him vision and he was able to see everything that had happened hundreds of years ago in the lands

[10] Sūratu 'l-ʿĀrāf (The Heights), 7: 91-93.
[11] Sūrah Hūd, 11: 94 -95.

they were crossing. He perceived these even as they were in the present and he informed his people of what he saw. He described to them how godlessness had spread among the Egyptians. He told them that they had become an evil people under the new Firʿawn, and the Chidlren of Isrā'īl had adopted their evil ways. He showed them the well into which Yūsuf ﷺ had been cast, the Lake of Lut and the site of the ruined cities of Sodom and Gomorrah. He showed them the tombs of Ibrahim ﷺ and Isḥāq ﷺ and Yʿaqūb ﷺ and he told them the stories of all these prophets of the past. "Man is created weak," he said, "and falls into every snare the accursed Shayṭān prepares for him. Again and again the prophets were sent to teach men righteousness and each and every time men returned to do the evil bidding of Shayṭān and their lower inclinations. In this way, they sell their souls for a slight price and lose everything in the bargain."

Shuʿayb ﷺ and his band of followers traveled for years, until they reached Babylon and Nineveh. They visited the place where Nimrūd had cast Ibrāhīm ﷺ into the fire and the place where the Ark of Nūḥ had landed. At last, they returned to their old country and found a new people settled there. They told them of all that had come to pass in that place and the believers bore witness. Then he led them on towards the south, past the cities of Ṣāliḥ ﷺ and Hūd ﷺ and the gardens of Irām and finally they crossed the great and stony deserts and came to the Kaʿbah which had forever been Shuʿayb's greatest longing. They drank from the water of the well Zam-Zam and prayed with grateful hearts to the Lord who had led them to His sanctuary.

Shuʿayb ﷺ stayed and settled there and preached to the tribes of that region who had forgotten what the prophets of old had taught them, and remembered not even the holiness of the place they lived in. They had, in time, begun to believe in all sorts of odd superstitions. They believed that man was descended from giant apes that had come out of Asia, great white apes, three times as tall as men, and they revered them as their ancestors. Shuʿayb ﷺ preached to them and taught them about Allah's creation and the honor bestowed upon mankind to be His representative on Earth and that this is his highest destiny, to become worthy of this station. Shu'ayb 🕮 was now very old but his voice was powerful and people came from far and wide to hear his words and many believed.

Shu'ayb 🕮 had nearly completed his 300th year when he felt death approaching. He lay down, and a few days later he surrendered his soul. The Muslims buried him in the vicinity of the Ka'bah, between the Maqām Ibrāhīm[12] and the Rukn.[13] May Allah's Mercy be upon his soul forever.

Āmīn.

---

[12]Maqām Ibrāhīm: The Standing Place of Ibrāhīm - a stone containing the imprints of Ibrāhīm's feet – located besides the Ka'bah. It is enclosed in a dome on four pillars and worshippers offer their prayers upon completing the circumambulation (*ṭawāf*).
[13] The Yemeni Corner of the Ka'bah.

musa: fir'awn comes to egypt

In Palestine, there was a young man named Walīd, the son of a blacksmith. He had a friend called Hāmān. They were both headstrong and willful young men. One day, Walīd quarreled with his father and was thrown out of the house. Walīd and his friend, Hāmān, took to the road and they led the life of adventurers and brigands, roaming the countryside and living from day to day. At last, they came to Egypt. There, they rented a field near to the gates of Cairo and stayed for a year, planting watermelon. That year, the harvest was good and their fruit was delicious. They bought animals and carts to transport the melons into the markets of the city but the guards at the city gates stood in their way and exacted the tax for the king. Walīd grew angry and began to argue with them. The more he argued the more the guards raised the tax and in the end he had to give in. So he paid the tax and entered the city with his melons. He and his friend went in to see the king and complain of the high tax they had been made to pay.

The king said to them, "If you were in my place you would do the same. And if a person argued with you, you would only increase the tax. If you own land, you can do the same."

Walīd said, "Yes, maybe you are right. But if I were to exact such dues, who would pay me? Give me a written authorization and the case is settled."

The king gave him written permission to levy whatever tax he wished on his land and to sell at whatever price he could obtain.

Walīd winked at his friend and said to him, "Now our fortunes are made."

After that year's melon harvest was sold, Walīd built a strong wall around his field and set up a number of gravestones to make the place like a cemetery. He made it known publicly that this lot was to be the new graveyard, and people brought their dead to be buried there. At first, Walīd charged them only a small fee. But one day, the king's daughter died and was brought there for burial and Walīd asked a very high price for the gravesite. They began to bargain with him and the price doubled. The more they argued, the higher the price rose. Finally they brought him before the king and Walīd showed him the writ he had received from his own hand, entitling him to charge whatever price he would. "Take it or leave it", he said to the king and the king paid what he asked.

In time, Walīd earned so much money off this profitable business of burying the dead that he built himself a regular palace and housed all his friends and associates in separate mansions and luxurious villas. He grew so rich that his lifestyle surpassed that of the king himself and he assumed the appearance of a lord. He still buried the poor without charge but from the wealthy he would demand exorbitant fees. The notables of the city began to complain of his excessive prices.

At last, the king summoned him to call him to account for his practices. Walīd entered the audience hall in a more regal attire than the king, himself. He was a handsome young man and so he made a good impression. He also had the gift of words. He knew how to twist and turn his phrases so that he always seemed to be in agreement with whatever the king said to him and yet get his own way. He was a born diplomat and a politician by nature. The king was not a complete fool and soon recognized these qualities in the man who stood before him. He said to him, "Is it not a shame that a man of your talents should waste his time dealing with what no longer can be changed, for the dead have no more say in the affairs of the kingdom. I invite you to become my vizier and advisor at court, you will accept the position." Walīd accepted, and so became the advisor of the king of Egypt.

For a while, all went well. His advice was good. The king was pleased and the affairs of the court and government flourished. But Walīd had secret ambitions which he discussed with no one but his trusted friend Hāmān. One day, in order to win the favor of the people, he decided to give back all the money he had made from his business with the people and he offered to pay all that year's taxes for them. People rejoiced and were full of praise for this generous official. When the king's Grand Wazir died, Walīd took his place and his influence, grew.

One day, the king asked Walīd, "How do I stand in public opinion, I wonder?"

"I will find out for you," answered Walīd.

He went out in disguise and listened to people's talk in the marketplaces but he knew very well what he would say to the king. "The people say, 'Our king is a good and just ruler and we are satisfied with him but he is not as generous as he used to be. Formerly, he would invite us once a year to a great banquet at the palace. Now he has grown rich and miserly and we love him not as we used to.' "

The king decided, at once, to remedy the situation and gave orders to prepare a great feast to which all were invited. He charged Walīd with the organization of this event and public notices were posted all over the city. The preparation continued, but secretly Walīd had all the food poisoned. Then he spread the rumor among the townspeople that the king had treacherous designs in inviting them all to the palace. He intended to poison all their chiefs and notables so that he could usurp their belongings and line his own pockets. The people took this warning seriously came hiding a knife or dagger beneath their robes. The food was served, and the guests were invited to eat but no one would touch the food. They said to the king, "We are suspicious of you. We will only eat after you have tasted the food first."

The food was then given to the slaves and dogs to sample. The first mouthful of food they tasted caused them to fall down and die. People saw their suspicions confirmed and fell upon the king and slew him. Then, they turned in gratitude towards Walīd and said, "Had it not been for your warning, we would all be lying here dead and poisoned now. You have saved us, you must become our king."

So, the treacherous Walīd became king and Fir'awn of Egypt. He took as his vizier his close friend, Hāmān, and for a while they governed the land justly and with success. They lowered the taxes and gave bread to the poor and lived in ease and splendor, themselves. After some time, Hāmān suggested to his friend, "Your rule is going well your hand is blessed with success. Why don't you make them believe that you are their god? Then your power over them will be absolute." Thereafter, Fir'awn came to be regarded as divine in the land of Egypt.

Centuries passed. Walīd lived for a very long time, for 450 years. The story of his origin and ascent to the throne was forgotten. No one lived who remembered the truth of the event or whoever did was quickly silenced. There was no one to dispute Fir'awn's divinity. The cult spread throughout Egypt and became the state religion. The Children of Isrā'īl had been living in Egypt for many years, since the time of Yūsuf ﷺ and the friendly reception they had received from the former Fir'awn had gradually cooled as they kept to themselves and did not mingle with the Egyptians or join in their cult of Fir'awn. They became oppressed and humiliated and were made to do slave labor. They were treated as the lowest of the low.

One night, Fir'awn saw a dream: Among the Banī-Isrā'īl, there grew a tree and it grew to a great height. He saw many people holding on to its branches. Suddenly all the people holding the branches fell upon Firʿawn and his palace and destroyed it utterly. Firʿawn was worried by this vision and called his soothsayers to interpret it to him. His wise men said, "It is clear. A man will be born to the Banī-Isrā'īl and will wrest the power from your hand." But they could not tell him when this event would take place. Firʿawn then gave orders for all the male children born to the children of Isrā'īl to be put to death that year. But the midwives hid the birth of babies saying, "The women of the Israelites are not like Egyptian women. They are strong and their offspring is delivered before the midwife comes to them." But the Egyptian soldiers killed any male children they could find. After a few years, they grew worried that they would run out of slaves if they killed all the male offspring, and so the infant slaughter was ordered in alternate years.

the BIRTH of musa

وَاذكُر فِى الكِتٰبِ موسىٰ ۚ إِنَّهُ كانَ مُخلَصًا وَكانَ رَسولًا نَبِيًّا

And mention in the Book Moses; he was devoted, and he was a Messenger, a Prophet.[14]

نَتلوا عَلَيكَ مِن نَبَإِ موسىٰ وَفِرعَونَ بِالحَقِّ لِقَومٍ يُؤمِنونَ إِنَّ فِرعَونَ

عَلا فِى الأَرضِ وَجَعَلَ أَهلَها شِيَعًا يَستَضعِفُ طائِفَةً مِنهُم يُذَبِّحُ أَبناءَهُم وَيَستَحيۦ

نِساءَهُم ۚ إِنَّهُ كانَ مِنَ المُفسِدينَ

Now Firʿawn had exalted himself in the land and had divided its inhabitants into sects, abasing one party of them, slaughtering their sons, and sparing their women; for he was of the workers of corruption.[15]

Mūsā's father was Imran of the house of Levi and his mother was Yohabith, descended also from Yaʿqūb's son Levi. His elder brother was Hārūn and he had a sister named Miryam. The name 'Mūsā' is derived from two words, 'Mū' meaning water, and 'Sā' meaning wood, which indicates that he came out of the water in a box of wood. The year Mūsā was born was a year of terror for the mothers of Isrā'īl because the soldiers were again making their rounds, killing the sons of Isrā'īl. At his birth, Mūsā radiated such light that even his own mother could hardly look him in the face. When the soldiers knocked at the door she swaddled the child and hid it in a corner of the house. She told the soldiers that she had been mistaken. She had not been pregnant after all and her illness had passed. But the

---

[14] Sūrah Maryam (the Virgin Mary), 19:51.

[15] Sūratu 'l-Qaṣaṣ (The Story), 28: 3-4.

soldiers did not believe her and demanded entrance to search the house. In her despair, Mūsā's mother threw him into the burning stove and closed the lid. Then she let them in. The soldiers searched the house and found nothing. They believed her then and left. When they had gone, Mūsā's mother said to her daughter Miryam, "Go and bring out your baby brother's body from the fire. He must have burnt to ashes by now." The girl looked in the oven and found the child unharmed, bathed in sweat but safe and whole. They praised the Lord and hid the child in the house for a whole year and this was easy for them for the child never cried.

After his mother had nursed him for a whole year, Mūsā began to raise his voice and the household grew afraid that the neighbors might betray them. His mother did not know what to do and prayed to the Lord for help. One day, she heard a voice calling to her from the Unseen, and this is one example of Divine Inspiration being sent to a woman. "Do not fear," she was told, "have a box made. Place the child within it and throw it into the river Nile. Your Lord will look after the rest."

Mūsā's mother obeyed the voice and went to a carpenter who would make for her such a box as she described. "What are you planning to do with such a box?" he asked her. She gave him no answer. The carpenter guessed the truth of the matter and followed her to find out for certain. There was a high reward for informers and severe punishment for any family that attempted to hide their sons. The child, his mother and the whole household were put to death and the house razed to the ground. The carpenter knew this but he thought only of his reward. When he knew for sure that his suspicion was correct he went to the officer on duty to inform. But when he tried to speak, his tongue twisted in his mouth and no sound came from his lips. He tried to make signs with his hands, but his muscles refused to obey him, and he appeared to be a paralytic, saliva dribbling from his open mouth. "Who is this man?" asked the Egyptian officer, and had him thrown out.

Once outside, he became well again, and lusting for the money paid to informers he went back in. But inside the police station, his strange condition returned and he could form no words. The soldiers threw him out once more and, regaining his health, he tried yet another time but could utter no sound. By now, the police were convinced he was a madman and they gave him a good beating before they threw him out into the street and warned him not to come again. Now his reason returned and the carpenter understood that this child must be a special child, that he could be none other than the boy about whom the prophecy pertained. He repented of his evil designs and made the box for Mūsā to be laid in and took it to his mother, revealing his knowledge to her. They placed the child in the box and at night took it down to the Nile and watched it float away.

Even though Mūsā's mother knew she was acting with divine guidance, she still felt a mother's pain at throwing her own child into the river and she lamented for him. She wept and cried until she was again addressed by the voice from the Unseen, "Fear nothing! We will protect him and he will be returned to your breast!" Mūsā's mother took heart and was patient. Now a branch of the river Nile was channeled off and flowed through the palace gardens, later to rejoin the mainstream. That day, Firʿawn and his wife Āsīyah were strolling in the gardens. Suddenly they noticed something bobbing up and down in the waters and Āsīyah said to her attendants, "Go and see what it is; if it is a living being, it shall be mine, if it is anything else, perhaps a precious treasure. It shall be yours." The slave girls ran and fetched the box out of the water, and tried to open it but try as they might could find no way to pry it open.

Firʿawn had a daughter from another marriage and she bore a blemish on her body for which no doctor could find a remedy. But the astrologers had predicted that on a particular day a creature will appear from the waters of the Nile, emerging from between two boards of wood. If the spittle of this creature is applied to the disease, it will pass away and there is no remedy but this. Now gradually the whole court had assembled around the box and not one was able to open it. Firʿawn's wife Āsīyah came and said, "Let me try to open it, perhaps I will succeed." She stretched out her hand and the box opened all by itself. As soon as she beheld the child in the box, Āsīyah's heart was filled with love and Mūsā looked up at her smiling. Light issued from his regard and he was sucking on the fingers of his right hand. Āsīyah lifted the child upon her lap and saw that from each of his fingers flowed a different sub-stance. From one finger came milk, from another butter, from a third honey, from the fourth water and from the fifth cream. When she withdrew his hand from his mouth Mūsā began to cry. She tried to comfort him but had no success. All the women held him in turn, but he continued to cry. Even Firʿawn himself held him in his arm, for he liked the child instantly in spite of himself, though he secretly feared it might be the child his astrologers had predicted would destroy him.

Firʿawn's daughter also took the crying baby in her arms, and when some of his saliva dribbled onto her arm her skin became cleansed and healthy in that spot. She began to collect his spittle and rubbed it on her whole face and body, and she was healed in an instant of the disease that had plagued her whole life. Now she said to her father, "Look at this miracle, this child is not the one predicted in your dream, but rather the one the astrologers foretold to me would occasion my healing. And see what has happened. I have become clean and no trace remains of my disease."

Āsīyah then said to her husband, "Oh my lord, we have no male children. Let us raise him as our son." Firʿawn answered her, "Take him then as your son." Had he only said, "Let us take him as our own son," he too would have become a believer and a follower of the prophet Mūsā but it was the Will of the Almighty that this was not to be, and it was destined from pre-eternity.

So Āsīyah kept the child. He would no stop crying, however, and they knew not what to do about this. It was as if Mūsā were making up for the whole year that he had never once cried. They offered him every sort of food. They brought wet-nurses from all over but he would accept neither food nor suckle.

Not far away, Mūsā's mother heard that Fir'awn's people had found something in the river which had caused a stir in the palace and she wondered whether it might be her baby son. Again she was addressed from the Unseen, "Be patient a little while longer, We will give him back to you very soon." She sent her daughter, Miryam, to find out what was happening and she learnt that they had found a child that would not stop crying and that even Fir'awn was occupied with trying to quiet him. This child would accept no wet-nurse and no food.

Miryam's heart leapt and said, "I happen to know a woman who had nursed the children of many noble families and no child has ever rejected her milk. If you wish, I will lead her to you."

They said, "What are you waiting for? This child is more than we can handle."

Miryam ran to fetch her mother and she took him to her breast. He drank and, fell asleep on her lap. Again, murmurs were heard in the palace that she must be the child's own mother and that he was indeed the child foretold to be Fir'awn's undoing as the woman was plainly of the Banī Isrā'īl. Āsīyah objected and said, "No, it is only that this woman has a great deal of experience with infants and her milk is clean and healthy; that is why he will take her breast and not that of any Egyptian wet-nurse." Thus, Āsīyah housed Mūsā's 🕮 mother, nicely in the palace. Yohabith was given her own apartments with attendants and her only office was to nurse her own baby son. The story is also told in the Qur'an:

فَالْتَقَطَهُ ءَالُ فِرْعَوْنَ لِيَكُونَ لَهُمْ عَدُوًّا وَحَزَنًا ۗ إِنَّ فِرْعَوْنَ وَهَٰمَٰنَ وَجُنُودَهُمَا كَانُوا
خَٰطِـِٔينَ   وَقَالَتِ امْرَأَتُ فِرْعَوْنَ قُرَّتُ عَيْنٍ لِّى وَلَكَ ۖ لَا تَقْتُلُوهُ عَسَىٰٓ أَن يَنفَعَنَآ أَوْ نَتَّخِذَهُۥ
وَلَدًا وَهُمْ لَا يَشْعُرُونَ   وَأَصْبَحَ فُؤَادُ أُمِّ مُوسَىٰ فَٰرِغًا ۖ إِن كَادَتْ لَتُبْدِى بِهِۦ لَوْلَآ أَن
رَّبَطْنَا عَلَىٰ قَلْبِهَا لِتَكُونَ مِنَ الْمُؤْمِنِينَ   وَقَالَتْ لِأُخْتِهِۦ قُصِّيهِ ۖ فَبَصُرَتْ بِهِۦ عَن جُنُبٍ
وَهُمْ لَا يَشْعُرُونَ   وَحَرَّمْنَا عَلَيْهِ الْمَرَاضِعَ مِن قَبْلُ فَقَالَتْ هَلْ أَدُلُّكُمْ عَلَىٰٓ أَهْلِ بَيْتٍ
يَكْفُلُونَهُۥ لَكُمْ وَهُمْ لَهُۥ نَٰصِحُونَ   فَرَدَدْنَٰهُ إِلَىٰٓ أُمِّهِۦ كَىْ تَقَرَّ عَيْنُهَا وَلَا تَحْزَنَ وَلِتَعْلَمَ أَنَّ
وَعْدَ اللَّهِ حَقٌّ وَلَٰكِنَّ أَكْثَرَهُمْ لَا يَعْلَمُونَ

So then the folk of Fir'awn picked him out to be an enemy and a sorrow to them; certainly Fir'awn and Hāmān and their hosts, were of the sinners. Said Fir'awn's wife, "He will be a comfort to me and thee. Slay him not; perchance he will profit us or we will take him for a son." And they were not aware.
On the morrow the heart of Moses' mother became empty, and she would have disclosed him had We not strengthened her heart, that she might be among the believers; and she said to his sister "follow him," and she perceived him from afar, even while they were not aware.
Now we had forbidden him aforetime to he suckled by any foster-mother; therefore she said, "Shall I direct you to the people of a household who will take charge of him for you and look after him?" So We returned him to his mother, that she might be comforted and not sorrowful and that she might know that the promise of God is true, but most of them do not know.[16]

[16] Sūratu 'l-Qaṣaṣ (The Story), 28:8-13.

musa's childhood and youth

Time passed. Mūsā grew to be a strong little boy and Firʿawn grew very fond of him. He used to place him beside himself on the throne and sought to have him near him all the time. One day, when Firʿawn was holding court and was expounding on his own divinity, the child Mūsā got up and overturned the whole throne, so that Firʿawn's crown flew to one side, his scepter to another and Firʿawn himself lay sprawling on the floor. The guards would have seized the child and put him to death instantly because Firʿawn had strong premonitions of the truth, but again the queen Āsīyah came running to his defense, saying "He is but a child, and he knows not what he does. His extraordinary strength honors us who have raised him but how can you assume that he acted with intention? Let us test him. Bring two plates and set them before him and let him choose. In the one we will place a red rose, in the other a piece of red glowing coal. Then let him pick. If he chooses the rose, we will know that he has understanding and can be held responsible but if he chooses the fire, then he is just a child and doesn't understand what is harmful and what is not." To this, Firʿawn agreed and they did as she suggested. The plates set before him, Mūsā was going to reach for the rose, but the angel Jibrīl stayed his hand and made him pick up the burning ember. He picked up the red hot coal and placed it in his mouth, and both his hand and mouth were badly burned. That is how Mūsā's tongue became gashed and twisted "You see," said Āsīyah to Firʿawn, "he knows not what he is doing and he had no bad intention when he playfully overturned your throne." So Mūsā's life was spared once more by Āsīyah's intervention.

Mūsā grew up at Firʿawn's court, and stayed there until he was thirty years old. His mother had revealed her identity to him and he knew his brothers and sisters he kept this knowledge to himself. It is also related by some that he was married and had two children.

One day, when he was out in the streets of the city, Mūsā witnessed a scene between an Egyptian and of one his own people. The Egyptian was forcing the man to do heavy, unpaid labor for him while the man begged him to let him go and earn a livelihood for his many children. But the Egyptian showed no mercy and dragged him along by force. Mūsā was moved by this injustice and also by sentiments of kinship. He stepped up to the Egyptian and pushed him lightly against the chest. At least he thought he had pushed him only slightly, but his strength was such that his whole hand went into the man's body and he fell down mortally injured and died soon after. There were no witnesses to the deed, the other man fled in fear, for the Egyptian was a man of rank. They searched for his murderer but could not find him. Mūsā kept silent, but regretted his deed though he had not done it willfully; he hadn't been aware of his own strength.

The next day he was out in the streets again and came upon the man whom he had helped the day before. This time he was acting the bully. He was dragging a poor man off to work in spite of his protestations. Mūsā stepped up to them and the man recognized him and cried, "Ah, it is you. Have you come to kill me today like you killed that Egyptian yesterday?" He let go of his victim and ran off to get the soldiers to arrest Mūsā. Mūsā feared Firʿawn and did not know what to do. The carpenter who had built the box Mūsā had been placed in as a baby was still alive and waiting only for the day when Mūsā would reveal himself as a prophet of Isrāʾīl. He now came running to Mūsā to warn him and advised him to leave the city immediately and to flee. This is mentioned in the Qur'an:

وَجَاءَ رَجُلٌ مِّنْ أَقْصَا الْمَدِينَةِ يَسْعَىٰ قَالَ يَٰمُوسَىٰٓ إِنَّ الْمَلَأَ يَأْتَمِرُونَ بِكَ لِيَقْتُلُوكَ فَاخْرُجْ إِنِّى لَكَ مِنَ النَّٰصِحِينَ

Then came a man from the furthest part of the city, running; he said, "Moses, the Council are conspiring to slay thee. Depart; I am one of thy sincere advisers."[17]

Mūsā departed and set out towards Madīan. He did not know the way, and would have lost himself in the desert but Allah sent two angels to guide him. They appeared to him as men, one went ahead of him, the other behind. The angel in front Jibrīl, shortened the road ahead of him while Mikā'īl rolled up the road behind them. In this way they traveled a month's distance in only a day and a night.

[17] Sūratu 'l-Qaṣaṣ (The Story), 28: 20.

musa in madian

They reached a well in the land of Madīan and the angels left Mūsā there to rest beneath a tree. He was very tired, and as he lay resting he saw a group of shepherds drawing water in buckets. Then he noticed two young girls, patiently waiting their turn, shy to mingle among the men at the well. He asked them why they had waited so long, for their sheep were bleating with thirst. Had they no brothers to do this job for them? They replied, "We have only our aged father and he does not see well, so we take the sheep to pasture." Mūsā then watered their sheep for them after the other shepherds had gone, or according to another account, he lifted a stone from a second well which fifty men could not have lifted and watered their sheep for them. The girls were surprised and happy, for in those days it was not the custom to be considerate of other people, let alone help women with their work and they ran home to tell their father. They were the daughters of Shuʿayb ﵇ the prophet.

Seeing them home earlier than usual he asked them, "Did you not water the sheep today? You have returned home early today."

His daughters answered him, "Oh father, we met a stranger at the well today and he helped us water the sheep. Were you not looking to employ a shepherd? We think he may be the man for you for he rose to help us even though he was tired and resting from his long journey."

قَالَتْ إِحْدَىٰهُمَا يَٰأَبَتِ اسْتَـْٔجِرْهُ ۖ إِنَّ خَيْرَ مَنِ اسْتَـْٔجَرْتَ الْقَوِيُّ الْأَمِينُ

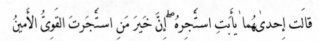

*"Said one of the two women, 'Father hire him, surely the best man
you can hire is the one strong and trusty.[18]*

Shu'ayb ☆ sent one of the girls to invite the man to the house. She approached Mūsā modestly and said, "Our father bids you come to the house and he will pay you for drawing water for us." Mūsā got up to go with the girl. At that moment Shayṭān, the ever-present, thought to himself, "This is my chance; if I can't tempt him now, I never will." So as the girl walked on, ahead of Mūsā, a sudden wind sprang up and lifted her skirts.

Mūsā lowered his gaze and said to her, "Girl, it is better you walk behind me."

"But how will you know which way to go?"

"Throw a stone ahead of me at every turn-off and I will know which direction to take," answered Mūsā.

When they reached the house, Shu'ayb ☆ greeted him and invited him for a meal to recompense his service.

Mūsā replied, "'I am a descendant of Ibrahim, the Prophet, and I accept no wages for my work."

Shu'ayb ☆ answered him, "I too am of the descendants of Ibrahim, and therefore I do not sit down to a meal before I have found a guest to share it with me."

So they agreed on the laws of hospitality and sat down together to eat. Mūsā told Shu'ayb ☆ his story and Shu'ayb ☆ set his mind at rest, saying that Madian was beyond Fir'awn's reign and that he was safe from him there. Then he went and spoke to his daughters about their guest. One of them said, "Father, I know he is a very strong and also a very good man. For at the well he lifted a stone which fifty men could not have lifted. As for his good character, when I was walking

---

[18] Sūratu 'l-Qaṣaṣ (The Story), 28: 26.

ahead of him on the way home, the wind blew and tugged at my skirts. Then he asked me to walk behind him and indicate the way by throwing a stone, in order not to gaze at what is forbidden."

Shuʿayb ﷺ then returned to his guest and said to him, "I wish to marry you to one of my daughters, provided you will herd my sheep for eight years."

Mūsā replied, "I will take the one who fetched me from the well, for she spoke well of me."

That is why we say: if someone has done good by you, repay him in kind and if you are not able to do that, at the very least speak well of him, for that is a form of *sadaqa*, charity.

the staff of musa

After they had agreed on the conditions, Shuʿayb ﵇ sent his other daughter into the next room where he kept his collection of staffs, to fetch a suitable stick for Mūsā to herd the sheep with. Shuʿayb ﵇ examined the stick she brought, feeling it with his hand, for his eyes no longer saw well and sent her back, saying, "No, this is not the night stick. Fetch another." She came with another one but her father said, "No, this is the same one, get another." So, she brought one stick after the other, but her father maintained it was still the same one and piled them to one side. At last, since there was no stick that seemed different to him, he gave him one of the sticks and said, "This one will do for you."

Mūsā took his shepherd's staff and left. As soon as he had departed Shuʿayb ﵇ realized that he had given him the one staff which meant the most to him and he fell into a state of great anxiety and concern about it. "This staff was given to me as a trust; it is none other than the staff our father Ādam ﵇ brought with him from Paradise and it has passed from the hand of one prophet to the next, down through the ages. I was charged to give it to no one but the prophet who is to appear and who will be called Kalīmullāh, The Word of God, and who will work great miracles with it. I must recover this precious trust and give him a different stick."

Shuʿayb ﵇ went after Mūsā and said, "Give me back this staff. I made a mistake, it is not meant for you but for another man." But Mūsā liked the stick and had a mind to keeping it. They would have argued about it, but just then a person approached and it occurred to them to ask for his arbitration. According to one tradition, the man told them to throw the stick to the ground and then to try to lift it up. They each wondered, for the stick was no heavier than a normal shepherd's staff. First, Shuʿayb ﵇ bent to pick up the stick but he found he could not lift it an inch off the ground. Mūsā then tried and raised the staff over his head with no difficulty. The arbitrator decided that Mūsā must be its rightful owner. Then he revealed himself to the two men; he was no man but an angel sent by the Lord of the Worlds, and he set Shuʿayb's heart at peace saying, "Oh Shuʿayb ﷺ, you may now rest, for you have completed your task. The staff has come to its owner, and you are relieved of that trust. Before you stands he who is known as Kalīmullāh in the Divine Presence. So give thanks and praise the Almighty."

Shuʿayb ﷺ was overjoyed at this news for he felt the closeness of God. His heart was always burning with longing for His Holy Presence, and this flame that was burning in Shuʿayb's heart had attracted Mūsā to him. Mūsā's rank is higher than Shuʿayb's for he was a Prophet as well as a Messenger while Shuʿayb ﷺ was only a Prophet. The Lord spoke to Mūsā without an intermediary and gave him the Law of the Tawrāt.

Mūsā went off to pasture Shuʿayb's sheep. Shuʿayb ﷺ called after him, "Oh Mūsā, don't lead my sheep towards the green fields; take them into the dry plains where everyone else grazes their sheep. In that luscious green valley dwells a terrible dragon who attacks and devours everything that comes near him. He spits poison and breathes fire and will destroy you and my flocks." Mūsā heard and obeyed, but as he went along he found he couldn't control his sheep; they strayed towards that perilous valley and nothing he did could stop them. All he could do was to follow them. As he sat watching them graze, a heavy sleep came over him which he could not resist. He drifted off into slumber, his staff by his side. After a while, he awoke and looked for his sheep. They had grazed to their heart's content and their bellies were full and bloated like the bellies of ships. Mūsā rose and reached for his staff and to his surprise he found it covered with dried blood. He looked for the trace of a fight and found pieces of the slain dragon scattered about the field. By the wisdom of the Almighty, Mūsā's staff had turned into a fierce rival dragon which had fought and killed the dreaded dragon of that valley.

Mūsā cleaned the staff and led his sheep homewards. He told Shuʿayb ﷺ what had happened and they both gave praise and thanks to the Lord, and Shuʿayb ﷺ said, "Oh Mūsā, it is indeed your very own staff; you must guard it well, for you are yet to see great miracles from it."

Musa is Sent to Fir'awn

Mūsā herded Shuʿayb's sheep for eight years, before he was married to his daughter, Zipporah.

He said to his father-in-law, "The agreed term is accomplished. With your leave I shall depart."

Shuʿayb ﵇ said, "Abide until the end of the year. Then you may go. All the lambs that are born female this year shall be yours."

That year there were only female lambs and so Mūsā's flock doubled in number. In the new year Mūsā again asked permission to leave but his wife had just given birth to a son and was unfit to travel. So, Shuʿayb ﵇ entreated him to stay another year that the ten years might be full and he promised him all the speckled lambs that were born that year. Now that year all the ewes gave twin births and all the lambs were speckled. In this way, Mūsā's flock grew very large and so the ten years were complete. Mūsā's wife was heavy with her second child and her time was near.

Mūsā took leave of his father-in-law and took the road towards Egypt for he wished to see his mother and family again, whom he had left behind when he fled from Firʿawn. Suddenly, the sky darkened and a great storm wind arose, blowing sand and rain and hail such that they were unable to maintain their intended course and soon lost their way in the desert. For several days they battled the storm and could find no shelter. They could light no fire nor erect a tent on account of the high winds and Mūsā's wife, Zipporah, went into labor. Their situation was growing desperate. Suddenly, Mūsā beheld a faint glow in the distance and said to his family, "I see in the distance what appears to be a fire."

فَلَمَّا قَضَىٰ مُوسَى ٱلْأَجَلَ وَسَارَ بِأَهْلِهِۦٓ ءَانَسَ مِن جَانِبِ ٱلطُّورِ نَارًا قَالَ لِأَهْلِهِ ٱمْكُثُوٓا۟

إِنِّىٓ ءَانَسْتُ نَارًا لَّعَلِّىٓ ءَاتِيكُم مِّنْهَا بِخَبَرٍ أَوْ جَذْوَةٍ مِّنَ ٱلنَّارِ لَعَلَّكُمْ تَصْطَلُونَ

"Perhaps I shall bring you news of it or a faggot from the fire, that haply you shall warm yourselves[19]

إِذْ رَءَا نَارًا فَقَالَ لِأَهْلِهِ ٱمْكُثُوٓا۟ إِنِّىٓ ءَانَسْتُ نَارًا لَّعَلِّىٓ ءَاتِيكُم مِّنْهَا بِقَبَسٍ أَوْ أَجِدُ عَلَى

ٱلنَّارِ هُدًى

"Perhaps I shall bring you a brand from it or I shall find at the fire guidance,"[20]

Mūsā set out in the direction of the fire and, as he came close to it, made out a bush which was enclosed in a shroud of light which resembled fire yet the tree was not consumed by the burning.

فَلَمَّآ أَتَىٰهَا نُودِىَ يَٰمُوسَىٰٓ إِنِّىٓ أَنَا۠ رَبُّكَ فَٱخْلَعْ نَعْلَيْكَ ۖ إِنَّكَ بِٱلْوَادِ ٱلْمُقَدَّسِ طُوًى

When he came to it, a voice cried, "Moses I am thy Lord; put off thy shoes; thou art in the holy valley of Tuwa."[21]

As soon as Mūsā had left his group, the storm died down and all was calm. His men set out to look for him, but they could find no trace of Mūsā or the fire, though they were expert in reading tracks. The Lord had veiled him from them. The Lord revealed Himself to Mūsā and for three days and nights he was engaged in communion with Him. Mūsā nearly succumbed to the awe and fear His Holy Presence caused in him and trembled, shook and was stricken by dumb terror.

In order to allay his fear, the Lord distracted his attention and asked:

---

[19] Sūratu 'l-Qaṣaṣ (The Story), 28: 29.

[20] Sūrah ṬāḤā, 20:10.

[21] Sūrah ṬāḤā, 20:11-12.

وَما تِلكَ بِيَمينِكَ يٰموسىٰ قالَ هِىَ عَصاىَ أَتَوَكَّؤُا عَلَيها وَأَهُشُّ بِها عَلىٰ غَنَمى وَلِىَ فيها مَآرِبُ أُخرىٰ قالَ أَلقِها يٰموسىٰ فَأَلقىٰها فَإِذا هِىَ حَيَّةٌ تَسعىٰ قالَ خُذها وَلا تَخَف ۖ سَنُعيدُها سيرَتَهَا الأولىٰ

"'What is that, Moses thou hast in thy right hand?" "Why, it is my staff," said Moses, "I lean upon it and with it beat down leaves to feed my sheep; other uses also I find in it." Said He, "Cast it down, Moses."

And he cast it down and behold it was a serpent sliding. Said He, "Take it and fear not; We will restore it to its first state."[22]

Thus, the Lord called Mūsā to be His prophet and upon his wish He granted prophethood, also to his brother, Hārūn, and sent them both to Firʿawn:

اذهَب أَنتَ وَأَخوكَ بِآياتى وَلا تَنِيا فى ذِكرى اذهَبا إِلىٰ فِرعَونَ إِنَّهُ طَغىٰ فَقولا لَهُ قَولًا لَيِّنًا لَعَلَّهُ يَتَذَكَّرُ أَو يَخشىٰ قالا رَبَّنا إِنَّنا نَخافُ أَن يَفرُطَ عَلَينا أَو أَن يَطغىٰ قالَ لا تَخافا ۖ إِنَّنى مَعَكُما أَسمَعُ وَأَرىٰ

"'Go to Firʿawn for he has waxed insolent; yet speak gently to him, that haply he may be mindful, or perchance fear: 'Oh our Lord;', said Moses and Aaron, 'truly we fear he may exceed against us, or wax insolent: 'Fear not,', said He, 'surely I shall be with you, hearing and seeing." [23]

Mūsā and his brother, Hārūn, came together and presented themselves at Firʿawn's gates but they were not admitted. Mūsā went again every day for one whole year and his patience was so great that he never once got angry at being refused. After a year, finally,

[22] Sūrah ṬāḤā, 20:17-21.
[23] Sūrah ṬāḤā, 20:42- 46.

they were admitted and came before Firʿawn's throne. He spoke to him as the Lord had commanded him speak:

فَأْتِيَاهُ فَقُولَا إِنَّا رَسُولَا رَبِّكَ فَأَرْسِلْ مَعَنَا بَنِى إِسْرَٰءِيلَ وَلَا تُعَذِّبْهُمْ ۖ قَدْ جِئْنَٰكَ بِـَٔايَةٍ مِّن

رَّبِّكَ ۖ وَالسَّلَٰمُ عَلَىٰ مَنِ اتَّبَعَ الْهُدَىٰ إِنَّا قَدْ أُوحِىَ إِلَيْنَا أَنَّ الْعَذَابَ عَلَىٰ مَن كَذَّبَ

وَتَوَلَّىٰ قَالَ فَمَن رَّبُّكُمَا يَٰمُوسَىٰ قَالَ رَبُّنَا الَّذِى أَعْطَىٰ كُلَّ شَىْءٍ خَلْقَهُ ثُمَّ هَدَىٰ

قَالَ فَمَا بَالُ الْقُرُونِ الْأُولَىٰ قَالَ عِلْمُهَا عِندَ رَبِّى فِى كِتَٰبٍ ۖ لَّا يَضِلُّ رَبِّى وَلَا يَنسَى

الَّذِى جَعَلَ لَكُمُ الْأَرْضَ مَهْدًا وَسَلَكَ لَكُمْ فِيهَا سُبُلًا وَأَنزَلَ مِنَ السَّمَاءِ مَاءً فَأَخْرَجْنَا

بِهِ أَزْوَٰجًا مِّن نَّبَاتٍ شَتَّىٰ كُلُوا وَارْعَوْا أَنْعَٰمَكُمْ ۗ إِنَّ فِى ذَٰلِكَ لَءَايَٰتٍ لِّأُولِى النُّهَىٰ

مِنْهَا خَلَقْنَٰكُمْ وَفِيهَا نُعِيدُكُمْ وَمِنْهَا نُخْرِجُكُمْ تَارَةً أُخْرَىٰ وَلَقَدْ أَرَيْنَٰهُ ءَايَٰتِنَا كُلَّهَا فَكَذَّبَ

وَأَبَىٰ قَالَ أَجِئْتَنَا لِتُخْرِجَنَا مِنْ أَرْضِنَا بِسِحْرِكَ يَٰمُوسَىٰ فَلَنَأْتِيَنَّكَ بِسِحْرٍ مِّثْلِهِ

فَاجْعَلْ بَيْنَنَا وَبَيْنَكَ مَوْعِدًا لَّا نُخْلِفُهُ نَحْنُ وَلَا أَنتَ مَكَانًا سُوًى

"We are the Messengers of thy Lord, so send forth with us the Children of Isrāʾīl and chastise them not; have brought thee a sign from thy Lord and Peace be upon him who follows the guidance!" "It has been revealed to us that chastisement shall light upon him who cries lies and turns his back." Firʿawn said, "Who is your Lord, Moses?" He said, "Our Lord is He who gave everything its creation then guided it." Firʿawn said, "And what of the former generations?" Said Moses, "The knowledge of them is with my Lord, in a Book. My Lord goes not astray, nor forgets. He who appointed the earth to be a cradle for you and therein threaded roads for you and sent down water out of the heaven and therewith. We have brought forth diverse kinds of plants. Do you eat and pasture your cattle? Surely in that are signs for men

possessing reason. Out of the earth We created you and We shall restore you into it and bring you forth from it a second time."
So We showed Fir'awn all Our signs, but he cried lies, and refused. "Hast thou come, Moses: he said," to expel us out of our land by thy sorcery? We shall assuredly bring thee sorcery the like of it; therefore appoint a tryst between us and thee, a place mutually agreeable and we shall not fail it, neither thou."[24]

They had one great Feast Days in Egypt and Fir'awn decided that this day should be the day of the contest. He sent out words to all sorcerers and magicians in the land that they should prepare for that day and assemble without fail. Four thousand sorcerers came and presented themselves before Fir'awn. They inquired about Mūsā and his magic and were told that Mūsā had only a staff which sometimes he could turn into a serpent.

Now, the magicians knew it to be one of the most elementary tricks of magic to turn sticks into snakes and they said to Fir'awn, "It will be an easy task for us, but what will be our reward?" Fir'awn promised them distinguished positions and many benefits that would make it well worth their while. So they accepted the challenge.

On the appointed day, they all assembled and the leaders of the magicians asked Mūsā, "Will you cast your staff first or shall we begin?"

Mūsā replied, "You may begin."

So the magicians began to work their magic and from their staffs and wands they introduced creatures which seemed to be alive and lay writhing and twisting on the ground. The onlookers were startled and held their breath as this entwined tangle advanced towards the prophet Mūsā. The monstrous illusion made a hissing sound and

---

[24] Sūrah ṬāḤā, 20: 47-58.

steam or smoke seemed to come from the mouths of those magical dragons. Mūsā and his brother were standing alone to one side and when it was Mūsā's turn to cast his staff he felt afraid. But why did Mūsā feel fear? Was it because the magicians had produced a thousand monsters by their magic and Mūsā only one staff to throw? No, Mūsā was not afraid of their magic for he was one of the greatest and most highly honored prophets and his fear was not fear of failure or lack of trust in the Lord Almighty. Mūsā feared simply that the people would not be able to distinguish between a true miracle and a feat of magic and he knew not how he should convince them. But Allah sent to him reassurance, and spoke to him:

قُلنا لا تَخَف إنَّكَ أَنتَ الأَعلىٰ وَأَلقِ ما فى يَمينِكَ تَلقَف ما صَنَعوا ۖ إنَّما صَنَعوا كَيدُ سِحرٍ ۖ وَلا يُفلِحُ السّاحِرُ حَيثُ أَتىٰ

"Fear not: surely thou art the uppermost. Cast down what is in thy right hand and it shall swallow what they have fashioned for they have fashioned only the guile of a sorcerer and the sorcerer prospers not wherever he goes."[25]

Just as that tangled knot of horror had drawn very close to him. Mūsā cast his staff and it turned into a large dragon which devoured all the smaller ones. The entire crowd witnessing this frightful event took to their heels and fled. As many as 18,000 people were trampled to death that day in the panic of the stampede. Firʿawn, himself, turned to flee and ran towards his palace which was built high and strong. The monster pursued him and opened its terrible mouth so wide that the whole palace rested between its jaws. The palace shook and Firʿawn fell off his throne a third time (once in his dream and a second time when Mūsā overturned his throne as a boy) and his crown fell off his head. All the days of his long life Firʿawn had never

[25] Sūrah ṬāḤā, 20: 68-69.

been ill. He had not known headache, a toothache or a stomachache and he used to empty his bowels only once in forty days. On that, he based his claims to divinity. But on this day, when Mūsā's dragon held the palace between its terrible jaws and threatened to crush it and all its inhabitants with its horrendous strength, Firʿawn rushed to the royal toilet forty times. Such was his fear.

Firʿawn screamed, "Catch him. Hold him. Stop him. Somebody do something!" But everyone was as helpless against the monster as Firʿawn himself. At last, Mūsā was ordered to recall the dragon and he stooped and caught hold of its tail. As he did so, it became as it had been before, a simple stick.

The magicians alone had not fled for they wished to observe this extraordinary event. They knew that if Mūsā's doing had been magic, everything would return to its former shape once the spell was broken. All their sticks would reappear. But when the dragon vanished, they saw only Mūsā's staff and none of their own sticks. From this, they understood that it had been a true miracle given to a prophet. All the magicians then believed and fell down in prostration before the God of Mūsā and Hārūn.

قَالَ ءَامَنتُمْ لَهُۥ قَبْلَ أَنْ ءَاذَنَ لَكُمْ ۖ إِنَّهُۥ لَكَبِيرُكُمُ ٱلَّذِى عَلَّمَكُمُ ٱلسِّحْرَ ۖ فَلَأُقَطِّعَنَّ أَيْدِيَكُمْ
وَأَرْجُلَكُم مِّنْ خِلَٰفٍ وَلَأُصَلِّبَنَّكُمْ فِى جُذُوعِ ٱلنَّخْلِ وَلَتَعْلَمُنَّ أَيُّنَآ أَشَدُّ عَذَابًا وَأَبْقَىٰ

Firʿawn said, "Have you believed him before I gave you leave? Why, he is the chief of you, the same that taught you sorcery, shall assuredly cut off alternately your hands and feet, then I shall crucify you upon the trunks of palm-trees; you shall know of a certainty which of us is more terrible in chastisement and more abiding."[26]

[26] Sūrah ṬāḤā, 20: 71.

But the magicians were no longer impressed by Firʿawn's might, and they answered, "Whatever you may do to us, it matters not, for we have found true faith in our hearts. Your power reaches no further than this world. All your torment and punishment touches us but briefly. We have found a path leading to eternal peace and a life everlasting. Allah has guided us to the truth and all your power is of no account."

The magicians had asked Mūsā whether he or they should cast their staffs first. That was the first sign of their recognition of his greatness and of respect for him. Therefore, the Lord gave their hearts such undaunted faith that Firʿawn's threats meant nothing to them and He gave them the strength to bear all his cruelty without fear.

According to one tradition, Mūsā had prayed to the Lord to vouchsafe security to the first people in Egypt who believed in him and the Lord granted his prayer. The magicians became part of Mūsā's nation and Firʿawn's punishment was averted from them. According to another narration, Firʿawn executed them and they became the first martyrs of that nation. Allah knows best.

Even after these events, Mūsā and Hārūn continued to preach to Firʿawn and they said to him, "Oh Firʿawn, you have lived on earth now for 400 years and yet you don't believe in Him who created the heavens and the Earth. Allah may increase your life and your kingdom for a thousand years if only you will believe in Him and worship Him truly." Firʿawn came very close to believing but his pride and his stubbornness were too strong for him to overcome. He consulted with his trusted advisor Hāmān and told him what the prophets had said to him but Hāmān said, "Oh Walīd, have you lost your mind? You are now a god to your people and your power over them is absolute. Will you then content yourself to become a slave and to worship another being? What more could you desire than what you already possess?" So Firʿawn remained stiff-necked and unyielding. For a long time Mūsā spoke to him gently as the Lord had commanded him, until one day he was ordered to use his stick. For men will heed words of reason at times but donkeys listen only to the stick.

The Lord ordered Mūsā to perform miracles that Firʿawn and his people might be warned. He struck the waters of the Nile with his staff and all the water turned to blood and the fish died and no one had any water left to drink or to wash. This condition lasted for eight days before it was lifted. Still, they would not believe. Next, came the plague of locusts followed by the plague of frogs, and then their cattle were stricken. Then, there was a plaque of hailstorms and famine. Still Firʿawn's heart remained hardened and he persisted in his unbelief, attributing all these plagues to natural causes. Finally, there came a plague of boils over the Egyptians and 70,000 died within one week. Then, people came to Mūsā and pleaded with him, "Oh Mūsā, please lift this plague from us before it destroys us all and we will believe and let your people go." But when the plague was lifted from them, they fell back on their promises and Firʿawn increased his oppression of the Banī Isrā'īl, making them responsible for all the disasters.

Mūsā spoke to the Lord, "My God, in spite of his unbelief You grant respite to Firʿawn. Explain the wisdom of this to me." The Lord spoke to Mūsā, "I have given him a period of grace for he has many good characteristics for which I love him and I do not hasten to destroy My creation, oh Mūsā. Firstly, he rules his people with justice. Secondly, he is a generous man and looks after the poor and thirdly, he has built up a city of great beauty. That he claims to be god in no way diminishes My Majesty. It is not important to Me."

One day, Firʿawn said to Mūsā, We will arrange a decisive contest between us to see whose religion is the true one. Let us both go to the Nile and order it to stop flowing. If it obeys my command, the proof of my claim will be proven." Mūsā agreed and they went to a certain place overlooking the river. Mūsā prayed his evening and night prayers and went to sleep. Firʿawn, however, went to his chamber and suspended himself from the ceiling by his beard and remained all night in that position, engaging in fervent supplication. He cried to the Lord, "Oh my God, I know of Your existence and I know I am less than nothing before You. I pray to You this one time not to abase me before the eyes of my people and Your prophet Mūsā. Please grant me this prayer just this once. Thereafter, You may send me to hellfire. Grant me tomorrow's success." He implored the Lord all night long and in the morning the angel Jibrīl appeared to him in the shape of a man.

Firʿawn, hanging from the ceiling, asked, "What do you want?"

"I have an urgent problem," answered the man which brooks no delay. For many years I have employed a servant in my house and I have always treated him well and honored him with position and rank. Now, instead of gratitude from him, I see that he has begun abusing it over the other servants in my house, abusing the power I gave to him and acting in my name without authority. What would be your verdict in such a case?"

Firʿawn answered, "Have him punished either by burning or by drowning."

"If I execute him as you say it is only just, but people will not believe me and will accuse me of murder; I must have your signature on this document, authorizing the sentence."

He extended a paper and a pen towards Firʿawn and Firʿawn signed the document, sentencing that disobedient servant to death by drowning, little knowing that he had signed his own death sentence. Then the angel disappeared and the Lord granted Firʿawn's prayer on that day.

In time, a lot of Egyptians began to follow the prophet and even at the court of Firʿawn there were believers. The queen, Āsīyah, was the first of the royal household to believe and she worshipped in secret with her following of slave-girls and servants. Though she was formally married to Firʿawn, Āsīyah remained a virgin throughout her life. On the Day of Judgment, she will be raised up and become the wife of our noble prophet Muhammad ﷺ.

One day, one of the servant women who had become a Muslim was combing the princess' hair and she happened to drop the comb. As she bent to pick it up, she pronounced the words of the Besmela (*Bismi'l-Lāhi 'r-Raḥmāni 'r-Raḥīm*). The princess heard these words and questioned the woman about them. The woman explained that she began every action in the name of Him who had created the heavens and the Earth and every living thing.

The princess said, "You mean, in the name of my father, Firʿawn?"

"Oh no," answered the woman, "God forbid! How can your father, who is a created being, have created the world? He is but a mortal like you or me."

And they began to argue. In the end the princess reported the woman to Firʿawn and accused her of heresy. Firʿawn had the woman interrogated and threatened to punish her severely if she didn't renounce her new faith but the woman was steadfast in her faith and said, "No matter what you may do to me, it will only affect my brief life here on Earth but He who has created both you and me will give me eternal reward in the life hereafter. I will never prostrate to any but Him, the Almighty."

This courageous woman had a husband and five children. Firʿawn had them brought before him and said to the maidservant, "You say your God has hell to punish the wrongdoers on the Last Day. I am god and I have prepared hell for you right now." He ordered a great cauldron to be set on the fire and when the water began to boil he had the woman's husband thrown into it and he was boiled until the flesh peeled off his bones. Then they threw in her children, one after the other. Yet, still, the woman refused to give up her faith in the

Almighty. Only when they grabbed her last baby from her, an infant of a few months and she heard the child cry for his mother's breast, did she momentarily hesitate. She suddenly felt a great pain within her and thought to herself, "So what if I prostrate before Firʿawn and pretend to have returned to worshipping him? I can still preserve my true faith within my heart. At least I will have saved the youngest of my poor, innocent children from this terrible fate." While she pondered, Firʿawn was watching her for signs of her weakening. The voice of that baby was suddenly heard loud and clear by all present and he spoke these words, by the Grace of the Almighty God, "Oh mother, don't worry or grieve for me or any of us. I see Paradise opening before me and the Huris are beckoning to me to enter. Have no fear of Firʿawn or his henchmen. They are like nothing before Allah Almighty. *Lā ilāha ill-L'lāh*!" Instantly, Firʿawn had the child thrown into the boiling cauldron and he died at once.

Then, the woman said, "Oh Firʿawn, I have served at your court for a long time. Now every condemned prisoner has the right of one last request. My request is that you throw me too into that kettle so that I may join my family and that you bury us together in one grave." Firʿawn granted her this request and it was done. On the night of the Miʿrāj of our Holy Prophet Muhammad ﷺ he was guided by the angel towards Jerusalem and suddenly he picked up a most lovely scent. He asked the angel leading him about this smell and the angel told him that they had just passed over the grave of that comb girl of Firʿawn's daughter. A garden of Paradise had been prepared for her and her family there and there they rest, enjoying its delights to this very day.

When the queen, Āsīyah, learned of what had been done to her faithful servant girl, she was very angry and reproached Firʿawn bitterly, "What has that poor woman done to you that you must act so cruelly and what crime have those innocent children committed?"

Firʿawn grew suspicious of his wife and said, "So, you too share her convictions?"

"Yes, I do," the queen admitted. "I have set my faith on the Almighty Lord whose reign is everlasting. This passing life is of no value to me, so you may take it."

Now Firʿawn loved Āsīyah and did not wish to hurt her but seeing his pride hurt before all the assembled court, he had to make a show of his power so as not to lose face. He ordered her to be crucified in a public place under the burning sun of Egypt. She was nailed to a cross and hung there for many days. Firʿawn would come every day and call upon her to relent and to forsake her faith in the invisible God and then he would spare her life. But Āsīyah gave him no reply. She uttered not a word. Even when Firʿawn ordered her to be whipped she did not sigh. Firʿawn made her eat salty barley bread and gave her no water. The sun burned down upon her fiercely and the flies infested her wounds; she was being eaten away while yet alive. Still, she clung to her faith and her heart remained whole. Firʿawn showed her no mercy and increased her torment.

One day, Mūsā passed by the place where she hung crucified and she winked at him and made a sign which he understood to mean, "Look at my condition. Can you do nothing to help me?" Mūsā raised his hands to heaven and prayed for her and asked the Lord to show mercy on that woman who was suffering such unspeakable torture for His sake. The Lord heard Mūsā's prayer and from that day on, Āsīyah felt no more pain. Firʿawn sought every day to increase her agony. He had the skin torn off her feet and legs up to her knees, but Āsīyah felt no more. She began to see the wonders of Paradise in front of her and the Ḥūrīs advanced towards her with refreshing foods and drinks, greeting her as their queen. The Lord lifted the veil from the hearts of the angels of the seven heavens and they grew aware of the suffering of this patient heart. The angels began to weep for her and their tears drenched the earth like rain.

Āsīyah then uttered the words, "Oh Lord, build for me a house in Paradise in Your Presence."

The angels heard her words and said, "That is no great reward to ask for all these sufferings."

The Lord then answered, "You must listen closely. She said 'in Your Presence'. That is the highest reward she can ask for and it is proportionate to what she has suffered."

He then ordered the angels to bring her soul to Paradise. Āsīyah died with a smile on her lips.

Her tormentors watched her die, and as they perceived only the outward aspect they said to the people, "Do you have, any doubt left that whoever follows this man, Mūsā, must have lost their minds? Only a mad person can die with a smile after having been tortured so long. Let this be a lesson for your all."

the exodus

With the death of his queen, Āsīyah, began the last forty years of Firʿawn's reign and he became a cruel tyrant in late life. In particular, his oppression was directed towards the people of Isrā'īl who believed in the message Mūsā brought to them. At last, Mūsā received the Divine Command to lead his people out of Egypt and out of slavery. The news spread among the Banī Isrā'īl. Some of them were prepared to follow Mūsā from the fullness of their faith while others wished only to be delivered from Firʿawn's cruel oppression. Forty days had passed since Mūsā received the command to lead his people away but for forty days no one could wake up on time. There was something holding them back in Egypt.

Yūsuf ﵇ had died in this land and his last request had been that the tribes of Isrā'īl should take him with them if ever they should leave Egypt. Everyone remembered this condition but none knew anymore where Yūsuf ﵇'s body lay. Finally, an Egyptian woman of Āsīyah's family told them where the grave was and they dug there and found the coffin. This woman wished to accompany the tribes when they left Egypt as did the carpenter who had built the box for Mūsā's mother.

Now the Command of the Lord came again and He ordered all the Israelites to slaughter a sacrifice and to paint their doors with blood as a sign, for He intended to smite the Egyptians once more. He sent the angel of death to all Egyptian houses that night to kill their firstborn. That night the Egyptians cried for there was not a house in Egypt that had not been visited by the angel of death, save the houses that were marked with the blood of the sacrifice.

That very night, while the Egyptians and cared for their dead, the Lord ordered the Children of Isrā'īl to leave. So Mūsā set out with the tribes by night and they numbered no less than 700,000 souls, including women and children. When Yʿaqūb had settled aforetime in Egypt with his family they had been only seventy persons.

Now, Firʿawn and the Egyptians could not follow them right away as they were occupied with the burial rites, but the following day he set out with his armies on horseback, with a great clatter of arms. The Banī Isrā'īl had come to the banks of the sea and behind them Firʿawn's armies were gaining on them. They began to lament and complain to their prophet, "Had we only stayed where we were. There, we were safe. Now look at us. We are dead men; before us the waters of the sea and from behind Firʿawn's host!" They blamed Mūsā for having brought them into these straights.

Mūsā was also perplexed and knew not what to do. Then, Yūshaʿ (Joshua) came up to him and asked him where he had been ordered to lead them. Mūsā pointed towards the sea with his staff and Yūshaʿ spurred his horse and the sea opened for him and he was gone. Next came the carpenter who had believed in Mūsā's mission first of all and he too disappeared in the sea. But the mass of people stood on the shore, wailing loudly. "What shall we do? Ah, we are lost!" Then Jibrīl appeared to Mūsā and ordered him to strike the sea with his staff.

The Children of Isrā'īl were divided into twelve tribes, descended from the twelve sons of Yʿaqūb. It was their custom that each tribe had separate wells and that they would not drink from each other's water nor would they travel on a road used by another tribe. When Mūsā struck the sea with his staff, it rose up on both sides as a mountain, leaving a dry passage in between, so that the sun touched the seabed. This will not happen again until the Day of Judgment. Twelve separate pathways became visible for each of the tribes of Isrā'īl to pass.

Firʿawn beheld this miracle from afar and he understood well that it was given to Mūsā but he said to his armies. "You see, the sea is rising up from respect of my majesty, and it is splitting a road in its midst so that I might pursue my enemy" But in his heart he knew very well that it was not so and he was afraid to advance towards the waters. Firʿawn was mounted on a magnificent stallion. Suddenly, the angel Jibrīl appeared riding a mare (called the 'Horse of Life') and passing close by Firʿawn's stallion rode ahead into the waters. Driven by nature, the stallion could not be refrained from following her and plunged after the mare. Seeing their king ride on ahead, the whole army followed him and the angel Mikāʾīl took the shape of an officer and urged them on. When the whole army was in the trough formed by the walls of the sea, the Lord ordered the sea to close in upon them and the mountains of water came crashing down and Firʿawn and all his hosts were drowned.

Some of the Israelites could not believe that Firʿawn was dead for they had heard all their lives that he was immortal and would never die. Mūsā prayed to the Lord and said, "Oh Lord, look at Your people and at the weakness of their faith. What shall I do with them?" So after three days the Lord made the sea expel the bodies of Firʿawn and his men and the Israelites could tell from his bloated corpse that indeed he had died and the sea would not accept him back.

Up to the time of our prophet Muhammad ﷺ the collecting of spoils and booty of war was not made lawful. Now some of the Israelites knew how to dive and swim and they fished out of the waters some of the precious ornaments Firʿawn and his army had worn even though Mūsā forbade it to them. They did not like to listen to what displeased them and took some of these things with them.

On their way, they passed by certain tribes and noticed that the idols they were worshipping were made of precious materials and said to Mūsā, "Why can't we see the God we are worshipping, oh Mūsā? Why don't we have such precious statues to adore?"

Mūsā said to them. "Oh my people the Lord of the Worlds has honored you above all other nations. He has saved you from Firʿawn and his hosts and you have witnessed miracle after miracle. Still, your hearts are inclined to idolatry. Still you don't understand that there is no God but He, the Living, the Eternal?" So the Children of Isrā'īl fell silent and continued on their way.

MUSA ON MT TUR

During the years that Fir'awn had ordered all the male infants of Isrā'īl to be slaughtered, there were some mothers who had hidden their children in a certain cave. The angel Jibrīl came to them and took them under his wing and they suckled on it and were fed that way. They grew up accustomed to the angel's presence and aware of him. One of these children was the man who came to be known as the 'Sāmirī'. One day, when the angel came to bring revelation to Mūsā, the Sāmirī perceived him, mounted upon his steed, the 'Horse of Life'. Nobody noticed when he bent to scoop up a handful of earth from beneath that horse's hooves for it was not visible to anyone else. Sāmirī hid this bit of clay from everyone.

Now, they had wandered as far as the mountain of Ṭūr (Sinai) and the Lord called Mūsā to the top of the mountain to converse with him. When he returned, the people said. "All the previous prophets have come with a scripture. Why do we have none? We don't know what is the right way for us and we want to know!" Mūsā returned to the mountain of Ṭūr and asked the Lord for a Book. The Lord answered, "They shall have their Book but let them be warned, if they do not hold to it and live by its laws they shall be struck by such punishment that they will become a lesson and a reminder for all the peoples of the world." Mūsā went and warned the tribes of the responsibility they were asking for but they insisted on their will.

Then, Mūsā was ordered to fast for thirty days and went into seclusion on the mountain of Ṭūr. The people didn't count the days of fasting correctly; they counted the nights as well, and when thirty days had passed they had already counted to sixty.

"He has not returned when he should have," They said.

"He has deceived us and gone away secretly," others said, "perhaps his prayer is not being answered because we disobeyed him when he ordered us leave behind the jewels and gold we took from the drowned men and which we carry with us. Let us burn them". They made a great fire and threw all these objects into it. As they were mostly made of metals, they did not burn but only melted.

At that time, the Sāmirī stepped forth. He was a jeweler and a goldsmith. He collected the molten metal and fashioned from it a golden calf. He sprinkled some of the clay on which the hooves of Jibrīl's 'Horse of Life' had stood, and the golden calf came to life. It walked among the people and lowed like a real calf. Sāmirī said to the people, "This is your god whom Mūsā forgot to show you before he left for the mountain."

Allah says:

فَأَخْرَجَ لَهُمْ عِجْلًا جَسَدًا لَهُ خُوَارٌ فَقَالُوا هَذَا إِلَٰهُكُمْ وَإِلَٰهُ مُوسَىٰ فَنَسِيَ

Then he(Sāmirī) produced for them a calf, of saffron hue, which gave forth a lowing sound. And they cried: This is your God and the God of Moses, but he hath forgotten.[27]

Mūsā's brother Hārūn had stayed with them and he tried his best to call people back from worshipping the golden calf. Never at any time have there lived two prophets among one people at the same time. But whatever he said to them could not dissuade them and they began threatening him. So Hārūn withdrew with 12,000 of the faithful and they busied themselves with worship and prayer.

As for the followers of the Sāmirī, they gathered around their living idol. He taught them ways of 'worship' which resemble very much today's New Year's carnivals. Their 'worship' consisted of drinking,

---

[27] Sūrah ṬāḤā, 20:88.

dancing and revelry and it was in every way perverted and idolatrous.

Mūsā fasted on the mountain for thirty days and when he was bothered by the foul smell coming from his mouth after so long a fast, the Lord instructed him to use a *miswāk*. "The smell from your mouth during the days of your fast is more pleasing to Me than the perfume of musk," The Lord said to Mūsā. Mūsā, then, fasted ten days longer; forty days in all. During those last ten days, he could hear the sound of trees being cut in Paradise from which the tablets of the Tawrāt were made. He also could hear the scratching of the Pen of Destiny as it wrote upon them. Great indeed, was Mūsā's closeness to his Lord at this time. Allah gave Mūsā knowledge of what was happening among his people in his absence:

قَالَ فَإِنَّا قَدْ فَتَنَّا قَوْمَكَ مِن بَعْدِكَ وَأَضَلَّهُمُ السَّامِرِيُّ

(Allah) said: "We have tested thy people in thy absence: the Samiri has led them astray."[28]

Mūsā, being the fiercest of all prophets, lost his temper and shouted at the Lord, "Oh God, they would not have strayed so far had You not let them!" But the Lord so loved Mūsā that He was not angered by Mūsā's speech. No other prophet ever dared to speak to the Lord in this way.

[28] Sūrah ṬāḤā, 20:85.

The Revelation of the Tawrat

Mūsā fasted for forty days upon the mountain, then he asked the Lord, "Who art Thou?"

And the Lord replied, "I am Allah beside whom there is no other God."

At that moment Iblīs appeared to Mūsā and tempted him.

He said, "How do you know this is the truth? How do you know it is really the Lord and not some figment of your imagination?"

"I know it is the truth for I perceive it with all my members and faculties. My whole being is suffused by this perception," Mūsā replied.

Sometimes we have such experiences in our dreams but the prophets' visions are in a waking state.

Mūsā encountered his Lord in a spiritual meeting and His words entered his perception as revelation. The Lord sent down a cloud of light upon Mūsā which covered him and barred Shayṭān from approaching. Mūsā entered the cover of this cloud and beheld the angels and the Throne. Jibrīl called to Mūsā and said, "The Lord has sent me to you to offer you hospitality. Mount my wing." He extended his wing and it was studded with heavenly gems the like of which are not found on Earth. Before Mūsā, no mortal had been invited to ride on the wing of this angel. Jibrīl, thus, transported him into the Presence of the Almighty Lord and the Lord spoke to Mūsā and he alone could hear His words. Allah Almighty then, ordered the angel to bring the tablets of the Tawrāt from the Garden of Eden. Upon them, the Lord had written ten lines with the Hand of Power.

According to a tradition from Prophet Muhammed ﷺ there are four things the Lord has revealed from His attribute of Power: the creation of Ādam, the revelation of the Tawrāt, the Ṭūbā tree in

Paradise and the Gardens of Eden. The tablets were ten times Mūsā's height and the angels carried them for Mūsā when he descended from the mountain of Ṭūr.

The Lord spoke to Mūsā, "I am your Lord, there is no God beside Me. You must take no partners. Whoever attributes partners to Me will surely burn in Hell. Mūsā, give thanks to Me. Be grateful to your parents and honor them. This is what your Lord has forbidden to you: do not steal or appropriate goods unlawfully; do not shed innocent blood. Adultery is a great sin in My eyes. Mūsā, whatever you wish for yourself you must also desire for your brother and all your people. Do not slaughter any animal without the mention of My Name, for if you do its meat will not be lawful to you. The Sabbath is a special day reserved for Me and you shall not work and there shall be no hunting on the Sabbath. This is forbidden to you and to all your people."

When Mūsā heard the Words of his Lord he felt a great desire to see the Lord with his own eyes.

He was so consumed by love for Him that he said, "Oh Lord, show Yourself to me that I might gaze upon You."

The Lord said, "No one has ever asked such a thing of Me. Oh Mūsā, how will you be able to support this vision? Where will you find the strength? If anyone were to behold Me as I am, his mind and senses would leave him and he would perish instantly."

Mūsā answered, "I would rather perish than live on without knowing You, my Lord."

The Lord said to Mūsā, "You can never behold Me directly but fix your gaze upon that mountain."

Mūsā did as he was commanded. First, the Lord sent one order of angels to Mūsā and they had the form of great bulls. Their hoof beats made the air tremble with thunder and lightning surrounded them. "You are asking a tremendous thing," they roared at Mūsā, as their bellowing voices caused the earth to quake. Mūsā began to tremble as he gazed at the angels who filled all the space to the horizon and believed that he would die. Indeed, had he been any other than Mūsā, he would have died there and then.

From another direction Mūsā beheld a different group of angels who had the shape of terrifying lions and they cried with one great voice, "*Lā ilāha ill-Llāh*! You have asked for an unheard of thing. You cannot even bear the sight of us, how then can you ask to behold the Lord?" And Mūsā nearly fainted. When he raised his gaze once again, he beheld yet another group of angels who resembled great falcons. The screeching and the flapping of their gigantic wings caused a violent storm around him as they arrayed themselves before him. Their presence was even harder to bear than that of the other angels. Behind him now, a fourth group of angels assembled and their shape resembled that of men of overpowering strength and they evoked more fear than all the others. They repeated their warnings and Mūsā nearly crumbled with awe. The angels were of the order of the Throne-bearing angels who resemble in form respectively the bull, the lion, the falcon and man.

When Mūsā's gaze was fixed upon the mountain, the Lord sent down a tiny bit of His own Light. It was the amount that might pass through the eye of a needle or perhaps much less than that. Revelation of the Divine Light split the mountain into seven parts, crushing and crumbling it into dust. Seeing this, Mūsā let out a scream and fell senseless to the ground. One account has it that the angel Jibrīl caught him as he fell and restored him to life. Another account says that Mūsā died and was given life a second time. When he regained consciousness Mūsā said "Oh Lord, I ask Thy forgiveness. I repent of my audacity."

This event is described in the Qur'an:

وَلَمَّا جَاءَ مُوسَى لِمِيقَاتِنَا وَكَلَّمَهُ رَبُّهُ قَالَ رَبِّ أَرِنِي أَنظُرْ إِلَيْكَ قَالَ
لَن تَرَانِي وَلَكِنِ انظُرْ إِلَى الْجَبَلِ فَإِنِ اسْتَقَرَّ مَكَانَهُ فَسَوْفَ تَرَانِي
فَلَمَّا تَجَلَّى رَبُّهُ لِلْجَبَلِ جَعَلَهُ دَكًّا وَخَرَّ مُوسَى صَعِقًا فَلَمَّا أَفَاقَ قَالَ
سُبْحَانَكَ تُبْتُ إِلَيْكَ وَأَنَاْ أَوَّلُ الْمُؤْمِنِينَ

When Moses came to the place appointed by Us, and his Lord addressed him, He said: "O my Lord! show (Thyself) to me, that I may look upon thee." Allah said: "By no means canst thou see Me (direct); But look upon the mount; if it abide in its place, then shalt thou see Me." When his Lord manifested His glory on the Mount, He made it as dust. And Moses fell down in a swoon. When he recovered his senses he said: "Glory be to Thee! to Thee I turn in repentance, and I am the first to believe." [29]

The Lord then forgave him. But it is said that the Light he had witnessed affected his face in such a way that it had become too piercing for any living creature to withstand. If he had looked at the mountain, it would have melted and had he looked upon men they would have been blinded or struck dead on the spot.

"Oh Lord," Cried Mūsā, "what shall I do now? Nobody can stand my gaze. How shall I fulfill my office as a prophet to my people if no one can bear to look at me?"

The Lord answered him and said, "Oh Mūsā, take the worn out clothes of the poor who are patient or from the learned for My sake

[29] Sūratu 'l-'Ārāf (The Heights), 7: 143.

and make yourself a veil. Neither will the fire then burn them nor the light cause them to melt away."

Mūsā did so and from that day on he wore a veil. No one saw his face any more after that.

When the Lord revealed Himself to the mountain and all about Mūsā fell into chaos and the terror seized him, Mūsā called to the Lord, saying, "Oh my Lord, if I remain here I will be consumed; if I go I will die. Oh Lord, send to me Your Support!" The Lord sent one ray of light from His Divine Throne and He veiled it in seventy thousand veils of light. Yet that one veiled ray split the mountain into seven pieces. Three of these pieces were flung to Medina, three to Mecca and one part is suspended between the heavens and the Earth where it will orbit until the Day of Judgment. One part became the Jabal Nūr near Mecca, and another Jabal Uḥud near Medina. This happened on a Thursday which was the day of 'Arafāt.

On Friday the Lord revealed the Tawrāt and gave it to Mūsā and it was written in the Hebrew tongue. The word Tawrāt means 'the Law' according to some sources. According to others it means 'that which is revealed from the Unseen'.

When the Lord gave the Tawrāt to Mūsā, He said to him, "Take what I have revealed to you, oh Mūsā, and be grateful for it. Take the Tawrāt to your nation and may they abide by it!" It is said that the Tawrāt consisted of eight hundred words. Some say 114,000.

Mūsā said, "Oh my Lord, where can I find You?"

The Lord answered, "You may seek Me in the hearts of those who have turned their backs on worldliness and are absorbed in contemplation of Me."

Then Mūsā asked, "Oh Lord, which of Your servants is dearest to You and most highly honored?"

The Lord answered, "It is he who forgives his enemy though he may have the means of seeking justice against him."

The Lord also said, "Oh Mūsā, even if all the creatures in the heavens and on Earth combined their forces to destroy one individual they would not be able to harm a single hair on his head, if it be not My Will." And He, the Almighty said, "Oh Mūsā, if ever you are afraid of any high and mighty one, make your ablution and his evil will not touch. For he who is in a state of ritual purity is in My charge and none can hurt him."

Hakim Menbih relates:

"I have read four verses in the Tawrāt.

The first: if a person reads the Holy Scripture and feels that it doesn't apply to him it is as if he was making light of Allah's Book, not taking His revelation seriously.

The second, if a person experiences some misfortune and complains of those who have done him wrong, it is as if he had complained against the Lord of the Worlds.

Thirdly, if an unliked thing happens to a person and he is angered by it, it is as if he were not content with the Lord's order of the world.

The fourth, if a person humbles himself before a rich man in the hope of attaining some profit, he has lost two thirds of his faith."

The Lord gave a description of the Tawrāt to his beloved Prophet Muhammad ﷺ. The Tawrāt consisted of one thousand chapters, each containing one thousand verses and the Banī Isrā'īl carried it with them on their journey on seventy camels.

Jābir bin 'Abd Allāh ﷺ relates that the Prophet Muhammad ﷺ told him:

> The Lord gave to Mūsā the tablets of the Tawrāt and upon them was written, I am the Lord, Allah. Attribute no partners

> to Me, for those who attribute partners to Me, I will burn them in the fires of Hell. Give thanks to Me, and honor your father and mother. Do not swear falsely by My Name and envy no one, for envy is the enemy of My Bounty. Be content with what I have given to you, for whoever is not content with his lot is not of My servants. Give your heart to none but Me alone and keep far from pride. Love your brother as you love yourself and keep the Sabbath.

ʿAbd Allāh bin Salām ﷺ relates:

> Allah Almighty says in the Tawrāt, "I will send a prophet from the line of Ismāʿīl ﷺ. His name will be Ahmad. Whoever believes in him will be rightly guided and My curse is upon him who disbelieves."

It is related from Abū Dardā ﷺ that Kʿab-ul-Ahbār ﷺ said:

> There is a verse in the Holy Tawrāt which says, "Know ye that the desire of the righteous is the meeting with Me and it is My desire to be joined with them. Whoever desires Me will find Me and who desires other than Me will not find Me."

Abū Dardā ﷺ replied, "I have heard these same words from our Holy Prophet ﷺ."

It is reported that the people of Isrā'īl were very upset when Firʿawn's host was drowned in the sea and they cried and asked Mūsā, "Who is the most learned person among us?"

Mūsā answered them and said, "There is none among you that knows more than I."

When Mūsā came down from the mountain with the tablets of the Tawrāt and found his people engaged in abominations and worship of the golden calf, he grew exceedingly angry and dashed the tablets to the ground so that they were broken and the words upon them flew back to the heavens.

The Qur'an relates:

أَلَمْ يَعِدْكُمْ رَبُّكُمْ وَعْدًا حَسَنًا أَفَطَالَ عَلَيْكُمُ الْعَهْدُ أَمْ أَرَدتُّمْ أَن يَحِلَّ عَلَيْكُمْ غَضَبٌ

مِّن رَّبِّكُمْ فَأَخْلَفْتُم مَّوْعِدِي قَالُوا مَا أَخْلَفْنَا مَوْعِدَكَ بِمَلْكِنَا

وَلَكِنَّا حُمِّلْنَا أَوْزَارًا مِّن زِينَةِ الْقَوْمِ فَقَذَفْنَاهَا

فَكَذَلِكَ أَلْقَى السَّامِرِيُّ

Then Moses went back unto his folk, angry and sad. He said: O my people! Hath not your Lord promised you a fair promise? Did the time appointed then appear too long for you, or did ye wish that wrath from your Lord should come upon you, that ye broke tryst with me?
They said: We broke not tryst with thee of our own will, but we were laden with burdens of ornaments of the folk, then cast them (in the fire), for thus As-Samiri proposed;[30]

Then he turned to his brother Hārūn, pulled him by the beard and shouted at him, as is related in the Qur'an:

قَالَ يَٰهَٰرُونُ مَا مَنَعَكَ إِذْ رَأَيْتَهُمْ ضَلُّوا أَلَّا تَتَّبِعَنِ ۖ أَفَعَصَيْتَ أَمْرِى قَالَ يَبْنَؤُمَّ لَا تَأْخُذْ

بِلِحْيَتِى وَلَا بِرَأْسِى ۖ إِنِّى خَشِيتُ أَن تَقُولَ فَرَّقْتَ بَيْنَ بَنِى إِسْرَٰءِيلَ وَلَمْ تَرْقُبْ قَوْلِى

Moses said, "What prevented thee, Aaron, when thou sawest them in error, so that thou didst not follow after me? Didst thou then disobey my commandment" "Son of my mother," Aaron said,

---

[30] Sūrah ṬāḤā, 20:86-87.

"take me not by the beard or the head. I was fearful that thou wouldst say, 'Thou hast divided the Children of Isrā'īl, and thou hast not observed my word.'"[31]

Hārūn said, "Oh my brother, don't pour blame on me and make me not ridiculous in front of our enemy. I tried to prevent this but they threatened me and nearly killed me, saying I was merely jealous of them. So I went aside with twelve thousand of the faithful and we worshipped the Lord and were loyal to our word."

Seeing Mūsā's wrath, a number of the others regretted what they had done and wished to repent. But in those days repentance was not as easy as it is today for the nation of Muhammad ﷺ. For us, it is enough to say, "Oh Lord, I repent of my sin and return to You. Do Thou forgive me?" The Lord forgives us in His endless mercy. In the time of Mūsā, however, the sinner's deed was written upon his forehead and he was unable to blot it out or erase its trace. Repentance required that a person leave his home and become an outcast or that he distribute all his wealth among the poor or that he put an end to his own life or that he be put to death. The Lord commanded that all the repentant sinners be put to death by the sword by those twelve thousand who had remained faithful. "Either they accept this as their atonement or they continue life as unbelievers and transgressors of the law."

This is related in the Qur'an:

[31] Sūrah ṬāḤā, 20:92-94.

وَإِذْ قَالَ مُوسَى لِقَوْمِهِ يَا قَوْمِ إِنَّكُمْ ظَلَمْتُمْ أَنفُسَكُمْ بِاتِّخَاذِكُمُ الْعِجْلَ
فَتُوبُوا إِلَى بَارِئِكُمْ فَاقْتُلُوا أَنفُسَكُمْ ذَلِكُمْ خَيْرٌ لَّكُمْ عِندَ بَارِئِكُمْ
فَتَابَ عَلَيْكُمْ إِنَّهُ هُوَ التَّوَّابُ الرَّحِيمُ

And remember Moses said to his people: "O my people! Ye have indeed wronged yourselves by your worship of the calf: So turn (in repentance) to your Maker, and slay yourselves (the wrong-doers); that will be better for you in the sight of your Maker." Then He turned towards you (in forgiveness): For He is Oft- Returning, Most Merciful. [32]

The repentant all accepted their punishment and the next morning, at sunrise, the sentence was to be carried out. The twelve thousand armed themselves with their swords. Their hearts were heavy though, for it was they were ordered to put to death their very own kith and kin. They nearly despaired of being able to carry out the Divine Command. The Lord sent down a thick black fog which enveloped them all so they could not recognize whom they were striking. From the early morning till late that afternoon the swords did their grisly task. Before the sun set it was done. Then the dense fog lifted and they could see the severed heads and blood drenched sands. Seventy thousand people were put to death that day.

Mūsā fell upon his face and cried to the Lord, "Oh my God, the Banī Isrā'īl are ruined now. There are hardly enough of us left to bury the dead."

"Are you not pleased with My Command?" asked the Lord.

---

[32] Sūratu 'l-Baqara (the Heifer), 2:54.

"Those who repented and suffered their punishment are now in Paradise, for I have forgiven them and those who carried out the judgment are promised Paradise, for they have obeyed Me. Could not you desire any better for them than that?"

Mūsā could not reply to his Lord. Henceforth, he began to teach his remaining people the commandments of the Tawrāt.

The Lord had revealed that they should pray fifty times a day and that they should give a quarter of their earnings as poor due. They were commanded to wash seven times to clean themselves from major impurity and if some impure matter (such as blood or excrement) soiled their clothing it was not sufficient to wash out that spot with water but rather they had to cut the part out of their clothing and bury it. If they committed a major sin, the punishment was death by the sword and their atonement was heavy before they could attain forgiveness. Adulterers, be they men or women, were to be buried in the sand up to their necks and stoned to death. People were to fast six months of the year and to break their fast only in the hour between dusk and nightfall. All the fifty daily prayers were to be prayed communally in their house of worship.

When Mūsā had informed them of their obligations, the people said, "But we cannot possibly fulfill all of that. It is far too heavy for us!"

Mūsā answered, "But you yourselves asked to be given the law of the Tawrāt. Now you refuse it?"

Mūsā ordered them to prostrate before the Lord but their pride prevented them and they said, "No, we can't and we won't, even if the Lord brings the mountain down on our heads!"

No sooner had they said this than the mountain of Ṭūr rose up in the air and hovered above threatening to crush them. Then, they obeyed and fell down upon their faces but their fear was not so great as to prevent them from peering out sideways with one eye to see whether the mountain had gone back to its place. This is the posture they assume in prayer to this very day when they perform a prostration once a year.

وَإِذْ أَخَذْنَا مِيثَاقَكُمْ وَرَفَعْنَا فَوْقَكُمُ الطُّورَ خُذُواْ مَا آتَيْنَاكُم بِقُوَّةٍ وَاذْكُرُواْ مَا فِيهِ لَعَلَّكُمْ تَتَّقُونَ

And remember We took your covenant and We raised above you (The towering height) of Mount (Sinai) : (Saying): "Hold firmly to what We have given you and bring (ever) to remembrance what is therein: Perchance ye may fear Allah."[33]

And what happened to Sāmirī? He, too, was punished but he was not forgiven as long as he lived.

قَالَ فَمَا خَطْبُكَ يَا سَامِرِيُّ قَالَ بَصُرْتُ بِمَا لَمْ يَبْصُرُوا بِهِ فَقَبَضْتُ قَبْضَةً مِّنْ أَثَرِ الرَّسُولِ فَنَبَذْتُهَا وَكَذَلِكَ سَوَّلَتْ لِي نَفْسِي

(Moses) said: And what has thou to say, O Sāmirī? He replied: "I saw what they saw not: so I took a handful (of dust) from the footprint of the Messenger, and threw it (into the calf): thus did my soul suggest to me." [34]

He was exiled from the community of men and for the remainder of his life no one was allowed to speak or listen to him and he became an outcast. He took to the hills in the wilderness and lived out his days among the wild beasts.

---

[33] Sūratu 'l-Baqara (the Heifer), 2:63.

[34] Sūrah ṬāḤā, 20:95-96.

قَالَ فَاذْهَبْ فَإِنَّ لَكَ فِي الْحَيَاةِ أَن تَقُولَ لَا مِسَاسَ وَإِنَّ لَكَ مَوْعِدًا لَّن تُخْلَفَهُ وَانظُرْ
إِلَىٰ إِلَٰهِكَ الَّذِي ظَلْتَ عَلَيْهِ عَاكِفًا لَّنُحَرِّقَنَّهُ ثُمَّ لَنَنسِفَنَّهُ فِي الْيَمِّ نَسْفًا

(Moses) said: Then go! And lo! in this life it is for thee to say: Touch me not! and lo! there is for thee a tryst thou canst not break. Now look upon thy god of which thou hast remained a votary. Verily we will burn it and will scatter its dust over the sea.[35]

[35] Sūrah ṬāḤā, 20:97.

the story of qarun

After the repentance and punishment of the guilty Mūsā turned to the object that had caused all this trouble and decided to burn the golden calf. But as the idol was made of metal it would not burn. Mūsā prayed to the Lord for advice and the Lord sent Jibrīl to reveal to Mūsā that a certain herb which grew on the banks of the Nile had the property of turning any metal that was burnt with it into gold and if gold were burnt with it the gold would turn to ashes. Mūsā sent one of his relatives to fetch this alchemical herb and his choice fell on his nephew Qārūn; his elder brother's son.

Qārūn was a greedy man and when he heard of the wonderful properties of this weed, he picked not only a handful of it as Mūsā had ordered but brought back a whole camel load. He gave Mūsā a handful, and the rest he dried and hid away.

The golden calf was then burnt with the help of this weed and its ashes were strewn into the Nile. Then, all the Israelites had to drink from the waters and by the Will of the Lord peoples inner condition became evident after they had drunk. If a person's faith was weak, his head turned into the head of an ox or an ass and he died shortly afterwards. Those of sound faith were unaffected by this drink.

وَأُشْرِبُوا فِي قُلُوبِهِمُ الْعِجْلَ بِكُفْرِهِمْ قُلْ بِئْسَمَا يَأْمُرُكُمْ بِهِ إِيمَانُكُمْ إِنْ كُنْتُمْ مُؤْمِنِينَ

And they had to drink into their hearts (of the taint) of the calf because of their faithlessness. Say: "Vile indeed are the behests of your faith if ye have any faith!" [36]

[36] Sūratu 'l-Baqara (the Heifer), 2:93.

Qārūn secretly busied himself with converting all the metal he could find into gold with the help of the alchemical weed and before long he had amassed a tremendous treasure this way. The keys alone to his treasure chests and safes filled seven camel loads. In the end he had so much gold that he hardly knew what to do with it. The doors of his donkey stables were made of gold, their reins and bridles were golden every button on his vest was made of yellow gold.

إِنَّ قَارُونَ كَانَ مِن قَوْمِ مُوسَى فَبَغَى عَلَيْهِمْ وَآتَيْنَاهُ مِنَ الْكُنُوزِ مَا إِنَّ مَفَاتِحَهُ لَتَنُوءُ بِالْعُصْبَةِ أُولِي الْقُوَّةِ إِذْ قَالَ لَهُ قَوْمُهُ لَا تَفْرَحْ إِنَّ اللَّهَ لَا يُحِبُّ الْفَرِحِينَ

Qarun was doubtless, of the people of Moses; but he acted insolently towards them: such were the treasures We had bestowed on him that their very keys would have been a burden to a body of strong men, behold, his people said to him: "Exult not, for Allah loveth not those who exult (in riches).[37]

One day, Mūsā taught his people the verses concerning the giving of zakat, the poor-tax. It became incumbent on them to pay one quarter of their earnings to the poor to make their possessions lawful to them.

Qārūn grew extremely wealthy but in his heart he was envious of Mūsā because Mūsā was loved and honored more by his people than was he. All his riches were nothing compared to the honor of prophethood. Mūsā came to Qārūn to remind him of the tax he was bound to pay by the law of the Tawrāt but Qārūn's avarice was so great that it hurt him to part with so much of his property. The Lord

[37] Sūratu 'l-Qaṣaṣ (The Story), 28:76.

revealed to Mūsā that, as a special favor and an exception, Qārūn should be allowed to pay only one fortieth of his fortune. Still, Qārūn was not happy with his Lord's decree. The Lord further eased his burden and let him know that even the hundredth part and finally even the thousandth part of what he owned would be enough to clear him of blame but the rich man could not bring himself to part voluntarily with even the smallest bit of his wealth.

Qārūn's envy and resentment grew every time the prophet reminded him of his duties and he began to talk ill of Mūsā and malign him in every way he could. He disobeyed the Divine Command to pay zakat, for he was too proud to follow another's orders. He began to spend of his wealth in order to gain influence over people and soon bought himself a considerable following. People are always easily corrupted when they are given what they desire. Qārūn organized fun fairs and festivities for his people and he entertained them with all manner of frivolous diversions on these occasions. He showered his guests with gifts of gold and coins to ensure they would return another time. Qārūn, himself, liked to ride around in a chariot, drawn by gold reined horses or oxen and surrounded by an entourage of white slave girls in scarlet wraps and naked to the waist. He loved to display his wealth and power and secretly dreamed of himself becoming king.

Many people were tempted by him to forsake the straight path and to lead a life of similar luxury and worldly pleasures. Their companions warned them and tried to dissuade them from following their desires and pointed to the prohibitions of the Law which Mūsā had brought to them when they had asked for it. But few people listened, for the seeds of corruption had already sprouted in their hearts.

Now a certain day had been fixed for Mūsā to speak before the whole assemble of the Banī Isrā'īl and all the tribes were going to be present. Qārūn had long been preparing for this day, intending to publicly discredit Mūsā, the prophet. He had bribed a loose woman who was with child to publicly identify Mūsā as the father of her child. The day came and a dais was set up and Mūsā took his place in the seat of honor. The assembly began.

فَخَرَجَ عَلَى قَوْمِهِ فِي زِينَتِهِ قَالَ الَّذِينَ يُرِيدُونَ الْحَيَاةَ الدُّنْيَا يَا لَيْتَ لَنَا مِثْلَ مَا أُوتِيَ قَارُونُ إِنَّهُ لَذُو حَظٍّ عَظِيمٍ

Then went he forth before his people in his pomp. Those who were desirous of the life of the world said: Ah, would that unto us had been given the like of what hath been given unto Qārūn! Lo! he is lord of rare good fortune.[38]

Qārūn stood up and said, "Oh Mūsā, I have a few questions concerning the Law. What is the punishment for a thief and how is the adulterer to be punished?"

Mūsā replied, "According to the Holy Law of the Tawrāt, the thief shall have his right hand cut off and the adulterer, if he be married, shall be placed in a well up to his neck. Then, he shall be stoned until the well is full up with stones and he either lives or dies."

"And if it was yourself, oh Mūsā, would the Law be any different, since you are a Prophet?"

"No," said Mūsā, "there is no exception to the Law of the Lord."

Then, Qārūn triumphantly called to the woman he intended to use as witness against Mūsā and asked her, "Who is the father of your child?"

It was agreed that she was to tell everyone that he was Mūsā, the prophet, but when she tried to speak these words, her tongue twisted and she could not voice them.

---

[38] Sūratu 'l-Qaṣaṣ (The Story), 28:79.

Qārūn then spoke for her and said, "This woman is too shy to speak out, so I will tell you. She has become pregnant through adultery. The father of her child is Mūsā, your prophet!"

When Mūsā heard this outrageous lie, he fell into such a rage that he trembled from head to toe. "Oh Lord," he cried, "will You let them utter such slander and calumny against me while I am Your servant and prophet? Are You not the Dealer of Justice? Exonerate me from their monstrous accusation!"

The Lord heard his cry and sent the angel Jibrīl to tell Mūsā to touch the belly of that woman with his staff. Mūsā did so and by the miracle power which the Lord gave to Mūsā, the child within her womb spoke up and his speech was heard plainly by all those present in the assembly.

"*Lā ilāha illa-Llāh, Mūsā Rasūlullāh*!" spoke the voice of the unborn child. "Listen, oh Children of Isrā'īl, Mūsā is your prophet and he is forever protected from committing major sins such as that which he stands accused of. My father is a certain shepherd who lives in a place I will describe to you."

They fetched this shepherd and the man confirmed that he knew the woman and that he was the father of her child. All the people ware overawed at the miracle they had just witnessed and the revelation of power and truth but Mūsā's fury was undiminished. The Lord said to Mūsā, "Oh Mūsā, I place the earth under your command so that you may punish him as you wish." Mūsā did give Qārūn a chance. "Do you repent of what you have done and do you retract your words? If you do not I will order the Earth to swallow you." Hearing these threats, Qārūn's following quickly changed sides and most ran back to Mūsā's camp. Qārūn, however, was stubborn and refused to repent. So, Mūsā ordered the Earth to swallow him. The Earth obeyed and swallowed Qārūn and his followers up to their ankles.

"Stop, stop!" cried Qārūn. "I will give you whatever you want me to pay in zakat. I will give you as much money as you wish for that is all you really want of me!"

"Swallow him!" Mūsā ordered the Earth a second time and the Earth swallowed him up to his knees.

"I will give you more," cried Qārūn. "I will give you a quarter of all I own"

Mūsā said to the Earth, "Swallow him!" The Earth swallowed Qārūn up to his navel.

"Oh, tell her to stop," cried Qārūn, "and I will give you even more; half of all my possessions! Is that not enough for you?"

"Swallow him!" said Mūsā and the Earth rose up to his neck.

"I will give you all that I own," cried Qārūn.

Those were his last words for Mūsā ordered the Earth to swallow him completely and his voice was not heard again.

فَخَسَفْنَا بِهِ وَبِدَارِهِ الْأَرْضَ فَمَا كَانَ لَهُ مِن فِئَةٍ يَنصُرُونَهُ مِن دُونِ اللَّهِ وَمَا كَانَ مِنَ
الْمُنتَصِرِينَ

So We caused the earth to swallow him and his dwelling place.
Then he had no host to help him against Allah, nor was he of those
who can save themselves. [39]

It is said that the punishment of Qārūn is yet continuing and the Earth is still swallowing him; little by little into the depths of molten lava. We should heed the lesson contained in this story and to take care which side we stand on. When Qārūn had disappeared in the earth, some people still grumbled and said, "Is it a wonder that Mūsā would not release him? Now that he is gone, all his gold is left to

[39] Sūratu 'l-Qaṣaṣ (The Story), 28:81.

Mūsā anyway." To silence these evil tongues Mūsā ordered the Earth to swallow up all of Qārūn's wealth, as well, so that both Qārūn and his gold went down together.

the promised land

One day, while the Banī Isrā'īl was encamped at the foot of Mt. Sinai, Mūsā saw in the distance a great cloud of dust. As it approached, he recognized it as his father-in-law, Shuʿayb عليه السلام, with his daughter, Mūsā's wife and her two sons. Mūsā rose to greet them and they rejoiced and they told each other all that had transpired since they had parted. They stayed together for some time and then Shuʿayb عليه السلام left Mūsā to pursue his destination.

The Banī Isrā'īl had been promised a land of their own and after some time, Mūsā gathered the tribes around him and said to them, "The Lord has ordered us to continue on our way and to seek the Promised Land and to enter it in peace or in war, as we will be shown." But people knew that the land Mūsā was leading them towards was inhabited by the Amalekites, a tribe greater in size and stronger than they and they were afraid to fight them. They said to Mūsā, "Let us send messengers into the land first to find out what conditions prevail there before we go forth." So messengers were dispatched, twelve in number, to scout out the Promised Land.

There was a great giant, ʿŪj ibn ʿUnq, who lived in Palestine, and he was the tallest man ever to have lived. His little finger was five and a half yards long. ʿŪj had been a young man in the time of Ādam عليه السلام and though he remained an unbeliever, the Lord had prolonged his life and sent him his provision. Now, ʿŪj saw the little men of Isrā'īl entering his land and scooped them up in his hand and brought them to the Amalekite queen who ruled over the land. This queen was a wise and just ruler and she regarded the Israelites carefully. "It will not do to have them killed," she thought, "then they are of no use to us. I will test them and then decide."

She presented them with a giant watermelon that had grown in the country, and ordered them to take it back to their leaders. None of the men could lift the fruit and they could not roll it all the way home. After discussing the matter among themselves they took a long pole and bored it right through the melon so that they could carry it on their shoulders. The queen realized that they were men of great intelligence and decided to welcome them into her realm so that the land would profit from their wisdom.

The twelve messengers on their homeward journey decided not to tell anybody at home about what they had seen in the land for they knew that if they told stories of the giant Amalekites and of 'Ūj, the Israelites would never agree to go there. When they came back to their people, however, only two of them were able to stick to their resolution and to keep silent. One of these men who showed strength of character was Yūsha' who later became a prophet. As a result of the stories they heard from the messengers, the Banī Isrā'īl said to their prophets, "No, Mūsā, we will not go there. You may go ahead with your Lord and fight for us. When all is settled we will follow."

As it is mentioned in the Qur'an:

قالوا يموسى إنّا لن ندخُلها أبدًا ما داموا فيها ۖ فاذهب أنت وربُّك فقتلا إنّا ههُنا
قعِدونَ قال ربّ إنى لا أملِكُ إلّا نفسى وأخى ۖ فافرُق بيننا وبينَ القوم الفسِقينَ

They said, "Moses, we will never enter it so long as they are in it.
Go forth, thou and thy Lord and do battle.
We will be sitting here."
He said. "Oh my Lord, I rule no one except myself and my brother. So do Thou divide between us and the people of the ungodly."[40]

[40] Sūratu 'l-Mā'idah (The Table Spread), 5:24-25.

Mūsā and Hārūn took their staffs and left their people. The giant ʿŪj was watching all this from afar and when he saw that both the prophets had gone, he lifted up a great rock and raised it over his head. Then, he loped along with giant strides, threatening to throw the huge rock and bury the whole nation of Isrā'īl beneath it. Mūsā and Hārūn perceived the giant advancing. It seemed like a great cloud of dust to them and they sought refuge with the Lord. The Lord strengthened their heart and sent a little bird against ʿŪj. This bird flew out of hell. It held a tiny pebble in its beak and with it pelted the giant ʿUj. This pebble, from hell, fell on top of the mountain ʿŪjwas carrying and burned its way through the rock, down into ʿUj's skull, through his brain and all the way down to his feet. ʿŪjfell down, slain and Mūsā was the cause of his undoing.

The prophets, Mūsā and Hārūn had not been gone long before their people realized what they had done and felt great shame and remorse for sending away the prophets whom the Almighty Lord had sent to them and to whom they were so deeply obliged. They decided to follow after them and fight alongside. The next day, they set out and traveled until nightfall when they set up their camp. When they awoke the next morning, they discovered they were still in the place they had set out from the day before. Again, they set out and wandered until evening and again they found themselves in their first place the next morning. Day after day, the same thing happened until they realized that it was the doing of the Lord. He was angered against them and they were trapped.

One day, they saw the prophets returning to them and were joyful and said, "Good news to you, oh people of Isrā'īl, the enemy is put down and we are free to enter the Promised Land." But the Lord had decided to punish the Children of Isrā'īl for their lack of steadfastness.

قَالَ فَإِنَّهَا مُحَرَّمَةٌ عَلَيْهِمْ ۛ أَرْبَعِينَ سَنَةً ۛ يَتِيهُونَ فِى الْأَرْضِ ۚ فَلَا تَأْسَ عَلَى الْقَوْمِ الْفَٰسِقِينَ

Said He, "Then it shall be forbidden for them for forty years, while they are wandering the earth; so grieve not for the people of the ungodly."[41]

The Lord imprisoned them there in the wilderness of Tih for a full forty years and they were powerless against His Will. They were condemned to roam the wilderness and always found themselves back at their starting place the next morning no matter in which direction they ventured. The desert of Tih lies between Palestine and the Red Sea; it is waterless and nothing grows there. They grew hungry and weary there and began to lament and yearn for the life they had left behind in Egypt. They forgot that they had been ill-treated captives and that Mūsā had led them out of slavery. All they could think of was food. Mūsā prayed to the Lord to remember them and the Lord sent down from heaven two kinds of food: Manna and Salwa. This is what they lived on for as long as they dwelt in the wilderness of Tih. The manna was a substance which rained down at night onto the scrubs and bushes of the desert. It was a light and flaky substance which they would gather in the morning for their breakfast. It was sweet and delicious and it is still found in that area today. Salwa was a small bird similar to a pheasant which fell down from the sky, and everyone ate his fill, but no more. It was not permitted for them to store up any of this heavenly food until the next day, except on the day before the Sabbath, for this day of rest no work was allowed and no birds fell from the sky.

[41] Sūratu 'l-Mā'idah (The Table Spread), 5:26.

the story of musa and khidr

One day, Mūsā was preaching about the wells of wisdom mentioned in the Holy Tawrāt, and his people were profoundly stirred by his words.

They sighed and asked, "Oh Mūsā, is there anyone wiser than you?"

Mūsā answered, "I think not, for the Lord has sent me to be your prophet in this time and He has given me all the wisdom there is to dispense."

The Lord was displeased with these words and addressed Mūsā.

"Oh Lord," said Mūsā, "show me this servant of Yours whose wisdom is greater than my own. Where can I find him?"

The Lord directed him towards the confluence of the two seas.

"And how will I know him, my Lord?"

"Take with you a big salted fish for your provision to last you along the way. In the place that salted fish comes back to life and swims away you will find My chosen servant."

"What will he look like?"

"He will be wearing a great cloak, like your own and you will know him by certain signs."

So Mūsā set out with his companion, Yūshaʿ (Joshua). They journeyed for some time until they came to a place where the two waters met and formed between them a small island. There, Mūsā was overcome with the irresistible urge to fall asleep, and while he slept Yūshaʿ, his faithful companion kept watch. Suddenly, the fish they carried with them and of which they had been eating came alive and with a swish of its tail slipped into the water and swam away. After a while, Mūsā awoke and they continued their journey.

When they sat down again to rest Mūsā said to Yūshaʿ, "Bring out the fish so that we might eat the other half."

Then, only Yūshaʿ remembered and said, "Oh my prophet, Shayṭān has made me forget what I ought to have told you as soon as you awoke. When you lay down to sleep the fish came to life and took off down the river."

"That is the sign we have been waiting for," said Mūsā. "Quickly, show me the place where this happened for there we will meet that servant of the Lord whose wisdom is greater than mine."

They retraced their steps, until they found the place where Mūsā had been overcome by sleep and there they saw a man sitting on the bank of the river, wrapped in his cloak. Mūsā gave him Salams and the man answered him with greetings of peace.

Mūsā then said to him, "Oh my Lord's special servant, will you not accept me as your companion and teach me of your wisdom?"

The man answered, "Thank Allah for the knowledge He has given to you and I shall thank Him for what He has given to me. He has bestowed on each a different sort of wisdom and you will not be able to carry my knowledge; You have neither the strength nor the patience." But Mūsā insisted that he teach him and said:

قَالَ سَتَجِدُنِىٓ إِن شَآءَ ٱللَّهُ صَابِرًا وَلَآ أَعْصِى لَكَ أَمْرًا ۝ قَالَ فَإِنِ ٱتَّبَعْتَنِى فَلَا تَسْـَٔلْنِى

عَن شَىْءٍ حَتَّىٰٓ أُحْدِثَ لَكَ مِنْهُ ذِكْرًا

"Yet thou shalt find me, if God wills patient and I shall not rebel against thee in anything." Said he, "Then if thou followest me,

question me not on anything until I myself introduce the mention of it to thee."[42]

Finally, the man agreed to try him and after Mūsā had sent Yūshaʿ back to his people, the two men set out in a boat down the river, Mūsā the prophet and Khiḍr, the Lord's special servant. The ferrymen, seeing their passengers were holy men charged nothing for the passage and asked only that they pray for them. As they were being rowed across, a sparrow chanced to alight on the rim of their boat and it took a tiny beak-full of water to drink. Khiḍr said to Mūsā, "All the knowledge which the Lord has given to us is as the amount of water that little bird held in its beak, compared to the vastness of the Sea of knowledge of our Lord."

When they had reached the other bank of the river and the boat people had gone off, Khiḍr began to pry planks off the boat and throw them one by one into the water, so that it leaked and began to sink.

Mūsā was disturbed and cried, "What are you doing? These people took us along for nothing and showed us goodness, and in return you are destroying their boat?"

"Did I not tell you that you would not have the patience to bear with me," said Khiḍr.

"Oh I forgot;" said Mūsā, "please forgive me. I will try not to forget again."

They continued their journey on foot. Before long they came upon a number of children playing by the roadside. One of them was a particularly charming youngster who smiled at everyone. Khiḍr, as he passed the child raised his hand and struck him so that he fell lifeless to the ground. Mūsā was appalled and could not help himself but to exclaim, "Oh servant of my Lord, what have you done? How

---

[42] Sūratu 'l-Kahf (The Cave), 18:69-70.

can it be righteousness that you slew an innocent child who has not yet reached the age of maturity so as to be held responsible for his actions? What can a child have done to deserve death as a punishment? Surely this is a gross misjudgment and a grievous error"

"Did I not warn you that you would never be able to put up with me?" answered Khiḍr.

Mūsā realized that he had broken his word a second time and grew ashamed and said, "Forgive me once more, my friend, and if I fail you again, I will agree to our parting of ways."

They continued on their way. At last, they came to a town and wished to stay there for the night but none of the townspeople would offer them hospitality nor were they given anything to eat, though they asked for food. They passed outside the city and came to a ruined building; one wall of which was on the verge of collapse. Khiḍr said, *"Bismi'l-Lāhi 'r-Raḥmāni 'r-Raḥīm"* and set to the task of repairing the wall, stone upon stone, until it stood firm again.

Mūsā puzzled over this and said, "For this, you could have taken wages then we would have had food and shelter for the night."

"Now is the time of parting between me and thee" said Khiḍr, for Mūsā had broken his word for the third time.

Mūsā saw that this was true and felt great remorse. "Nevertheless," said Khiḍr, "I will now explain to you the meaning behind my actions so that you might learn from them. But first we must sit down to eat, for we are both hungry and tired from the journey."

As they sat down to rest, a deer came springing out of nowhere and Khiḍr halted it with a wave of his hand. The deer fell to the ground, slaughtered and skinned, one half of it ready cooked, the other half raw. "The roasted half is for me," said Khiḍr, "for I have done my work for the sake of Allah Almighty, and He in His endless bounty has rewarded me. The raw half of the deer is for you, since you saw fit to ask for reward for your labor, hence you must also work to prepare your own provision."

"But how shall I do this?" cried Mūsā who was very hungry and tired. "How shall I find firewood and cooking gear in the dark? Come, let us share your roasted half which is ready to eat now and which smells so delicious surely it will suffice us both."

Khiḍr said, "Alright, eat of it if you may." Mūsā reached out to take a piece of the roasted meat but when he put it in his mouth he found it had become raw again in his hand and was dripping with blood. Every time he took a morsel and tried to eat it, the same thing would happen and he could not eat a single bite. "It seems you must cook your own meal after all," said Khiḍr. So Mūsā went and collected wood to cook the meat while Khiḍr finished his own meal and performed his devotions.

When they had both finished eating Khiḍr took the remains of the meal and wrapped them up in the deerskin. He stroked the bundle with his hand and the deer became whole and alive again and sprang off into the woods. "Now, I will explain to you the hidden wisdom of my actions," Khiḍr said. "The first case in which you showed no patience was this: By the river, there lived several brothers who jointly possessed a boat. They ferried passengers across the river and made a profit from this occupation. These people were good to us and took no money for their services and are believers in the Almighty. But unknown to them there was a greedy king further upstream who had sent out his men to seize by force all boats that looked sturdy and functional and in a state of good repair. He would have appropriated the boat these good people owned and they would have been left with nothing. Therefore, I helped them by damaging their boat a bit and making it look shabby and neglected, so the king's henchmen would not cast their greedy eye on it. The second instance was the innocent child I slew. It was shown to me that his parents were steadfast believers, while it was written for that child to become a great sinner and that his criminal actions would cause his parents great pain in the future. So, the Lord ordered me to remove him from this world while he was yet in a state of innocence and unable to cause his parents grief through his Godlessness. The Lord revealed to me also that He meant to give the couple another child who would be the ancestor of seventy prophets. The third episode occurred in this town which refused us hospitality. Although, the inhabitants of the town are evil people, yet I repaired this wall, for the Lord informed me that among them are living two orphans whose father was a righteous man. Underneath this wall there is a buried treasure which rightfully belongs to them, it is their inheritance. Had the wall been allowed to cave in, the people of this town would have found this treasure before the two orphans came of age and they would have been left empty handed. In this way, I secured a future for them. In every case, I acted not on my own but upon the Command of my Lord, Allah Almighty." Having spoken these words Khiḍr departed, and Mūsā saw him no more.

Musa's Conversation with the Lord

It is related that Allah spoke to Mūsā, "Is there anything you have done for My sake?"

Mūsā replied, "Oh my Lord, I have prayed; I have fasted; I have performed Dhikr and I have given alms."

The Lord said, "Prayer is your proof; fasting is Paradise for you; alms giving is shadow and Dhikr is light for you. But what have you done for My sake alone?"

Mūsā replied, "Oh Lord, show me what to do, so that I may perform an action for Your sake only."

The Lord told him, "When you love a person, love him for My sake and if you do not love a person, then feel that way for My sake."

It is related that the Lord said to Mūsā, "Oh, Mūsā, make My servants love Me and tell them of My favors, so that they might learn to love Me."

Mūsā said, "Oh Lord, what is the reward of a person who stands in prayer while his people are asleep?"

The Lord answered, "Mercy will rain upon that person and his heart will be enlightened and his supplication will be accepted. I will write one hundred times the reward of one *raka'at* prayed during the daytime for each *raka'at* he prays at night and I will build a palace of gold for him in Paradise."

Again it is related that the Lord said to Mūsā, "Oh Mūsā, verily I have honored the nation of Muhammad with three holy names and no nation have I honored so highly before this. If a person in need invokes Me, calling upon these holy names, surely I will grant his prayer."

Mūsā asked, "And what are these holy names?"

"They are *Bismi'l-Lāhi 'r-Raḥmāni 'r-Raḥīm,"* said the Lord.

A blind man was with Mūsā and heard Mūsā say these names so he repeated them and the Lord restored his eyesight.

Mūsā said, "Oh Lord, You have made me Your speaker (Kalīm) and You have made Muhammad Your Beloved (Ḥabīb). Tell me what is the difference between us two?

The Lord said, "Oh Mūsā, the meaning of Kalīm is that all his works are performed for My good pleasure and the meaning of Ḥabīb is that all My works are for his sake. One loves the Lord, and the other is beloved by the Lord."

The Lord also said to Mūsā, "Oh Mūsā, if you remember Me, I will remember you." And the Almighty said, "Oh Mūsā, I have built a house for the sons of man and I have made it a safe haven for them. This house is made of light and its place is in the hearts of man. Its foundation is knowledge and its roof is faith. It is lit by yearning in the daytime and by love at night. Its pastures are righteousness and its mountains certainty. Its gardens are aspiration. Its thunder is fear and its lightning is hope. In its clouds are virtue and its rain pity. The trees are obedience, their leaves fulfillment and their fruits wisdom. The rivers are experience, the days are understanding and the nights are ignorance. This house has four doors: knowledge, forbearance, patience and gratitude."

Mūsā asked of the Lord, "Oh Lord, how can I know a servant whom You love from a servant against whom You are angry?"

The Lord answered, "Oh Mūsā, when I love a servant, I implant in him the remembrance (*dhikr*) of Me and both heaven and Earth will remember him and I protect him from disobedience and safeguard him from punishment. But when I am angry with a servant, I cause him to be heedless and to forget the remembrance of Me and he will be disobedient and I will make punishment come upon him lawfully."

Mūsā asked, "What are the signs of a servant who has earned Your Wrath?"

The Lord said, "Oh Mūsā, his heart is full of pride, his tongue speaks harsh words, his eye stares at what is forbidden and his hand is tight."

Qūt-ul-Qulūb says:

"The Lord said to Mūsā, "Oh Mūsā, tell My servants: he is My friend whose inner qualities are better than his outward ones and he is my enemy of whom the reverse is true."

When Allah drowned Firʿawn and his men, Mūsā asked the Lord to reveal to him some way to show gratitude for the Lord's favor to him. Allah told him to repeat the words *lā ilāha illa-Llāh*. Mūsā asked for more than this but the Lord said to him, "Oh Mūsā, if I were to place all the heavens and the Earth on one side and these words upon the other, these words would tilt the balance to their side."

Mūsā asked the Lord, "You have given me miraculous powers and a staff from the branches of Paradise. You have sent down Manna and Salwa from heaven for me and You have destroyed Firʿawn and all his men for My sake. Can there be any servant of Yours more highly honored in Your sight than I?"

The Lord replied, "There is one prophet and his nation who are more highly honored than any other creature to whom I gave life. This is my beloved Muhammad and his nation."

One day, Mūsā asked the angel, "Does my Lord ever sleep?"

The Lord ordered Mūsā to take two vessels filled with water and to hold them aloft, continuously. Finally, Mūsā was overcome with sleep and the vessels tumbled down and broke, spilling the water. The Lord then said to Mūsā, "Oh Mūsā, now you see, if ever I were to sleep, the heavens and the Earth would fall and break, spilling their contents, just as those earthenware jugs have done."

It is related that Mūsā asked the Lord, "Is there a place which is dearer to You than any other?"

"Yes," Answered the Lord, "There is such a place."

"And who inhabits this place, oh Lord?"

"Three groups of people enter that place, oh My prophet: Those who are patient with the trials I send to them, those who are grateful for what I have given them and those who are content when I send death to them."

The Lord said to Mūsā "There are five attributes which belong to Me and five belonging to you. Lordship is Mine and servanthood is yours. The bestowal of favors is Mine and gratitude is yours. Answering is Mine while asking is yours. The decree of destiny is Mine and patience with it is yours. Majesty belongs to Me and obedience to you." Then the Lord said, "I have placed five things within five others, yet people seek them always in other places. I have placed knowledge within poverty and people seek it in satiety. Secondly, I have placed satisfaction in the abandonment of desires, yet people seek it in their fulfillment. Thirdly, I have placed honor within obedience while people seek it at the threshold of the mighty. Fourthly, I have put wealth within contentment and people seek it in the accumulation of riches. Fifthly, I have put comfort and ease in the eternal life to come and people seek it in this passing worldly life."

Allah said to Mūsā, "Oh Mūsā, if a person obeys his parents and he disobeys Me, I will still write him in the book of the repentant and those deserving Paradise but if a person disobeys his parents, I will write him among the disobedient, even if He obeys My Commands."

Mūsā asked the Lord, "What is the distance between the Throne and the Divine Court?"

The Lord replied, "It is 10,000 times the distance between east and west."

One day Iblīs came to Mūsā and said, "Oh Mūsā, the Lord has chosen you among all His servants to be His prophet. He has also created me but I sinned and fell from my station on account of my disobedience. Now I wish to repent; please pray for me and intercede with your Lord on my behalf."

Mūsā prayed to the Lord that He might accept the repentance of Iblīs.

Allah Almighty replied, "Tell Iblīs to go to Ādam's grave and to prostrate himself before it. Then I will accept his repentance."

Iblīs heard what the Lord had said and he flew into a rage and cried, "What! When Ādam was alive I did not bow before him, how much less I will do so now that he is dead and gone." Iblīs again refused to obey his Lord and his repentance was not accepted.

The Lord asked Mūsā, "Oh Mūsā, do you wish for My Grace and Mercy to be closer to you than the words to your tongue and closer than the white to the black of your eye?"

"Oh my Lord, I do wish for that."

"Then you must frequently give *ṣalawāt* to My beloved Muhammad Muṣṭafā," said the Lord.

It is related that Mūsā said to the Lord, "Oh Lord, from Your Power You have created Ādam ﷺ and You bestowed upon him so many favors. How did he thank You for all that?"

The Lord answered, "He knew that everything came from Me."

"Oh Lord, show me one way, one action through which I might attain Your satisfaction!"

"Oh Mūsā, if you show yourself satisfied with what I have decreed for you, then I too will be satisfied with you." And the Almighty said, "Whoever remembers Me, I will remember him. Whoever obeys Me, I will obey him and whoever loves Me, I will love him too. Whoever seeks Me will find Me."

The Lord said to Mūsā, "You must teach the poor who seek Me with the same zeal with which you apply yourself to teaching the rich and powerful. For if you make a distinction, oh Mūsā, the knowledge which you have taught will become as a grave for you and cover you like the soil and on the Day of Judgment, your excellence will be diminished. Go and visit the sick and wash the robes of the poor!"

After this Mūsā went once a month to visit the sick and to wash the robes of the poor and humble.

Mālik ibn Dīnār relates that the Lord spoke to Mūsā:

"Oh Mūsā, fashion yourself a pair of sandals of tin and sheathe your staff with iron. Then go from house to house and from land to land in search of knowledge, until your shoes and your staff are worn out! Study My creation and learn from it!"

Mūsā said, "Oh Lord, You have given me the Tawrāt and spoken with me on Mount Ṭūr. There are four things I fear and my hope is set on one. I fear the bitterness of poverty and the throes of death. I dread the punishment of the grave and the Day of Judgment. My only hope is that You give my heart a love that will remain forever pure and untouched."

The Lord said to Mūsā, "Oh Mūsā, if you fear poverty keep the prayer of Ishrāq, you will be safe from poverty. If you fear the agony of death, pray the Awwābīn prayer (between Maghrib and 'Ishā). If you fear the punishment of the grave, pray two or four *raka'at*s during the night and if you fear the Day of Judgment, fast during the month of Rajab. And Mūsā, there are three things I will give to you if you can avoid three others: Keep your tongue from uttering lies and slander and I will give you great honor. Secondly, keep away from bad company, and I will choose for you righteous companions. Thirdly, stay away from foods that are doubtful or forbidden and I will give you wisdom."

The Lord said to Mūsā, "Oh Mūsā, there are four things you must not ask of Me, for I have not given them to those who went before you nor will I give them to those who are to come. Ask Me not for wealth so that you might revel in the glory of its possession and men submit to you on account of your riches. Secondly, do not ask of Me knowledge of the Unseen, for no one can know it except what I reveal. Thirdly, ask Me not to cut off the hearts of mankind from the hope of redemption for I am their Creator and I have cast their lots and surely they will die and be resurrected. Even the hearts of sinners are not cut off from hope. Fourthly, do not ask Me for permanence in this world for I am the King of all Eternity and everything in this world is of passing and perishing nature."

The Lord said to Mūsā, "Even if all the seven seas were ink and all the trees were pens, even if all of mankind, jinn and angels were scribes and wrote down 70,000 pages, they would not have completed the description of even the first of the stations of hell."

Mūsā asked, "How far, then, is it to hell?"

"It is a road of 4,000 years and each year has 4,000 months. One month has 4,000 days and each of these days has 70,000 hours; each hour is as 1,000 years which you know. Tell your people to please each other, then I will bring them into Paradise."

"Oh Lord, what if they cannot make each other happy?"

"Then let them please Me," said the Lord. "There are four things by which they can please Me: If they repent while their hearts are beating, if they ask for pardon with their tongues, if their eyes cry tears of remorse and if all their members engage in service for My sake."

It is reported that there lived a person in the time of Mūsā whose great pride lay in being the son of nine great forbears. The Lord ordered Mūsā to say to him, "Including you and your forefathers, there will be ten more persons in hell."

The Lord said to Mūsā, "There are two things you ought know and keep from the knowledge of two other things: Know that I, your Lord, am One but ask not to know how I am, for I have no 'howness. Know also that I am the Provider and Sustainer but ask not to know how and from where I give. And Mūsā, go not to the dwellings of the evildoers and oppressors even if they are ill and do not go to the funerals of My enemies for he who keeps friendship with My enemy is My enemy as well."

Muʿazzim Jābir relates:

The Lord spoke 400 words to Mūsā in three days. His last words were, "Obey your father and your mother." Mūsā asked the Lord nine times, "Oh Lord, what is Your final injunction?" The Lord said "Obey your mother," nine times and once He said "Obey your father." The Lord also said, "If a person obeys his parents in this world, I will give him honor during his life and I will make his sojourn in the grave and on the Day of Gathering, I will show him mercy and guidance and I will show Myself to him without intermediary. Oh Mūsā, the satisfaction of parents with their child is My satisfaction and their anger is also my anger. Even if a person performs good actions throughout his life, yet is disobedient to his parents, I will not accept his worship and I will not grant him safety from Hell."

And it is related that Mūsā said to the Lord, "I am a stranger and a poor man and I am ill."

The Lord said to him, "Oh Mūsā, to the stranger there is no friend like Me and for the indigent there is none who dispenses his bounties such as I and for the sick man there can be no doctor such as I."

The Lord said to Mūsā, "Your nine greatest faults are these: pride, covetousness, envy, speaking, eating and sleeping too much, love of wealth, fondness of flattery and lack of thankfulness."

It is related from Ibn Masʿūd:

"The Sūrah of Tabāraka (al-Mulk) was revealed in the Tawrāt. The Lord said to Mūsā that whoever recited this sūrah during the night will find safety from the punishment of the grave."

The Lord said to Mūsā, "Whenever you achieve a profit in your dealings, think of the Last Account whenever you feel desire for the pleasures of this world, remember death and whenever you are visited by affliction, pray to Me. When you sit down to eat, remember those who are hungry and when you are about to commit a sin, remember Hell. When you fall ill, give *sadaqa* (alms) and you will find healing. If you are rich, enrich also your people."

The Lord said, "Oh Mūsā, you have come to know My treasures. Leave off asking things from mankind? You have come to know My Kingdom, do not depart from My gate. You have come to know that My enemies are not dead, so do not give yourself over to complacency. As long as you have not cleansed yourself from all impurity, do not busy yourself with the defects of others. While you have not yet entered Paradise, do not deem yourself in safety."

This constitutes Mūsā's conversation with the Lord when he went up to the Mount of Ṭūr. He brought the verses of the Tawrāt to the Banī Isrā'īl and continued to teach them what the Lord revealed to him. They dwelt in the desert of Tih and the years went by.

One day, his people came to him and complained of the unchanging diet of Manna and Salwa which the Lord sent to them from heaven. They desired a change and asked Mūsā to pray to the Lord to send them the foods they had known in Egypt, the lentils, onions and garlic. Mūsā grew very angry at their ungratefulness and said, "Go then. Return to Egypt and eat there whatever you desire. Have you forgotten that our imprisonment in this desert is alone your doing. Had you only gone ahead into the promised land as you were ordered by the Lord, you would now have milk and honey and lack for nothing!"

وَإِذْ قُلْتُمْ يٰمُوسَىٰ لَن نَّصْبِرَ عَلَىٰ طَعَامٍ وٰحِدٍ فَادْعُ لَنَا رَبَّكَ يُخْرِجْ لَنَا مِمَّا تُنبِتُ الْأَرْضُ
مِن بَقْلِهَا وَقِثَّائِهَا وَفُومِهَا وَعَدَسِهَا وَبَصَلِهَا ۖ قَالَ أَتَسْتَبْدِلُونَ الَّذِى هُوَ أَدْنَىٰ بِالَّذِى هُوَ
خَيْرٌ ۚ اهْبِطُوا مِصْرًا فَإِنَّ لَكُم مَّا سَأَلْتُمْ ۗ وَضُرِبَتْ عَلَيْهِمُ الذِّلَّةُ وَالْمَسْكَنَةُ وَبَاءُو
بِغَضَبٍ مِّنَ اللَّهِ ۗ ذٰلِكَ بِأَنَّهُمْ كَانُوا يَكْفُرُونَ بِـَٔايٰتِ اللَّهِ وَيَقْتُلُونَ النَّبِيِّـۧنَ بِغَيْرِ الْحَقِّ ۗ ذٰلِكَ
بِمَا عَصَوا وَّكَانُوا يَعْتَدُونَ

And when you said, "Moses we will not endure one sort of food; pray to thy Lord for us, that He may bring forth for us of that the earth produces-green herbs, cucumbers, lentils and onions." He said, "Would you have in exchange what is meaner for what is better? Get you down to Egypt; you shall have there that which you demanded."[43]

[43] Sūratu 'l-Baqara (The Cow), 2:61.

the story of the cow

There lived in that time a rich man who had no children of his own. He took his brother's sons into his house and raised them as his own. He looked after them well and gave them the best education and in his will he left them all he had. Within their hearts, however, there was the seed of evil and they were unable to appreciate what their uncle had done for them. For if man's heart has no understanding, whatever you may do for him will be in vain. As the boys grew up they grew tired of waiting for their uncle's death so that they might possess all of his wealth. They secretly murdered him one night and dragged his body to the borderline between two neighboring villages and left him there.

The next day, they pretended to be searching for him and made a great show of being worried about their uncle. In the end, shepherds found the body in the field where they had laid him. Everyone was puzzled by this heinous crime because he had been a good man and had no enemies. The villagers began accusing the neighboring villagers of the deed and a dispute arose between them, and it would soon have come to blows. At last, someone thought of calling prophet Mūsā to settle their problem for them and people were sent out in search of him.

Now, not far away, there lived a poor widow with her only son who was the pride and joy of her life. His father had possessed a yellow calf, and when he felt that he must die, he had gone to the woods and prayed to the Lord, "Oh Lord, soon You will call me to surrender my soul and I return to You with pleasure. But what is to become of my wife and my young son? This yellow calf I will leave in Your trust and I leave You my family to look after." Before he died, he said to his wife. "Wife, if ever your poverty becomes too hard and pressing on you, tell our son to go to a certain place in the woods and to call out for help. Then, by the Will of God, it will come to him." Then, he lay down and died.

After his father's death, the boy earned a meager livelihood from collecting firewood and binding it into bundles which he carried on his back to the nearby markets. However little he earned from this hard work, he divided it into three parts: two thirds he would give to his mother to expend on the needs of their household and the other third he would give to those poorer than himself.

One day, he came home from work having injured his back with the heavy burden he carried. He said to his mother, "If only we had a beast of burden to help me with this work, it would be so much easier." That night, they both did not sleep; the boy was sleepless from his pain and his mother from worry about him. At last, she remembered what her late husband had said to her before he died. She told her son, "Your father has left something for you. Go into the woods to such-and-such a place and call out. Your father's beast will come to you there." The boy did as his mother bade him and called out at that clearing in the woods. At once, the yellow cow came out of the woods. She was tame and licked the boy's hands and face, as if she had always known him, although she had been living as a wild animal in the woods all this time. The boy happily led her home. He asked his mother for permission to sell the cow and set out for the market town. On the way, he met a man who offered him twice the price he had thought of asking for the animal. The boy grew confused and said he must first ask his mother. The woman was overjoyed, for it was a very high price. He set out again with the cow and met the same man again. This time he offered him a price three times as high as his original bid. Again, he went home to consult his mother and she said, "Oh, my son, go now and sell the cow and accept whatever price you are offered. You have my permission, for they are offering you very good money."

So the boy set out once more and again he met the man he had met before and he told him that he accepted his offer. The man then said, "I may seem to you to be a man but in reality I am an angel of the Lord. This is what you must do. After a short while you will meet some men who will want to buy your cow from you. As its price you must name all the gold which its hide will hold, and you must accept no less than that." The boy understood and the angel disappeared from his sight.

Meanwhile, the troubled villagers had found Mūsā and asked him to allay their conflict. "Perform a miracle for us." They said, "Raise up the dead man and let him point out his own murderer. Then our case will be solved and we shall believe in all you tell us and obey your Lord. Mūsā raised his hands in supplication and prayed to the Lord and the Lord spoke to him, "This is My Command. Let them slaughter a cow and divide it into two parts. With the tongue and the tail let them strike the dead man's body and My Wisdom will be known." Mūsā informed the people of the Lord's Command but they were skeptical and began to question Mūsā's revelation, as it is written in the Qur'an:

وَإِذْ قَالَ مُوسَىٰ لِقَوْمِهِ إِنَّ اللَّهَ يَأْمُرُكُمْ أَن تَذْبَحُوا بَقَرَةً ۖ قَالُوا أَتَتَّخِذُنَا هُزُوًا ۖ قَالَ أَعُوذُ
بِاللَّهِ أَنْ أَكُونَ مِنَ الْجَاهِلِينَ قَالُوا ادْعُ لَنَا رَبَّكَ يُبَيِّن لَّنَا مَا هِيَ ۚ قَالَ إِنَّهُ يَقُولُ إِنَّهَا بَقَرَةٌ لَّا
فَارِضٌ وَلَا بِكْرٌ عَوَانٌ بَيْنَ ذَٰلِكَ ۖ فَافْعَلُوا مَا تُؤْمَرُونَ قَالُوا ادْعُ لَنَا رَبَّكَ يُبَيِّن لَّنَا مَا لَوْنُهَا
ۚ قَالَ إِنَّهُ يَقُولُ إِنَّهَا بَقَرَةٌ صَفْرَاءُ فَاقِعٌ لَّوْنُهَا تَسُرُّ النَّاظِرِينَ قَالُوا ادْعُ لَنَا رَبَّكَ يُبَيِّن لَّنَا مَا
هِيَ إِنَّ الْبَقَرَ تَشَابَهَ عَلَيْنَا وَإِنَّا إِن شَاءَ اللَّهُ لَمُهْتَدُونَ قَالَ إِنَّهُ يَقُولُ إِنَّهَا بَقَرَةٌ لَّا ذَلُولٌ
تُثِيرُ الْأَرْضَ وَلَا تَسْقِي الْحَرْثَ مُسَلَّمَةٌ لَّا شِيَةَ فِيهَا ۚ قَالُوا الْآنَ جِئْتَ بِالْحَقِّ ۚ فَذَبَحُوهَا

وَما كادوا يَفعَلونَ وَإِذ قَتَلتُم نَفسًا فَادّٰرَءتُم فيها ۖ وَاللَّهُ مُخرِجٌ ما كُنتُم تَكتُمونَ فَقُلنا

اضرِبوهُ بِبَعضِها ۚ كَذٰلِكَ يُحيِ اللَّهُ المَوتىٰ وَيُريكُم ءايٰتِهِ لَعَلَّكُم تَعقِلونَ

"And when Moses said to his people, 'God commands you to sacrifice a cow.' They said, 'Dost thou take us in mockery?' He said, I take refuge in God, lest I should be one of the ignorant.' They said, 'Pray to the Lord for us that He may make clear to us what she may be.' He said, 'He says she is a cow neither old, nor virgin, middling between the two; so do that which you are bidden.' They said, 'Pray to thy Lord for us and ask that He make clear what her color should be.' He said, 'He says she shall be a golden cow, bright in color, gladdening to the beholder.' They said, 'Pray to thy Lord for us that He makes clear to us what she may be. Cows are much alike to us and, if God wills, we shall then be 'guided.' He said, 'He says she shall be a cow nor broken to plough the earth or to water the tillage, one kept secure, with no blemish on her.' They said. Now thou hast brought the truth' and therefore they sacrificed her, a thing they had scarcely done. And when you killed a living soul. and disputed thereon and God disclosed what you were hiding so We said, 'Smite him with part of it' Even so God brings to life the dead and He shows you His signs, that haply you may have understanding."[44]

Meanwhile, the boy had led his cow to market and it fulfilled all these conditions perfectly, in that t was of the right color, had been raised in the woods and had never been employed in service. Also, it was the right age and had not calved. People asked its price and the boy answered as the angel had told him to say, "This is a special cow, unlike others. Therefore, its price is also special. Its skin must be stripped and made into a bag. Then this must be filled to the brim

[44] Sūratu 'l-Baqara (The Cow), 2:67-73.

with gold. That will be its price. No less." People grumbled but Mūsā reminded them of their promise so in the end they accepted. They filled the cow's hide with gold and paid the poor widow's son. Then Mūsā took the tail and the tongue of the animal and struck the dead man with these parts. The dead man sat up in his grave and pointed to his murderers. Justice was done. People witnessed the miracle they had demanded and the poor boy's fortunes were made. He had made his mother pleased with him and therefore Allah's Pleasure was on him, too.

the death of harun عليه السلام

Mūsā and Hārūn went out into the desert one day and came to a place where a tree grew that they had never seen before. Beneath the tree was a settee on which lay mats and cushions, inviting them to rest in the shade. Hārūn had grown very old and was tired and when he saw the readymade bed he lay down upon it to rest his weary bones. In his sleep, the angel came to him and Hārūn surrendered his soul. Mūsā looked on and saw what had happened and as he watched, the tree, the couch and his brother's body all disappeared from view. Mūsā then said to the Lord, "Oh Lord, how shall I explain this to my people when I return to them?" Indeed, when Mūsā returned to the people without his brother, Hārūn, they instantly were suspicious and muttered amongst themselves, "We were fond of Hārūn and Mūsā knew this and was jealous. Hārūn was a great prophet and his tongue was sweet. Mūsā must have done away with him and hidden his body in the desert where no one can find him." Mūsā protested, but suspicions persisted and people demanded that he show them proof of his story.

He led them to the place in the desert where the tree and the couch had stood, but there was nothing to be seen. "How should we believe what you tell us;" they accused Mūsā, "how can a tree grow in one instant and disappear in the next? And what of a readymade bed?" While they were yet grumbling, the Lord gave them proof of Mūsā's truthfulness. He made the tree grow again and the bed with Hārūn's body on it appeared in that spot, before their very eyes. Hārūn's soul returned to him also and he spoke, "Oh my people, do not think ill of my brother, Mūsā. My appointed time had come and I went to the meeting with my Lord. Know that the Lord loves the 'righteous' and do not speak against my brother Mūsā, ever." Having spoken these words, the vision dissolved and the desert was as it had been before.

People then said, "Now we believe that you were true. We did this only to try you."

Musa's عليه السلام End

One day, Mūsā fell ill and suffered greatly from his disease. He disliked ill health, extremely, and prayed to the Lord not to ever let him fall ill before he died nor to send death to him before he asked for it. The Lord granted his prayer and sent Jibrīl to bring out the shirt of health from the stores of Divine Treasures. This shirt was given to Mūsā and he wore it and never fell ill again.

Mūsā also prayed, "Oh Lord, do not give me death until I am lying in the grave which I have dug for myself." The Lord granted him this wish also.

One day, the Angel of Death came to Mūsā to take his soul. But the Lord had vouchsafed to Mūsā that He would not take his life until he had dug his own grave. Mūsā was passing along the road one very hot day when he saw some people digging a grave. He stopped to watch them and it occurred to him that this grave would provide cool and welcome shade from the burning heat. Just then, the people turned to him and asked him, "It is so hot and we are very tired. Perhaps you can tell us whether we have dug long enough? This grave is intended for a person of exactly your size and stature." Mūsā climbed into the grave in order to test it. He, then threw out a few handfuls of earth so that it fit him perfectly. At that very moment, ʻAzrā'īl appeared and wished to take his soul. Mūsā struck him violently with his fist, so that he lost an eye but the Lord gave him a new one at once. Then, Mūsā died and his life on earth had been 120 years.

After his death, the shirt of health which he had worn all his life was taken from him and the angel Jibrīl came to the Lord and asked to put it back into the Divine Treasure House. Allah Almighty said,

"Whatever has gone out of My Treasure Houses once, does not enter them again. Give it to the sun." So Jibrīl clothed the sun in it. Therefore, all those who are ill, feel better during the day when the sun is shining and at night they feel worse. Every morning, the sun rises in its cloak of health which it will wear until the Day of Judgment.

yushaʿ

The prophet Yūshaʿ is mentioned several times in the Holy Qur'an, though not by name. He was 82 years old when he succeeded Mūsā and had held the station of prophethood for twenty-eight years. He taught according to the Tawrāt, Mūsā had received from the Lord, and led the Children of Isrā'īl into the Promised Land. Yūshaʿ was a descendant of Yūsuf عليه السلام, through Ephraim and Nūn. He had been a young man when the tribes left Egypt and all his life he was Mūsā's faithful companion and servant. Yūshaʿ was a soldier of strength and courage but he was learned in the Scripture, as well. The Lord gave him wisdom and granted him prophethood. Yūshaʿ accompanied Mūsā to the foot of Mount Nebo when the Lord called him there. Mūsā ascended to the heights from where he overlooked the Promised Land which he was not destined to enter. On Mount Nebo's summit, Mūsā received the Lord's last Commands to him. When he returned to Yūshaʿ he informed him that he, Yūshaʿ, was to succeed him and lead his people into the promised land when the days of their punishment had ended.

Together they returned to the tribes and Mūsā told them what he had told Yūshaʿ and confided his flock to his care. He handed him the Holy Ark and the Scrolls of the Tawrāt and preached his last sermon. Mūsā's grave has been long forgotten but with all probability it is situated in the hills of the east bank of the Jordan. May peace be upon his inspired soul.

Mūsā was not yet buried, however, when the tribes got together to accuse Yūshaʿ of having murdered him, just as they had accused Mūsā of murdering his brother Hārūn, aforetime. Yūshaʿ confronted them, and he was every bit as severe as Mūsā had been. He called them to order and firmly exhorted them to obey and follow him, for had Mūsā not told them he was to lead them into the promised land?

Yūsha‘ immediately began the preparations for the march to their destination. On the third day, he received the Divine Command to have all the males of the tribes circumcised with knives of stone. Most of the older men who had left Egypt had died during the forty years in the wilderness and while roaming the desert they had not found opportunity to circumcise the young. When they had healed from their operations, Yūsha‘ assembled all men able to carry weapons and ranged them in battle order.

They set out on their march and soon reached the Jordan Valley which they could not cross on account of its depth and steepness. They were forced to halt and immediately his men began to grumble against Yūsha‘.

"If only Mūsā were with us still, he would know how to lead us out of this impasse."

Yūsha‘ turned to them and spoke, "You must understand that I have not led you here of my own will but because my Lord has ordered me to. The forty years of roaming have now come to an end. Have you not noticed that for some days the heavenly provision of Manna and Salwa has ceased to rain from the skies? That is a sign that the exile has ended and I have been ordered to lead you into the Promised Land. So be patient and trust in Allah Who has appointed me to be your prophet now that Mūsā has gone."

Then Yūsha‘ prayed and waited for inspiration to come to him. It came to his heart that the Lord had parted the seas for Mūsā and all of Banī Isrā'īl had passed through the waters safely. He was inspired to now lead his people through the waters of the Jordan in the same way. He went ahead and told his men to follow him. They were doubtful at first but when they saw that the waters parted for Yūsha‘ they took heart and followed him. They all passed through, dry, and when they reached the plains of Jericho on the far side of the river they fell down and praised Allah Almighty. Some of the men claimed this was the first miracle of their prophet Yūshaʿ but others knew of another, earlier one. It had happened once that Yūshaʿ had passed into the land near Jericho with a band of scouts on the Ḥawā of the Sabbath and they had encountered a group of hostile warriors. It was late in the day when they engaged in battle and they knew that if they could not achieve victory by sunset, the Sabbath would be upon them, making battle unlawful for them. At that time, Yūshaʿ had prayed to the Lord to halt the sun in its course in order to give them time to fight off the enemy before nightfall and the Lord had granted his prayer. This had been the first miracle of Yūshaʿ.

Of all the men who had been young when they left Egypt only Yūshaʿ survived and the husband of Mūsā's sister, Kilaf, who never strayed from the straight path. He became the right hand of Yūshaʿ and always fought close by his side. In due course, the Israelites took all the land that had been promised to them by Allah, from the Mediterranean Sea to the lands of Shām. They settled there, and divided the land among the tribes of the twelve sons of Yʿaqūb according to the command of the Lord. They encountered fierce resistance from the tribes of Kanaan who were a strong and war-like people. The Israelites were as yet inexperienced in the ways of war, having sojourned for so long in the uninhabited desert. But Yūshaʿ was a great leader and an able general and he knew neither fear nor hesitation. Under his command, they soon conquered all the small kingdoms of the area and set up a rule of peace. Jerusalem was taken after a siege that lasted six months and all the idols in the city were dragged down and destroyed, while the conquered kings looked on in fear.

One day, it happened that their fortunes turned against them and the Israelites lost on the battle field. Yūshaʿ, at once, understood that this must be a sign from Allah and that his men must be guilty of some misconduct or transgression. He assembled all his men in ranks and commanded them to renew their allegiance to him as their leader and prophet. He took the hand of each and every one of the soldiers, and in this way he found the man who had broken the law. His hand remained stuck to his own and he could not wrench it free. The soldier was questioned and he confessed to having taken some of the booty to which by law he had no right and had hidden his loot, secretly. He repented after his confession and thereafter, the Israelites were again victorious in battle.

Five of the enemy kings united to fight against Yūshaʿ and the Banī Isrāʾīl. They knew that it was their custom to end a battle by nightfall and so they intended to detain them until it was dark and in that way gain victory over them. The day waned and still they were so engaged in battle that an interruption would have meant defeat. So Yūshaʿ prayed to the Lord as he had prayed before. "Oh Allah, give order to the sun who is under Your Command to stay his course, that he might not set until we have defeated the unbelievers. Thereafter, the name of this field shall be, 'the heavens rise' for the day was lengthened" The Lord heard his prayer and the sun was stopped just as it was about to set, not for one hour or two, but for a whole day. Night did not fall but the full moon rose in spite of this, pale and white, in bright daylight. As it set again, the Banī Isrāʾīl achieved victory and the battle was won. Now even the most stubborn doubter believed in the prophet Yūshaʿ. The men were ordered to fetch their families from the encampment at the Dead Sea and they settled in the land, living by the Law that Mūsā had taught them.

Once more, the Divine Command came to 'Yūshaʿ: He was ordered to purchase the field that had belonged to Ibrahim Khalīl-ur-Rahman (by Hebron-Khalīl) which was his gravesite and the burial-ground for many other prophets. There, he was to bury the body of the prophet Yūsuf 🕮 which they had carried with them all the way from Egypt. In this way, Yūsuf 🕮's last wish was fulfilled.

the story of zimri and cozbi

The tribes of the land of Kanaan were overcome by military might with Divine Aid but they were yet plotting to destroy Isrā'īl from within. They began to invite people to the sacrifices of their gods and sought occasion to introduce the men to the young girls so that they might be seduced. The soldiers of the Israelites were very much taken by the beauty of the women of Kanaan and would soon have forgotten their commandments and abandoned themselves to worldly pleasures. One of the tribal chieftains, Zur, had a very beautiful daughter by the name of Cozbi.

He perceived a chance of destroying the Israelites and one day he called his daughter to him and said to her, "Oh my daughter Cozbi, you have witnessed what all the sons of Isrā'īl have done to our land. Do you wish to see them destroy our cities as well and lead us off into slavery?"

Cozbi replied instantly, "Who could wish for such a thing, oh my father?"

"Will you then do as I tell you, Cozbi, for you have the means of saving your people."

"But what can I possibly do, father, being that I am but a frail woman?"

"If only you were willing, you could be the undoing of 100,000 men."

"May my soul be ransomed for you, oh father;" she said, "I am ready to do anything you say."

"Your soul has nothing to do with this. Do you not know that your beauty is the subject of many a song and ballads are sung about your charms? How many princes have asked for your hand in marriage and I have refused them all, holding out for the best bargain. At last this day has come."

"Oh father, help me to understand your speech," said Cozbi.

Zur then said, "You must know that among the sons of Isrā'īl it is counted as a crime to consort with other than one's own wedded partner and it is forbidden for them to take foreign women as their wives. Anyone found guilty receives the death penalty at once."

"What a strange thing. Why does their god mix into the affairs of the heart?"

"That, I don't know but I do know that it is our only chance against them. We must try to corrupt their morality. That way we can divide them against each other and incite them to oppose their prophet and leader, Yūshaʿ. It has come to my knowledge that one of their officers, a certain Zimri, the son of Salu, is greatly enthralled by the beauty of women. If he were seduced to transgress the law, all his men would follow his example and rebellion would break out in their ranks. In that way Yūshaʿ's power over them would be broken and it would be a good thing for us."

"Now finally I have understood father. Leave the rest to me. I will complete the task to your satisfaction."

She went off to prepare herself. Then she descended into the marketplace which was frequented by the soldiers of the Israelites, holding a basket in which she displayed her goods. She spoke to no one until she had found the man she was sent to look for, Zimri the son of Salu. She approached him, offering him her wares. Once she cast upon him a ravishing glance, all sense of reason left Zimri and maddened by desire for the girl, he half pushed, half dragged her off to his tent. When his men saw that their leader had taken it upon himself to disobey, they followed his example and went ahead and took foreign women as well.

Word soon spread to Yūsha'. Yūsha' hoped to stop the evil ways from spreading and called Zimri to him. He came, accompanied by his mistress, and spoke to the prophet in a mocking and disrespectful tone.

"You know that you are doing what is forbidden and you know also what is the punishment, oh Zimri. You are a bad example to your men. The Wrath of Allah is not far away."

"Now that we have finally reached and settled in the Promised Land, Allah is not concerned with us anymore," retorted Zimri.

"You are still young, Zimri. You don't know what the Wrath of God brought upon your fathers in the days of old. Repent now and turn away from evil, lest you draw Divine Anger upon yourself and your people."

But Zimri had neither eyes or ears for other than the woman whom he adored and gave no heed to the prophet's words. People saw him leaving Yūsha''s tent unharmed and took it for a sign of permission. They all went and followed his example. Before a month had passed, the whole tribe of Zimri who lived in the border region of Kanaan took to leading a dissolute life. They engaged in immoral activities with a frenzy, as if they had been deprived of a vital necessity.

The Wrath of Allah was not long in coming. Soon an epidemic broke out among them that slew no less than 70,000 of their number. The survivors of that plague understood that it had come as punishment for their betrayal and came running repentant to the prophet Yūsha', crying to him to save them.

"How should I save you? You have brought the plague upon yourselves by your godlessness. I can advise you only to carry out judgment against the transgressors amongst you."

This, none of the people dared to do and they answered half heartedly, "You are a prophet. The Shariah is in your hands. If you will not apply it, who will?" So the plague continued to rage among them. Phinehas, the son of Eleazar, son of Hārūn was sent to the north to report on the conditions in the land. He was a man of courage and strong faith. When he saw the effects of the general immorality and the plague that it caused, he set his mind to extinguishing its root. He took his spear in his hand and went unaided to the tent of Zimri and his mistress. He killed them both with one thrust. Then he brought out both bodies from the tent, impaled on his lance and showed them to the people. "This is how we punish immorality according to the Law," he said, "for the sake of the Almighty Lord." Whereupon, the soldiers went out and put to death all those indulging in forbidden pleasures and Allah Almighty took from them the dreadful disease which had visited them. Again, all the people of Isrā'īl renewed their oath. They promised not to turn from the path of righteousness and to observe the Law of Mūsā.

The Story of Bala`am

Yūsha''s conquests proceeded to the north, until the armies of the Israelites had come close to the borders of Shām. Yūsha' sent out scouts who brought back reports that there were only minor kingdoms in that area whose kings were stricken with fear of the invaders and had no intention of allying their forces. They also brought back word of a certain Bala'ām, son of Be'or, who they reported, was living in the land and had great influence over the regional chiefs.

This news came as a surprise to all of Isrā'īl, for Bala'ām was born of the sons of Isrā'īl and had left Egypt with them. Besides Yūsha' and Kilaf, he was the third survivor of that generation. He had been a man of great learning, for Mūsā had taught him, and was one of those whose prayers were answered by the Lord. Later, something within him had become twisted and he rebelled against Mūsā, along with Qārūn, who had promised him a great reward if he would utter a curse against the prophet. The Lord Almighty did not leave him to speak his imprecation and his tongue curled up in his mouth and was thus maimed. In the course of events, he left the tribes and went off alone, settling at last in the lands of Shām among the unbelievers. There, he was greatly respected for his wisdom and learning and because his supplications were always answered, even though he had gone so far astray and his tongue remained twisted. None of the Israelites could understand how this could be, but Yūsha' said to them, after hearing the reports, "The wisdom of the Lord is inscrutable. Don't trouble yourselves about this Bala'ām. If his prayers are acceptable to the Divine Presence to this very day, there must be a hidden reason for it. Allah never accepts a prayer uttered against a believer: See what happened to this Bala'ām when he tried to curse the prophet Mūsā. We don't know what the Lord holds in store for him, yet."

The messenger had also reported that Bala'ām lived alone and had not married, for the women of the land despised him on account of his short stature. Bala'ām lived alone with his donkey as if she were his wife. The words of their prophet gave the Muslims courage and they prepared to march out against the enemy.

In a village in the land of Shām, an old, wizened man was sitting by a brook while his donkey stood nearby. Whenever the donkey looked towards the man, her eyes became red and bloodshot with anger and hatred. The man rose and looked towards the mountains, straining to see, as if expecting somebody to come from that direction. But try as he might, he could make out nothing. This man was Bala'ām, the son of Be'or. He had heard of Yūsha''s victories and the advance of the armies of the Israelites and had grown restless and fearful. He remembered all that had befallen him of old and now was filled with regret. He would have gone forth to meet Yūsha' and beg forgiveness of him but he had not the courage to do so. He had considered fleeing even further to the north and settling in an unknown land but he was old, and felt uneasy about moving to a strange place where no one knew him or of his special characteristics. So he just stayed on and waited. Several times in the past he had been on the verge of a decision and had called to his donkey to make ready to go but the beast had only looked up at him with her blood tinged, hateful eyes. The Lord had given to her the power of speech. On certain occasions she spoke out spitefully against her master. Bala'ām, of course, was stupefied to hear his donkey speak to him and began to tremble. The donkey made use of his confusion and landed a kick on his backside so that Bala'ām tumbled over. As he picked himself up, he heard sounds of footsteps approaching. Looking, he saw a crowd of people, notables and envoys from the Lords of Shām who greeted Bala'ām with deference and signs of great respect. They bore valuable gifts and honored him in every way. The kings of Shām were expecting an attack by the Israelites and knowing themselves to be too weak to withstand their forces, they had come to Balaʿām to ask him to bless them and to curse the armies of Yūshaʿ, for whomever Balaʿām cursed, was cursed, and whomever he blessed was blessed.

Now they approached Balaʿām with sweet words, "Oh Balaʿām, surely you have heard that Yūshaʿ, who shows his enemies no mercy, has taken up position behind yonder mountain and we are now going out to face him in battle."

"Yes indeed, I have heard," replied Balaʿām. "Nobody can survive the onslaught of his armies."

They continued, "He has destroyed all our neighbors, the Amalakites, the Kanaanites, the Amorites and the Midianites. All of them fell before him and were vanquished. How then shall we stand against him and hope to fight a victorious battle?"

"I know all this and I am not interested," said Balaʿām.

"Is it not true," they asked, "that once, long ago, you uttered a curse against their prophet Mūsā? Surely they have not forgotten this. You are guilty in their eyes and if they find you here and discover your identify, you will be the first to die. It is in your own interest to help us win against them this day."

"Help? How should I help you? I am old and withered. I will barely be able to save myself."

"You can help us, indeed. You must go out onto the battlefield ahead of our army. While facing them, you must curse them in the name of their God. Everyone whom you curse, is cursed. That way we will be able to overpower them."

Balaʿām trembled in the depths of his being and said, "No, that I cannot do. I can and may not speak a curse against them."

He felt sincere remorse at what he had done aforetime, and the oldest allegiance in his heart began to stir. But the envoys had expected something like that and they winked at each other, signaling that they would try a different tactic.

They began, "Oh Bala‘ām, you are an old man now and your life has not been easy. Are you content, then, to live out the rest of your days in hardship and poverty? We could easily change these conditions for you, if you were only willing."

Bala‘ām broke out into shameless laughter and said, "When I mount upon this donkey, it is as if I have mounted upon the whole of mankind, for I am of the sons of Isrā'īl and all of mankind is condemned to bear my burden. Don't worry. I will look after myself and pursue my own kind of pleasure. Allah answers the prayers of a person like me, but He does not give me power. That is why I am angry at heart and full of bitterness. Don't let yourself be fooled by the lies of Isrā'īl. In the future they will all be like me and they will make the nations spit blood!"

One of the envoys tried to appease Bala‘ām and began to speak to him softly, "Bala‘ām, leave off your idle dreams and unwholesome cravings and live in real life at last. If you help us just this one time we will set you up in comfortable villa, surrounded by green parks and gardens, replete with sparkling fountains and a host of slaves to see to your needs There will be beautiful maidens for you and wine flowing in streams. This sordid life with your donkey will be over for you for good."

Bala‘ām looked up and sneered, "Your women have always held me in contempt," he said, "because I am shorter than they."

The man smiled and said, "We have thought of a solution for that as well. The girls we will provide for you will be no older than ten years of age. If you stretch yourself a little bit you should be well able to reach to them."

Now, Bala‘ām could not entirely reject this offer off-hand. It did appeal to him in a secret corner of his dark heart and he began to soften. He made them swear a solemn oath that they would keep their promise if he agreed to help them as they wished. It was their custom, on swearing an oath, that each man pierce his thumb and squeeze out a drop of blood into a vessel. Their blood was then mixed and they would each lick it up in turn. In this way their oath was sealed. Bala'ām participated in this ceremony, thus promising to do their bidding. The envoys departed, reminding Bala'ām to be at the appointed place of the meeting of the armies the very next morning. Bala'ām set out promptly with his donkey, already dreaming of the luxurious life promised to him after his accomplished feat. But he began to have trouble with his donkey. It ran off ahead of him and he could barely catch up with it. He tried to mount it but it would not stop for him to do so.

When, finally, he succeeded, the donkey ran on at a great pace, until suddenly its feet sank into the ground as If it had stumbled into a bog. It fell and could raise itself only with difficulty. By now it was late in the afternoon and Bala'ām had not covered even a tenth of the distance. He realized that even, if he were to ride hard all night long, he would scarcely reach the battleground by the morning. He addressed his donkey and asked her, "You know a lot of things, oh my little donkey. Tell me what to do now?"

Unexpectedly, his donkey spoke to him harshly, saying, "Oh you arch-misguided one. Just look at yourself! Has the punishment of the Lord not been enough for you that He made your tongue hang outside your mouth for that you attempted to curse His Holy Prophet! Now you have set out again to do the same thing. What do you think will happen to you this time? Do you think the Lord will reward you? Many years ago you fled here to live among the idolaters and you took me into your service. I have served your every purpose, even standing in as a wife! You can hardly be said to be a human being. You are a low and despicable creature! Yet in spite of all your misdeeds, the Lord is infinitely great and merciful. No matter what a man has done, if he seriously repents and turns back from sin, he will find forgiveness. Oh Balaʿām, repent! Return to your Lord, He will forgive you and place your tongue back in your mouth and stop all your drooling and slobbering. How can you trust in the promises of the godless? Who could drive a single nail into a piece of wood if it be not His Will? Even Qārūn with all his knowledge and wealth and multitude of slaves was powerless against the Might of the Lord. The earth swallowed him. That was his end which you did not know."

Balaʿām heard but did not believe. He could not believe he was hearing his donkey speak. He thought he was listening to his own thoughts and imaginations and misgivings. He began to scream out loud to enhance his courage. "Oh yes, I will press on and be on time for the meeting of the armies. Then I will hurl my curse against the Banī Isrā'īl and they will be defeated. And then I will retire into my palace and my harem of delightful ten-year olds! Oh my donkey, then I will divorce myself from you!" Such was his frivolous speech.

But the donkey spoke again and tried to shake him into consciousness, "Balaʿām, did you not see how I stumbled and fell a little while ago? And do you not see how I can scarcely walk ahead even now? One step ahead and two steps back."

Balaʿām replied, "Yes, come to think of it, I have noticed. What are you doing that for?"

The donkey said, "It is because I can perceive those angels whom you cannot see. They are all around, preventing me from stepping ahead. They are trying to prevent you from reaching the mountain before daybreak."

But Balaʿām was too far gone into his dream for these warning words to reach him and remained unimpressed. He was now possessed by a strange form of pride and ambition. He yelled with all the air in his lungs, "I will proceed to curse them. Who could stop me?"

The donkey then said, "Woe to thee! The angels have now withdrawn. from the path. It is now clear to lead you towards your destination where, you will find your just desserts. I can carry you ahead now at the speed which you desire but know that you are hastening towards your punishment."

All along the way the donkey reminded Balaʿām of the events that had taken place before his time and how the Wrath of Allah had destroyed the unbelievers and transgressors, hoping that he would yet change his mind before they reached the mountain.

By the early morning, they had arrived. The two armies were arrayed against each other and were about to sound the charge. Balaʿām dismounted from his donkey, enveloped in his dreams of palaces and young virgins. The commanders of the idolaters applauded his coming with triumphant cries and a great clamor, while Yūshaʿ regarded this lost son of his people with a sorrowful heart. Balaʿām's pride was swelled by the applause afforded to him and he marched on, his head held high. He climbed to the top of a boulder in order to appear taller and then began to speak. He spoke for a long time, singing his own praises. Then, he raised his hands towards heaven, ready to speak the words of imprecation which he had prepared so well for that day, "Oh Lord, make Yūshaʿ and his armies perish on this day!" But these words, try as he might, would simply not come out of his mouth and instead he ended up voicing the opposite of what he had intended to say, damning the unbelievers and praying for Yūshaʿ's victory. After he had finished speaking, his tongue which he had been incapable of withdrawing into his mouth since the time he had cursed Mūsā, now became so swollen and distended that it swung pendulously down to his navel. Balaʿām could speak no more. He only made unintelligible sounds in his throat. He slid down from the rock he had so proudly climbed like a beaten dog with his tail between his legs and crawled over to Yūshaʿ's side. He no longer had the means of expressing himself in human terms but Yūshaʿ had understood all he needed to know. Upon a sign from him, the charge was sounded and the battle began. The enemy was easily beaten and put to flight, their morale having been badly shaken by the two events. The outcome of the battle was that all the kingdoms of the region passed into Yūsha''s hands. He controlled all the land up to the foot of the Toros mountain range.

Some months passed. One day, Bala'ām was brought before Yūsha'. They told him that Bala'ām only howled and groveled like a dog at their feet and had come to Yūsha' expecting the order to execute the creature. But Yūsha' thought otherwise, "Leave him as he is," he said to them, "so that people might behold him and take a lesson from his subhuman condition. He is an example for all of Isrā'īl. Allah Almighty had given him great knowledge and had he remained steadfast on the way to what heights and exalted stations might he not have attained! But he chose instead to follow the way of Shayṭān, the accursed. He was obsessed by the love of worldly possessions. As a result, everything was taken from him. All his rewards have gone and who knows for how long he is destined to crawl over the face of the earth in this degraded fashion! Truly, it is a thing to be feared"

Some of Yūsha''s people wished to know more. "What then, should we learn from his example? What does it mean for us?" they asked.

"Have you still not understood? Allah Almighty teaches you, thereby, to hold fast to the Tawrāt and the knowledge conveyed to you through His prophet Mūsā, so that you might live in peace in the Promised Land. But if you let yourselves be seduced by greed and lust for worldliness, surely you will he driven out into exile and degraded. Perhaps your tongue will not be made to hang down to your navel, but punishment is sure to reach you. Only He, the Almighty, knows what He has written for you. If you let Shayṭān dominate you, he will strip you of the honor that has been given to the sons of Ādam. He will twist your minds and make you do as Bala'ām did to his donkey."

"May Allah protect us!" they cried out.

"Yes, may Allah protect us all and preserve our reasoning. He will not let this happen to you as long as you walk in His way. But how many prophets have come and gone, always with the same message of truth to mankind? After my time, how many more are yet to come? I do not know. Yet man has always forgotten again and again."

'One day the last prophet of all will appear, as it is written in the Tawrāt. He will bring a revelation for all people on Earth. He will be the final messenger. After him there will be no new revelation till the end of time. This has been revealed to you. So teach your children, your sons and grandsons, to believe in him and to honor his name until the time he appears. Let them adhere to the Scriptures and abide by the Law and all their works will be made easy for them. If you don't follow these injunctions, you will be crushed under a mountain of sin and you will have to bear that burden in this world and the next and you will not be forgiven."

As Yūshaʿ spoke these words to the Children of Isrāʼīl, tears welled up in his eyes and his voice became harsh with sorrow.

His followers asked him, "Oh Yūshaʿ, what causes you to grieve? Is it that you are seeing visions of the future and is it as terrible as the lot of Balaʿām?"

To this, Yūshaʿ gave no reply and said only, "Set him free!"

They let Balaʿām go and he took a few steps away from them. Then turned and crept back. Thus, he turned round and round in indecision for in truth he had no place to go to. At that moment, he heard an ass braying in the distance and he made his way towards it. When he reached the ass, he lay on his stomach and began munching the grass as he saw the donkey doing.

Again, Yūshaʿ addressed the men, saying, "Pay heed to my words. Don't ever adopt the ways of the beasts. You are born the sons of Ādam. Perhaps they may appeal to you at times and you might think you have gained but in the end you will find yourself abased and degraded like Balaʿām. I haven't the authority to slay him and put him out of his misery. This is in the hands of the Lord. Each man has his own mind and conscience and every human being is born into this world as a Muslim. His upbringing and environment leads him astray. See what has happened to Balaʿām the son of Be'or. Be wary of the way you tread. I don't know how long Balaʿām will yet have to live in this fashion but his life is not ours to take. Every remaining day of his life is a punishment for him. After him there will come many more Balaʿāms but I pray that they might not be from your descendants. Oh sons of Isrā'īl, I pray that men may not look on you with disgust and loathing, watching you crawl through the dust on all fours like the lowly beasts."

Yūshaʿ was farsighted and provident and tried to warn the Banī Isrā'īl of what he foresaw of the future.

This story is also mentioned in the Qur'an an in these verses:

وَاتْلُ عَلَيْهِمْ نَبَأَ الَّذِىٓ ءَاتَيْنَٰهُ ءَايَٰتِنَا فَانسَلَخَ مِنْهَا فَأَتْبَعَهُ الشَّيْطَٰنُ فَكَانَ مِنَ الْغَاوِينَ وَلَوْ
شِئْنَا لَرَفَعْنَٰهُ بِهَا وَلَٰكِنَّهُۥٓ أَخْلَدَ إِلَى الْأَرْضِ وَاتَّبَعَ هَوَىٰهُ ۚ فَمَثَلُهُۥ كَمَثَلِ الْكَلْبِ إِن تَحْمِلْ
عَلَيْهِ يَلْهَثْ أَوْ تَتْرُكْهُ يَلْهَث ۚ ذَّٰلِكَ مَثَلُ الْقَوْمِ الَّذِينَ كَذَّبُوا۟ بِـَٔايَٰتِنَا ۚ فَاقْصُصِ الْقَصَصَ لَعَلَّهُمْ
يَتَفَكَّرُونَ سَآءَ مَثَلًا الْقَوْمُ الَّذِينَ كَذَّبُوا۟ بِـَٔايَٰتِنَا وَأَنفُسَهُمْ كَانُوا۟ يَظْلِمُونَ مَن يَهْدِ اللَّهُ فَهُوَ
الْمُهْتَدِى ۖ وَمَن يُضْلِلْ فَأُو۟لَٰٓئِكَ هُمُ الْخَٰسِرُونَ وَلَقَدْ ذَرَأْنَا لِجَهَنَّمَ كَثِيرًا مِّنَ الْجِنِّ وَالْإِنسِ ۖ
لَهُمْ قُلُوبٌ لَّا يَفْقَهُونَ بِهَا وَلَهُمْ أَعْيُنٌ لَّا يُبْصِرُونَ بِهَا وَلَهُمْ ءَاذَانٌ لَّا يَسْمَعُونَ بِهَآ ۚ أُو۟لَٰٓئِكَ
كَالْأَنْعَٰمِ بَلْ هُمْ أَضَلُّ ۚ أُو۟لَٰٓئِكَ هُمُ الْغَٰفِلُونَ

And recite to them the tiding of him to whom We gave Our signs, but he cast them off and Shayṭān followed after him, and he

became one of the perverts. And had We willed, We would have raised him up thereby; but he inclined towards the earth and followed his lust. So the likeness of him is as the likeness of a dog; if thou attackest it lolls its tongue out or if thou leaves, it lolls its tongue out. That is that people's likeness who cried lies to Our signs. So relate the story; haply they will reflect.
An evil likeness is the likeness of the people who cried lies to Our signs and themselves were wrongful. Whomsoever God guides, he is rightly guided and whom He leads astray, they are the losers.
We have created for Gehenna many jinn and men. They have hearts, but understand not with them.
They have eyes, but perceive not with them. They have ears, but they hear not with them. They are like cattle? Nay, rather they are further astray. Those, they are the heedless.[45]

The land that the Israelites had conquered was divided into twelve provinces. Each of the twelve tribes dwelt in their own land and each tribe had its own leader. The Tawrāt was taught and learnt and the people prospered and multiplied and could not have wished for a better life. The prophet Yūsha' lived apart from the people, on his own, but he was informed of all that went on in the land. There was, however, one point which worried him. The Israelites had destroyed and torn down all the temples of pagan worship, but they were very reluctant to teach the unbelievers about the one, true God. They began to ill-treat the people they had conquered and made them work hard and suffer cruelty as if they sought to venge themselves on them for what their fathers had suffered at the hands of the Egyptians. Although it was forbidden to them, they took to drink and gambling and used their God-given ingenuity to devise what was forbidden. They learned how to make liquor out of every fruit and tree and invented games and gambling bits of carved wood and polished stone. Yūsha' saw that it was the beginning of no good and

---

[45] Sūratu 'l-'Arāf (the Heights),7:175-179.

called the leaders of these games and diversions and counseled them to steer clear of these transgressions. He was more than amazed at the strange answer they came up with in their own defense.

"Oh Yūshaʿ, we know full well the harm contained in these things. But you see, we are not producing them for our own people but for those we have conquered. For, if we don't keep their minds busy with such distractions they will awaken to opposition and cause us a lot of trouble. We are poisoning them in order to keep our own people free to lead a clean and god-fearing life."

When he heard their twisted reasoning, Yūshaʿ grew very angry and turned on them, "Oh sons of Isrāʾīl, this is not righteous conduct, nor one befitting a people from which have sprung such a number of blessed prophets. No man was created for evil and no one's purpose on Earth is an evil one. Is not the All-Merciful God, the Creator of all men, believers and unbelievers? Be careful, lest not those weapons your guile has devised be turned against you and you become your own victims. Should you not be teaching the people you have conquered with the help of the Almighty, His Holy Name, instead of trying to perpetuate their corruption and misguidance?"

Again they gave Yūshaʿ a strange answer, "What do they have to do with our God? He is the God of Isrāʾīl, and they have no part in that."

"Be quiet," cried Yūshaʿ, "You are committing sacrilege. Have you already forgotten the forty years in the desert? Do you think you are safe from punishment for your iniquity? No, Allah may strike you again at any time if you adhere not to the path of righteousness."

They said, "You, Yūshaʿ, because you are a descendent of Yūsuf 劤, still hold against us what our forefathers, Yūsuf's brothers, did to him! You bear a personal grudge; that is all. Or else, you have not yet forgotten the time we accused you falsely of having murdered Mūsā."

"I have forgotten and forgiven," said Yūsha'. "Allah Almighty showed all of Isrā'īl the truth in their dreams at night. Was that not vindication enough?"

But the men of Isrā'īl were possessed by pride and their bad characteristics took hold of then. The pride of race was strong and they would not marry from among the people. All extramarital relations were forbidden and punishable by death. But they cheated anyway and took the children born to them illegitimately and raised them in their families.

Their enemies were now largely subdued and the tribes turned and began to look at each other with envy. Rivalry and hatred broke out between members of different tribes. They often came to Yūsha' to complain that a certain party possessed more or was living in better conditions than they were. But Yūsha' told them again and again that the land had been divided up already by Mūsā under Divine Command and that justice had been done to everyone and none was preferred above the other. For a while, this placated them but Yūsha' could see that they would soon be at each other's throats the very first opportunity they found. Yūsha' tried to explain these dangers to the Israelites but he discovered they were no longer content with being tribal chiefs. They wished to be feudal lords and kings. The disease of worldliness was spreading rapidly among them.

Yūsha' was by then nearly 110 years old but he was still vigorous and strong. He often retired to the Ephraim mountains and climbed their high peaks to be alone with his Lord. From the highest peak he could see all the way from the Jordan valley and the Dead Sea to Lake Tiberius in the north. In those days, nearly 3,000 years ago, all the land was green and verdant and soothing to the eye. There, in solitude, Yūsha' took account of his life and tried to recognize his errors. He prayed and fasted and asked the Lord for forgiveness. One morning, he got up early and went to his favorite spot on the mountain. When he had arrived at the summit, he suddenly heard a voice. At first Yūshaʿ thought it must be a shepherd but soon he realized he was wrong. It was an old man who was talking to himself as he wandered, speaking of his innermost thoughts and feelings. Yūshaʿ listened to him, half amused, half curious. The man spoke thus, "Why all this wandering towards an uncertain goal? What a foolish bird that leaves its nest! I left behind me a Paradise. Will I ever find any way back to it? Will my old feet carry me over all that distance back to my home? Ah, surely before I reach it, the rocks will have rolled over me and buried me underneath them." He then paused and looked wistfully all around him. Then he continued, "Ah, how much this land resembles my own homeland! How ungrateful of me to leave it behind and wander away. Never again will I catch sight of it again. How much this land resembles my own. The blue waters of one sea and the green waters of the other. It is like a smaller version of my own country. Oh, that I could spend my last years in a country like this."

At this point, Yūshaʿ interrupted him and called out, "Good morning, stranger and may your morning be a good one!"

The man was startled and made as if to flee. "So there is no peace for me even here," he muttered under his breath.

But Yūshaʿ persuaded him to stay a little while and to tell him more about his beloved homeland as he had heard him talking to himself from his memories. The man asked him, "Does this mountain belong to you?"

Yūshaʿ replied, "How can anything on Earth belong to us? Everything is from Allah, the Creator of the heavens and the Earth. In truth, all belongs to Him, alone, and to Him is our return."

Now the stranger was interested to know more about Yūshaʿ and Yūshaʿ spoke to him. He told him his whole story and the fates of the Children of Isrāʾīl. He spoke for a long time. Then they sat down to share bread and water. Thereafter, they still did not part company but stayed together for some days for they felt sympathy and kinship for each other. The stranger understood the truth of Yūsha'''s message and accepted the faith in the unity of God. One day, Yūsha' asked the stranger to finally tell him about his country which he had been musing about the first day they met.

"You mentioned that this land is similar to the one you have left. How is that? Explain it to me."

The man thought for a while, then he said, "Is not that river we see flowing in the valley below, the Jordan River? And to the north we see the Lake Tiberius, while to the south there is the Dead Sea. Both bodies of water connected by the Jordan. Is it not so? So we can regard the Jordan River as a straight between two seas. My country about which you have asked lies to the northeast of the Toros Mountains. You must cross the mountain range and turn towards the northeast. Then, you will cross a great many mountains, plains and rivers and one day you will reach my country. It is just like what we see before us here, except that it is much greater, wider and the water much deeper. There, on the south end lies my mountain and I was used to calling it 'Dev Mountain'. Life was peaceful there and untroubled. My people were good and kind and lived as brothers with one another. Yet something possessed me and forced me to wander. I tore myself loose and began to travel, as a rock that tumbles from its bed and keeps on rolling."

Yūsha' listened carefully to his description, then he sighed and said, "Truly a paradisiacal place where there is no strife and contention between people. How could you ever leave it?"

"Oh my friend, I was young and I let myself be distracted by the desires and restlessness of my youth. If only you knew what I found at the foot of the mountain. A venomous breed of people, a veritable nest of snakes and scorpions. From their evil, I have been fleeing ever since. When I met you, I had resolved to return to my home at last, that God-willing I might die there. Having met you and learned all you taught me, my life's wanderings now make sense to me and I shall return home a fulfilled man."

"Then depart now and peace be with you," said Yūsha'. "I would fain accompany you but as I am a prophet I can take not a step without my Lord's permission. He has commanded me to stay here with my own people."

The stranger understood, but his heart was heavy at the parting. At last, he got up and picking up his staff, saluted Yūsha' one last time and turned towards the northeast. Yūsha''s heart was sore at the parting, for again he was left alone without a companion and he knew this was to be his fate. Now, the land the stranger had described to Yūsha' was the Bosphorus which connects the Black Sea with the Sea of Marmara, where the city of Istanbul is now located. The mountain he came from lies on the eastern shore, the Anatolian side, close to the entrance into the Black Sea.

Two more years passed and again it was spring on the plains of Jericho. Yūsha' had been a prophet to his people for twenty eight years and he sat once more on his favorite spot on the Ephraim mountains and delved into his memories. Suddenly, he was overcome by a longing to know what had become of the stranger he had met so briefly and who had, nevertheless, become his friend. He also sensed with certainty that his time in the world was drawing to an end. He descended from the mountain peak to take leave of his people and to counsel them one last time. Conditions in the plains had deteriorated as the Israelites had readily adopted the unholy ways of the people they had conquered. Idols were being set up again, slave-markets sprang up and the men fought each other over the possession of the youngest and most beautiful slave-girls. The conquered Amorites and Amalakites spread the word that soon their idols would begin to multiply and take up their reign anew. They said to the Banī Isrā'īl, "What good is this practice of yours of paying Zakāt? You work for your earnings and someone else enjoys the profits? Surely this can't be justice. Listen to us. Until the idols resume their reign, better hide away your earnings and make them appear minimal. That way you won't be obliged to pay the poor-tax!" The Israelites listened and gladly took that advice.

Yūsha' descended from the mountain and stayed among his people for some days, gathering about him all the priests and leaders. He admonished them one final time to obey Allah and His Commands and to worship none but Him, alone. He reminded them of history and the tribulations of his people. He warned them against adopting the customs of the idolaters and of doubting the truth that had been revealed to Mūsā and to the prophets who went before him. The Israelites were moved and wept and promised to follow and to hold fast to the Tawrāt.

Yūsha' said to them, "Oh my people, I have grown very old amongst you and perhaps this is my last address to you. I have seen you weep before this and make promises which you haven't kept. Your state is not favorable. You have come to a crossroads now. One road is the path of righteousness and light, the other is that of wrong doing and sinfulness. There are those among you who work at both your inward and outward destruction. Step on your ego while it is still weak and small. Let it not grow into a monster which you can no longer control. Don't look down on people with contempt. Allah has created all men to be free and they should live and die in freedom. Before the Lord, all men are equal. Wealth doesn't confer rank upon man but his works do. Do not oppress others. Treat them as your brothers and remember the times when you were oppressed and enslaved. Be not a stiff-necked people, for if you persist in stubbornness you will be made to bear a yoke, like the oxen who plough the fields. I have spoken to you many times and I say it again, for my duty as a prophet commands me to do so even if it displeases you. This is Allah's word to you. After me, many prophets are yet to come. They will teach men about the Unity of Allah and the religion of Islam. According to mankind's degree of maturity, the Law revealed to them will be perfected also. The final prophet whose name is Ahmad will bring the last revelation, a book containing the most perfect law and answers to all questions. This book will be valid on earth until the end of time. The coming of this prophet has been revealed in the Tawrāt which Mūsā has brought to us. It is our duty to teach our children and our children's children to expect his advent and to believe in him when he appears. I now testify to my belief in the prophet of the last times. Do you the same. Prepare your sons to be ready for him and to join forces with him."

After this address, Yūsha' retired again into his place of seclusion and was not seen again by his people. He died that same year. When the tribes of Isrā'īl learnt of his death, they buried him at his favorite mountain retreat in the Ephraim Mountains, on the summit of the mountain of Timah-Sarah, may his soul rest in peace.

Since then, nearly 3,000 years have passed. On the eastern shore of the Bosporus near the entrance to the Black Sea there is a hill which is called Mt. Yūsha'. Opposite from it, across the straight there lies another hill called 'Telli Baba'. These two hills are considered to be burial places of patron saints who are regarded as the guardians of the gates of the 'Dāru 'l-lslām' (Homeland of Islam). But who are they? Telli Baba is supposed to have been a soldier in the army of Mehmet the Conqueror, who was slain while drawing his bowstring.[46] But how did the name "Mt. Yūsha'" originate? Could it possibly refer to the prophet Yūsha'? Or is it another saint of the same name? There are various accounts of this subject. Of old, the hill was called 'Dev Mountain'. On its summit one finds a grave, seventeen meters long and four meters in width. This is said to be the grave of Yūsha' who died fighting on the hilltop. The dimensions of the tomb are not realistic; they are symbolically referring to the man's

[46] Turkish: *tel* - string, wire.

spiritual rank. The hilltop is crowned with beautiful, age-old poplar trees.

Yūshaʿ traveled only as far as Shām and the foothills of the Toros mountains. He never came as far as Istanbul. In order to reach the Bosporus he would have had to fight the Hittites in Anatolia, and this certainly did not take place.

The spiritual history, however, suggests another possibility. After the death of their prophet Yūshaʿ, the Israelites fell into ever greater corruption, disobeying the Law of the Tawrāt and reverting to idol-worship. They slew their prophets, imprisoned their priests and betrayed again and again the trust that had been given them. The soul of Yūshaʿ felt remorse at having chosen this spot on the mountains of Ephraim as his burial site, from where he had to witness the undoing of his people. His soul also saw into the future and perceived the coming of bloodshed and iniquity in the Holy Land. He foresaw his people's denial of the Last Prophet, whose coming he had foretold. Yūshaʿ's soul felt disgust at all this ungodliness and he prayed to the Almighty to remove his resting place from the lands in which such an unholy people dwelt. The place of his choice was one which resembled his original burial ground, as had been described to him by the stranger whose name he never knew. The man who had spoken to Yūshaʿ about Dev Mountain. Perhaps Allah Almighty heard his prayer and granted Yūshaʿ that site as his spiritual resting place (*maqām*). Another curious fact is this: The grave at first was facing Jerusalem, but after the conquest of Mecca and the cleansing of the Kaʿbah of the idols it turned in the direction of Mecca.

May Allah grant his soul eternal peace. Amin.

the loss of the ark

After Yūsha' had passed away, the Lord did not send another prophet to the Israelites for over eighty years. During this period they fell away from the Law of the Tawrāt and forgot their prophets' teachings. For this, they were punished by the Lord at the hands of the unbelievers who raided their flocks and their fields, plundered their houses and villages and led their children off into captivity. The Israelites suffered much at their hands and became despondent, living in fear of their enemies. They were unable to choose a king and leader from among themselves, for each tribe vied for the kingship and there was no unity among them. They deplored their fate and prayed to the Lord to send them guidance.

Their greatest enemies were the giant tribe of the Amalakites[47] and their kings, the Jālūt or Goliath. (As the kings of Egypt were called Fir'awn and the kings of the Babylonians Nimrūd, so the kings of the Amalakites were called Jālūt). The largest tribe of Isrā'īl was the tribe of Yehūdā. They were the keepers of the Ark of the Covenant. Whenever they went to war they carried the Ark ahead of them and it gave the soldiers strength and courage. As to what was contained in this Ark, Allah only knows. Some say it contained the broken shards of the tablets Mūsā had brought down from the mountain which he had smashed in his anger at seeing his people worshipping the golden calf. The holy words had flown from the tablets but the shards remained. Others relate that it contained the staffs of Mūsā and his brother Hārūn or their sandals and their cloaks. Some say that it held the heavenly foods, *manna* and *salwa* or some fragments of the stone of Mūsā upon which he had laid his clothes. Yet others

[47] Arabic: al-'Amālaqah.

maintain that the Ark was completely empty, that it was filled only with the breath of the holy spirit of the Tawrāt, which gave to it its power. Allah knows best.

One day, the tribesmen of Yehūdā learnt that the Amalakites were planning a major attack on them and they sent out word to their brother tribes to assemble their forces and to help them against their enemy.

But none of the tribes were willing to stand by their brothers and they said, "The holy Ark is with you. You can rely on its strength and protection. We have barely the strength to fend for ourselves."

The men of Yehūdā were very disappointed at their brothers' refusal to come to their aid and said, "Oh, if among a hundred of our number there were only one man of true courage."

They meant to say, "one man of perfect faith," for when a man has faith he feels no fear in the face of death. Jālūt also learnt of the tribes' refusal to help Yehūdā andcame out in great force to the battle. Yehūdā was outnumbered and surrounded in battle and defeated. The men fled and the Ark fell into the hands of the enemy. They carried off this valuable trophy to King Jālūt who ordered that it be set up in their temple among the other idols, and they said, "We have captured the god of the Israelites" and rejoiced.

When they went the next day to the temple they saw that their chief idol had toppled down and that the captured Ark was standing on top of it. Jālūt ordered that the Ark be nailed to the ground and the other idols be set on top of it. This was done but again, when they went in the next morning they found the Ark on top and the idols broken to bits on the ground. They began to worry and removed the Ark from the temple and stored it in other places, but whatever they did with it, it brought them harm. Either their crops withered or their animals died. A slave-girl who was an Israelite told them, "This Ark will bring you only misfortune as long as you keep it with you. You must return it to its owners." But this they were unwilling to do, knowing that possession of the Ark gave strength and blessing to their enemies. So they kept it and the drought and death among their flocks continued. Finally, they banned it to a remote village and left it there with the unwitting inhabitants. These, however, soon became aware of the fact that any person who as much as looked at the Ark would fall ill and break out in boils. Jālūt was told of the outbreak of an epidemic, and people appealed to him to free them of the 'cursed' thing he had placed in their midst. Jālūt promised a handsome reward to any person able to solve the problem. The, Israelite slave-girl spoke up and said, "I have told you before there is no other solution than that you return the Ark to its rightful owners. Nothing else will lift this bane." Jālūt, himself, went to the stricken village and as soon as he set eyes upon the Ark, he too fell ill. Then, he was convinced and asked the girl how best they could rid themselves of the Ark. "Place it upon an ox-cart and send the animals off towards Yehūdā. The oxen will return after a day or two, and you will know, then, that the Ark has been removed," she said. This they did and the oxen set out straight for the east. By the wisdom of the Almighty, the Ark fell from the cart into a grassy field after the oxen had gone for a day and a night. The animals then broke free of their yoke and trotted off homewards. The Amalakites guessed that they were now freed of the Ark but instead of rewarding the slave-girl, they put her to death so that she would not reveal their shame.

The Ark had fallen into a field belonging to two young men whose mother was widowed and blind. Soon a number of curious people assembled around the unknown object that lay in the field and they tried to look inside it to see what it contained. But whoever set hand the Ark was struck down dead on the spot. When the two young men, the owners of the field arrived, they found the ox-cart and the Ark and a number of dead bodies there. They concluded that the box must contain something of importance. They believed, however, that if they went and reported the matter, they would be accused of murder, so they decided to quietly bury the bodies, burn the cart and carry the Ark off into their house, where they hid it from the world. This, then they did. The two brothers were Israelites. A short while after they had hidden the Ark in their barn all their affairs mysteriously began to prosper: Their fields yielded hundredfold, all their flocks suddenly gave twin births, until their old, blind mother became suspicious and asked them whether anything unusual had happened to them. But they denied and didn't tell her their secret, fearing she might betray the matter, and the wondrous Ark might be taken from them.

So the Ark remained with them for several years and during this time their mother gradually regained her eyesight and she was glad and praised the Lord. But her two sons by now had realized that all their fortunes were due to the Ark, and they termed it the 'magic box of Mūsā and Hārūn'. They became irreverent and greedy and the more blessings they received the less they thanked the Lord, and their faith gradually dwindled. The Lord's punishment came upon them one day when they went out to their fields and an enemy raid came upon them. They were surrounded and slain and their old mother remained behind to mourn them. She wept and prayed for their souls for she understood that greed had corrupted their hearts. Meanwhile, their land passed into the hands of the Amalakites and with it the Ark.

In the years that followed, Banī Isrā'īl increased in numbers, but they were weak because of their disunity and suffered much tribulation at the hands of their enemies. In despair, they remembered their Lord and gathered around their priests and wise-men to pray for the Almighty to send them a prophet who might help them recover the Ark, for they realized that their weakness of faith had led to this serious loss.

Shamwīl's عليه السلام Birth

The prophet Shamwīl[48] was born in the year that the Ark was lost. He is mentioned in the Holy Qur'an, and although not by name, (The Cow: 246 - 249), the scholars agree that it is a reference to Shamwīl, the prophet. Shamwīl was the son of Elkanah from Ephraim and his wife Hannah who, for a long time, could bear no children. In the sadness of her heart she had prayed to the Lord to grant her a son and vowed to give her son to the service of the temple. The Lord heard her prayer and she bore a son at Ramah. She named him Shamwīl, which means 'the Lord has heard (the prayer).' When he was weaned, his mother gave him to the priest, Eli to be instructed in the Tawrāt, according to her vow and Shamwīl grew up to be a learned and God-fearing man. When he was twenty-nine years old, he received the call of prophethood and the first man to hear of it was Eli, the priest.

Word soon spread through all Isrā'īl that the Lord had sent a new prophet but many people didn't believe, saying they wanted the proof of a miracle or that the prophet should have come from their own tribe. Shamwīl began to travel throughout the land, according to the Almighty's command and he preached and taught whoever would listen to him. But many times he was ridiculed and reviled and even stoned. Four years passed in this way. At last, conditions had become so intolerable in Isrā'īl that the heads of the tribes turned to the prophet Shamwīl to help them choose a king from among them to lead them in a decisive battle against Jālūt, in order to regain the Ark. They promised to abide by his decision.

---

[48] Arabic: Shamwīl.

This is told in the Holy Qur'an:

أَلَم تَرَ إِلَى المَلَإِ مِن بَنى إِسرٰءيلَ مِن بَعدِ موسىٰ إِذ قالوا لِنَبِىٍّ لَهُمُ ابعَث لَنا مَلِكًا نُقٰتِل
فى سَبيلِ اللَّهِ ۖ قالَ هَل عَسَيتُم إِن كُتِبَ عَلَيكُمُ القِتالُ أَلّا تُقٰتِلوا ۖ قالوا وَما لَنا أَلّا نُقٰتِلَ
فى سَبيلِ اللَّهِ وَقَد أُخرِجنا مِن دِيٰرِنا وَأَبنائِنا ۖ فَلَمّا كُتِبَ عَلَيهِمُ القِتالُ تَوَلَّوا إِلّا قَليلًا
مِنهُم ۗ وَاللَّهُ عَليمٌ بِالظّٰلِمينَ

Hast thou not regarded the Council of the Children of Isrā'īl, after Moses, when they said to a prophet of theirs, "Raise up for us a king, and we will fight in God's way."
He said, "Might it be that, if fighting is prescribed for you, you will not fight?" They said, "Why should we not fight in God's way, who have been expelled from our habitations and our children?" Yet when fighting was prescribed for them, they turned their backs except a few of them; and God has knowledge of the evildoers.[49]

[49] Sūratu 'l-Baqara (The Cow), 2:246.

Talut is Chosen King

The prophet Shamwīl asked the heads of the tribes to give him time whilst he waited for a revelation from the Lord. They left him and Shamwīl retired to pray.

There was a man of the tribe of Bin Yamīn whose name was Kish the son of Abiel. He had a son who was a very tall and handsome man. His name was Ṭālūt (Saul). One day, when Ṭālūt was herding his father's camels, some of them strayed. Ṭālūt went to look with his servant. They came to the city of Shamwīl, and decided to go and pay their respects to the prophet so that he might help them find their lost animals. They approached the prophet and asked him for help. Shamwīl, however, did not answer them at first, for the angel had appeared to him who informed him of Allah's Will concerning Ṭālūt. Then Shamwīl said to Ṭālūt, "Oh Ṭālūt, Allah has chosen you to rule over all Isrā'īl and to be their king! May you always remember His favor, and may your rule be blessed!" Ṭālūt was very much surprised and couldn't believe this news for the tribe of Bin Yamīn was held in low esteem by the other tribes. Bin Yamīn had been Y'aqūb's youngest son. Ṭālūt voiced all his concerns, saying that his tribe, his house and family were of low rank and order and none would look up to him, much less obey him.

Shamwīl answered, "I know all that but it is the Will of the Lord."

Ṭālūt then said, "And by what sign shall we know that you speak the truth?"

Shamwīl replied, "Before you have reached your father's house, the beasts you have been looking for will have been found."

This turned out to be true and Ṭālūt stayed with Shamwīl the prophet and ate with him. Then Shamwīl blessed Ṭālūt and annointed him. Shamwīl then called the chiefs of the tribes and informed them of the Lord's Will.

وَقَالَ لَهُمْ نَبِيُّهُمْ إِنَّ اللَّهَ قَدْ بَعَثَ لَكُمْ طَالُوتَ مَلِكًا ۚ قَالُوا أَنَّىٰ يَكُونُ لَهُ الْمُلْكُ عَلَيْنَا

وَنَحْنُ أَحَقُّ بِالْمُلْكِ مِنْهُ وَلَمْ يُؤْتَ سَعَةً مِنَ الْمَالِ ۚ قَالَ إِنَّ اللَّهَ اصْطَفَىٰهُ عَلَيْكُمْ وَزَادَهُ

بَسْطَةً فِى الْعِلْمِ وَالْجِسْمِ ۖ وَاللَّهُ يُؤْتِى مُلْكَهُ مَنْ يَشَاءُ ۚ وَاللَّهُ وَاسِعٌ عَلِيمٌ

*"Then their prophet said to them, 'Verily, God has raised up Saul
for you as king"*
*They said, 'How should he be king over us who have better right
than he to kingship, seeing he has not been given amplitude of
wealth?'*
*He said, 'God has chosen him over you and has increased him
broadly in knowledge and in body. God gives the kingship to
whom He will and God is All-Embracing, All-Knowing.'"*[50]

When the commotion had quieted down a bit, Shamwīl reminded them of their promise to accept the decision of Allah and that Allah gives power to whom He wills regardless of rank or heritage. The chiefs then demanded proof of the truth of this claim. Shamwīl said to them:

وَقَالَ لَهُمْ نَبِيُّهُمْ إِنَّ ءَايَةَ مُلْكِهِ أَنْ يَأْتِيَكُمُ التَّابُوتُ فِيهِ سَكِينَةٌ مِنْ رَبِّكُمْ وَبَقِيَّةٌ مِمَّا تَرَكَ

ءَالُ مُوسَىٰ وَءَالُ هَٰرُونَ تَحْمِلُهُ الْمَلَٰئِكَةُ ۚ إِنَّ فِى ذَٰلِكَ لَءَايَةً لَكُمْ إِنْ كُنْتُمْ مُؤْمِنِينَ فَلَمَّا

فَصَلَ طَالُوتُ بِالْجُنُودِ قَالَ إِنَّ اللَّهَ مُبْتَلِيكُمْ بِنَهَرٍ فَمَنْ شَرِبَ مِنْهُ فَلَيْسَ مِنِّى وَمَنْ لَمْ

يَطْعَمْهُ فَإِنَّهُ مِنِّى إِلَّا مَنِ اغْتَرَفَ غُرْفَةً بِيَدِهِ ۚ فَشَرِبُوا مِنْهُ إِلَّا قَلِيلًا مِنْهُمْ ۚ فَلَمَّا جَاوَزَهُ هُوَ

---

[50] Sūratu 'l-Baqara (The Cow), 2:247.

وَالَّذِينَ ءَامَنُوا مَعَهُۥ قَالُوا لَا طَاقَةَ لَنَا الْيَوْمَ بِجَالُوتَ وَجُنُودِهِۦ ۚ قَالَ الَّذِينَ يَظُنُّونَ أَنَّهُم مُّلَٰقُوا
اللَّهِ كَم مِّن فِئَةٍ قَلِيلَةٍ غَلَبَتْ فِئَةً كَثِيرَةً بِإِذْنِ اللَّهِ ۗ وَاللَّهُ مَعَ الصَّٰبِرِينَ

"'The sign of his kingship is that the Ark will come to you. In it a Shechina from your Lord and a remnant of what the folk of Moses and Aaron's folk left behind, the angels bearing it. Surely in that shall be a sign for you, if you are believers.'"[51]

(*Shechina* (Arabic: *sakīnah*) the blessings of God.)

The chiefs had all heard the story of the Ark having landed in the house of the old widow and her two sons but their land had since passed into the hands of Jālūt, so they were perplexed and said to Shamwīl, "How should this be? Thus far we have thought of you as a man of sound reason but now we are in doubt. How should the Ark be brought to us if it is in the hands of our enemies? Moreover no one knows for sure where it is? Surely this is madness."

Shamwīl said, "The Ark will be borne by angels and it will be left on the threshold of Ṭālūt's house."

The chiefs agreed that if this were to really happen it could be counted as a kind of miracle, and together they proceeded to the house of Ṭālūt. When they arrived there, nothing was to be seen. So they waited and before long they heard a rustling sound in the air. When they looked again they could not believe their eyes for there was the Ark, standing right before them. No one had seen it coming. Having experienced such a plain miracle, their spirits rose and their faith was reborn as was their courage and confidence. All the young men were now willing to assemble in the army under Ṭālūt's leadership and before long, more than 100,000 had been mustered. They pledged their allegiance as they assembled around the Holy

---

[51] Sūratu 'l-Baqara (The Cow), 2:248-249.

Ark, and Shamwīl blessed them. Then, they marched off to do battle against Jālūt.

Now, the miracle had at first inspired them with courage but as they marched forward, approaching the dreaded enemy whose king was held by his men to be an immortal and a god, their courage began to fail and a number of them lagged behind, before finally turning back. Reports reached them that the terrible Jālūt was approaching with 80,000 men. Fear struck their hearts. To provide them with more incentive for battle, Ṭālūt promised to give his daughter in marriage to the man who would slay Jālūt and that he would make him his successor to the throne. So they marched on and the heat of the day grew. Water is scarce in that region and both man and beast suffered from an incredible thirst. When they finally reached a river of sweet water, the soldiers would have fallen on the water and gorged themselves, but Ṭālūt, their commander, knowing how harmful it is for a very thirsty man to drink his fill, stopped them and ordered them to drink no more than they could scoop up in their hand, lest they become unfit for battle. This, too, is described in the Qur'an:

فَلَمَّا فَصَلَ طَالُوتُ بِالْجُنُودِ قَالَ إِنَّ اللَّهَ مُبْتَلِيكُم بِنَهَرٍ فَمَن شَرِبَ مِنْهُ فَلَيْسَ مِنِّى وَمَن لَّمْ
يَطْعَمْهُ فَإِنَّهُ مِنِّى إِلَّا مَنِ اغْتَرَفَ غُرْفَةً بِيَدِهِ ۚ فَشَرِبُوا مِنْهُ إِلَّا قَلِيلًا مِّنْهُمْ ۚ فَلَمَّا جَاوَزَهُ هُوَ
وَالَّذِينَ ءَامَنُوا مَعَهُ قَالُوا لَا طَاقَةَ لَنَا الْيَوْمَ بِجَالُوتَ وَجُنُودِهِ ۚ قَالَ الَّذِينَ يَظُنُّونَ أَنَّهُم مُّلَٰقُوا
اللَّهِ كَم مِّن فِئَةٍ قَلِيلَةٍ غَلَبَتْ فِئَةً كَثِيرَةً بِإِذْنِ اللَّهِ ۗ وَاللَّهُ مَعَ الصَّٰبِرِينَ

"And when Saul went forth with the hosts he said, 'God will try you with a river. Whosoever drinks of it is not of me, and whoso tastes it not, he is of me saving him who scoops up with his hand. But they drank of it, except a few of them and when he crossed it and those who believed with him, they said, 'We have no power today against Goliath and his hosts.' Said those who reckoned they should meet God, 'How often a little company has overcome a

numerous company, by God's leave! And God is with the patient.''[52]

But of the 70,000 soldiers, only 4,000 obeyed his orders; all the others filled up their bellies with water. When the time came to move on, only these 4,000 men felt fit to march; the rest lagged behind, making excuses.

[52] Sūratu 'l-Baqara (The Cow), 2:249.

Dawud عليه السلام slays Jalut

Now among Ṭālūt's men there was one man from Bethlehem from the tribe of Yehūdā whose name was Jesse. This is his lineage: Jesse Obed Bo'az Salmon, Nahshon, Amminadab, Ram, Hezron, Perez, Yehūdā, Yʿaqūb. Jesse had eight sons who bore armor with him in addition to his youngest son, Dāwūd who was but a lad of thirteen and tended his father's flocks. He would bring food to his brothers who were soldiers in Ṭālūt's army. Dāwūd was of medium height and ruddy complexion. He had reddish hair and beautiful eyes. He was also given to song and when he sang, whoever listened was so entranced by his voice that he wished his song would never cease. This was Dāwūd whose name in Hebrew means 'beloved' and he was the first to be both a prophet and a king of Isrā'īl.

When Dāwūd saw the men of Isrā'īl preparing for war against Jālūt, he wished to go with them but was too young to bear armor. He had also been ill, recently, and knew his father would never allow him to accompany the soldiers.

Dāwūd said to his father, "Oh father, I am very good with my slingshot. I always hit my target."

His father replied, "Very good, my son. Allah has given you a special tool. You will be a good hunter." He spoke to his son as one might speak to a child when one tries to humor him.

But Dāwūd continued, "Oh father while I was in the mountains, I encountered a great mountain lion and I overcame him and rode upon his back, holding on to his ears. I wasn't in the least afraid." Again, his father smiled and took his words for the words of a mere boy. But Dāwūd was very serious and tried once more to tell his father of his strength and courage and of his true faith. He said, "Oh father, when I am at prayer in the wilderness all the birds and wild beasts of the mountain assemble round me to pray with me and we worship together." Again Jesse patted him on the head and made little of his words. Seeing that he had failed to convince his father, Dāwūd asked him openly to let him go to battle along with his brothers.

His father answered, "Oh my youngest son, you will do a lot of fighting yet in your time but now you are still too small. You must stay with your mother."

Dāwūd's 'eyes filled with tears and this his father could not bear, so he conceded that Dāwūd should accompany the army to carry the provisions for his brothers.

They set out together and caught up with the army which was one day's march ahead of them. Word had come to Shamwīl of the defection of the men at the river and he prayed to the Lord to send aid to Isrā'īl and to give the few brave men victory over the enemy. The Lord heard his prayer and Shamwīl sent to Ṭālūt a suit of mail, ordering him to have all the men try it on. "The man it fits shall be anointed and chosen by the Lord." By now, they had come close to the hosts of Jālūt and they beheld the giants from a distance and fear filled their hearts. Ṭālūt ordered all his men to try on the suit of mail the prophet Shamwīl had sent but it fit none of them. Dāwūd's father and brothers tried it on but it was too large for them. Ṭālūt began to despair for he feared he would be unable to fulfill the order of the prophet. He asked Jesse whether he had other sons. Jesse answered, "I have none other than these, save a young lad who is coming after us with our provisions. But he is still green and unfit for battle."

At that very moment, Dāwūd came running up, bearing his father's and his brother's food. He was breathless from running and he said, "Pardon me, father, for having come so late but I was delayed on the road by a very strange thing. I was making my way here when I heard a voice calling to me from the ground. The voice came from three stones that said to me, "Pick us up and take us with you for we are parts of the stone of Mūsā." So I stopped to do so and this is why I have come late."

"You see," said Jesse to Ṭālūt, "he is but a child."

Ṭālūt regarded Jesse's youngest son and saw that he was small and frail from illness but as it was the prophet's command that every man should try on the suit of mail so, he ordered Dāwūd to try on the armor. How great was their wonder when the suit fit Dāwūd perfectly though it had been too large for every other man. Ṭālūt, now anointed his forehead and sent him to the front row.

The armies of Jālūt had now drawn close and when the small troop of Ṭālūt's men beheld them their hearts quaked and trembled, so terrible were they and so great their number. Dāwūd marched ahead and faced them fearlessly. His father and brothers began to grieve for him in advance and wondered what they should say to his mother for they were certain he would be killed. Jālūt laughed and sneered when he saw the small group of Israelites that had come forth to face him but when he beheld the boyish figure of Dāwūd marching ahead of them all he felt, for the first time in his life, deadly fear, though he could not explain why.

However, despite his anxiety, he spoke belittling words to Dāwūd, "Oh child," he said, "you are not even a youth. Go home to your mother and leave this fighting to grown men. My heart feels pity for you."

Dāwūd gave the shortest of answers, "No!" he cried.

Placing the three stones he had picked up on his way in his slingshot, he aimed and hurled them at the giant. By the Will of Allah they melted together and struck Jālūt on his forehead. They pierced his skull and entered his brain and Jālūt fell like a tower and was slain. The men of both armies were thunderstruck with surprise. Then,

Dāwūd signaled for the battle to begin and the small army of Israelites fell upon the mighty army of Jālūt. Having lost their god-king and general, they were in a state of wild panic and confusion. By sundown, they were completely routed. Dāwūd also fought in the battle but the only booty he carried off was the head of Jālūt on the tip of his spear. So with the help of the Almighty, the Israelites overpowered a mighty foe, as it is written in the Holy Qur'an:

وَلَمَّا بَرَزُوا لِجَالُوتَ وَجُنُودِهِ قَالُوا رَبَّنَا أَفْرِغْ عَلَيْنَا صَبْرًا وَثَبِّتْ أَقْدَامَنَا وَانصُرْنَا عَلَى الْقَوْمِ الْكَافِرِينَ فَهَزَمُوهُم بِإِذْنِ اللَّهِ وَقَتَلَ دَاوُودُ جَالُوتَ وَآتَاهُ اللَّهُ الْمُلْكَ وَالْحِكْمَةَ وَعَلَّمَهُ مِمَّا يَشَاءُ ۗ وَلَوْلَا دَفْعُ اللَّهِ النَّاسَ بَعْضَهُم بِبَعْضٍ لَّفَسَدَتِ الْأَرْضُ وَلَٰكِنَّ اللَّهَ ذُو فَضْلٍ عَلَى الْعَالَمِينَ

"So, when they went forth against Goliath and his hosts, they said, 'Our Lord, pour out upon us patience and make firm our feet and give us aid against the people of the unbelievers' And they routed them, by the leave of God, and David slew Goliath and God gave him the kingship and Wisdom and He taught him such as He willed.
Had God not driven back the people, some by the means of others, the earth had surely corrupted: but God is bounteous unto all beings."[53]

When news of the victory reached the towns, most people could not believe it at first and the soldiers who had turned back were biting their nails with regret. The tribesmen who had refused their help to Yehūdā thought it was a rumor circulated by Ṭālūt, and they came to the prophet Shamwīl in anger demanding to know the truth. Shamwīl said, "If this was not the truth, where are the armies of

[53] Sūratu 'l-Baqara (The Cow), 2: 250-251.

Jālūt? They must be here by now, for who is there to stop them? You will see our armies return victoriously before three hours have passed." The chiefs were still doubtful, but before long a messenger arrived who had been on the battlefield and who confirmed all they had already heard. Shamwīl looked at the chiefs as if to say, "Was there anything else you wanted to know?" but they hung their heads, ashamed of their faintheartedness. The messenger had mentioned that in three hours the victorious army would reach the town and so quickly they made ready a feast to welcome their heroes. The women were overjoyed to welcome back their valiant men who had saved their lives and honor. Soon the Muslim army came in sight and the townspeople lined the streets. Shamwīl sat in the place of honor, radiant as the sun, surrounded by the tribal chiefs as by a wreath of dark clouds. At the head of the procession, marched King Ṭālūt, followed by Dāwūd carrying the head of Jālūt on his spear. As they passed, cries of great cheering broke out and Ṭālūt believed that the applause was for him. When he heard the words of the women's songs, all his gladness was poisoned for they sang not of his glory, but of the greater glory of Dāwūd.

"Ṭālūt has slain his thousands but Dāwūd has slain his ten thousands." This was the beginning of his great and consuming jealousy of Dāwūd for he understood then that people loved not him but Dāwūd who was only a boy of thirteen and favored by the Lord.

Talut's Envy of Dawud عليه السلام

Ṭālūt could not forget the people's preference for Dāwūd. Although, he regarded this as a slight to his person he hid his jealousy in his heart and guarded it well, outwardly making the greatest show of affection for Dāwūd. He kept him by his side and made sure they were always seen together in public. The poison of envy was eating its way into his heart and Shayṭān had possession of him. Six months had passed since Dāwūd had slain Jālūt and still Ṭālūt hadn't rewarded him for his heroic feat as he had promised. There was a very rich man at the time named Adriel of Meholath who had asked for the king's eldest daughter, Merab, offering Ṭālūt a palace full of gold for her. Ṭālūt was not a man to refuse such an offer and his daughter Merab was of like mind. So Dau'd said to Ṭālūt, "Who am I a poor man from a poor family to become the king's son-in-law?" Merab was quite content with the outcome and married Adriel, the rich man. Her younger sister however, Michal, was inclined towards Dāwūd and Ṭālūt was told of this. The news pleased Ṭālūt for he conceived in his heart a plan to rid himself of Dāwūd.

One evening, Ṭālūt went to see his younger daughter, Michal, in her palace and found her eyes full of tears.

"What ails you, my child? Tell me quickly so that I might punish he who has hurt you," he said.

His daughter answered, "Oh father, you don't understand. Was it not the Almighty who raised you to this station when you were nothing? Why then do you not abide by His Law and fulfill your promise?"

"What makes you say this, oh my daughter?" she replied. "Today I was feeling restless and I strolled out into the fields under the open sky. There, I chanced upon Dāwūd who was all alone, playing his harp and singing to his Lord. I hid myself and listened to him. Oh father, if you could only have heard that song. Your heart would have melted away as did mine. All the heavens and the Earth held their breath and listened to him and when he paused to perform his devotions, the birds and the beasts gathered around and prayed with him. My heart has been touched by his song and I am sick with longing."

وَلَقَدْ ءَاتَيْنَا دَاوُۥدَ مِنَّا فَضْلًا ۖ يَـٰجِبَالُ أَوِّبِى مَعَهُۥ وَٱلطَّيْرَ ۖ وَأَلَنَّا لَهُ ٱلْحَدِيدَ

"And We gave David bounty from Us: '"Oh you mountains, echo God's praises with him, and you birds'"[54]

The fires of jealousy that Ṭālūt had sought to extinguish were rekindled at his daughter's words. He controlled himself and asked her to tell him what else she knew of Dāwūd.

"Everyone says he is very fair-spoken and wise," she said, and His judgment is just and fair. His wisdom is far beyond his years. They say it is his practice to fast one day and to eat the next he spends half the night in prayer and devotion. His piety is renowned."

Ṭālūt laughed and said to his daughter, "I have understood, my child. You are enamored of Dāwūd. But why is it that you insist on praising so much of his spiritual virtues when what is attractive to young girls is mostly the physical aspect of a person? Anyway, I will see what I can do for you. I wished to marry him to your sister but he insisted that he was too poor and unfit to be the son-in-law of the king of Isrā'īl."

"Is then lack of possessions the measure of a person's worth, father?" cried Michal. How can you think that way? My regard for you, father, will not change even if I am given all the gems in the world."

---

[54] Sūrah Sabā (Sheba), 34:10.

"Yes," Ṭālūt said quickly, "I am of the same opinion, but you know it is the custom. Perhaps, tomorrow things will change. Maybe it will be the girls' parents who pay the dower. But for now it is as you and I know it, so what can we do?"

"The people will become suspicious of a king who doesn't keep his word. Already they are talking about you. If you prefer you may marry one of my sister's to him. I am concerned mainly that you fulfill your promise and that Dāwūd's light enters our palace."

Ṭālūt left his daughter and thought all night long about what she had said and he saw that she was right. However, Shayṭān had entered his heart and he was loathe to do it. He returned to Michal and informed her of his intention to make Dāwūd his son-in-law. "But", He said, "I can't force him. He is poor and if he refuses on the grounds of his poverty, what can I do?" Michal said, "May it please Allah to make things easy for him."

Soon after this, it was reported to the palace that Dāwūd had been seen in the market-place, fashioning iron coats of mail for the soldiers and that he did this without the help of a fire or a furnace. He simply melted the iron in his hand as if it were candle-wax.

وَعَلَّمْنَٰهُ صَنْعَةَ لَبُوسٍ لَّكُمْ لِتُحْصِنَكُم مِّنۢ بَأْسِكُمْ ۖ فَهَلْ أَنتُمْ شَٰكِرُونَ

"And We taught him the fashioning of garments for you, to fortify you against your violence;"[55]

وَلَقَدْ ءَاتَيْنَا دَاوُۥدَ مِنَّا فَضْلًا ۖ يَٰجِبَالُ أَوِّبِى مَعَهُۥ وَٱلطَّيْرَ ۖ وَأَلَنَّا لَهُ ٱلْحَدِيدَ

"And We gave David bounty from Us: 'Oh you mountains, echo God's praises with him and you birds' And We softened for him iron: 'Fashion wide coats of mail, and measure well the links.'"[56]

---

[55] Sūratu 'l-Anbīyā (the Prophets), 10: 80.

Michal was gladdened by this news and hoped that Dāwūd would be able to save money to pay for her bridal gift. She thanked the Lord for giving him this miraculous strength and power. She went, herself, into the marketplace to see Dāwūd's work, but she was disappointed. She saw Dāwūd at work making suits of mail for the soldiers with his bare hands but he took no money for his work or only a token sum. Barely enough to pay for his daily bread, let alone her bridal sum. That evening, her father Ṭālūt had invited all the heads of the tribes of Isrā'īl to the palace to discuss Dāwūd's future and Dāwūd was present among the assembly.

Ṭālūt spoke to him, "Oh my son, it has made me very happy to see that you have seriously begun to think about making a living for yourself and your future family. Fashioning armor is a well-paid craft and I see you are doing well at it. For how long have you been practicing this profession?"

"For six days now," Dāwūd replied.

"And how many coats of mail are you able to complete in one day?" asked Ṭālūt.

"Twenty," said Dāwūd.

Ṭālūt found this incredible, but all those present confirmed this and told also how Dāwūd worked with his bare hands and without the use of fire. In this way, he was able to complete his work quickly.

"So if you can sell so many suits of mail, you will be ready to pay the bridal gift for my daughter very soon?" asked Ṭālūt.

Dāwūd answered, "What bridal gift, oh my king? There was a time when you had promised your daughter to the man who would slay Jālūt but you kept not your word. Once you offered me the hand of

---

[56] Sūrah Sabā (Sheba), 34:10.

your eldest daughter but I was not in a position to accept because of my poverty. I have given up the idea of becoming the king's son-in-law for I can't pay the bridal price. The Lord has given me the skill of melting iron in my hand and I fashion the soldiers' armor for the Lord's good pleasure and as a service to Isrā'īl not for my own personal gain. I am not allowed to take more than I need for my dally bread."

The chiefs of Isrā'īl took Dāwūd's side for they felt that he had spoken justly and it cut Ṭālūt to the core. He said, "Yes, my son, you are right and I am also right. As king of Isrā'īl, I have the right to ask a bridal gift for my daughter. So let it be from the spoils of war. I will place you at the head of the army. Go and fight the Philistines and bring me one hundred of their foreskins. Then I will give to you my daughter, Michal." To this Dāwūd agreed and the assembly was concluded.

Now Ṭālūt had thought that Dāwūd might fall at the hands of the Philistines and he sent him on this expedition without the protection of the Ark. People marked this fact well and grumbled against the king. "Clearly, Ṭālūt is envious of Dāwūd for he has sent him to war against a fierce enemy without the protection of the Ark. He wishes for his death and with him thousands of our men will perish." But Allah Almighty protected Dāwūd and gave him victory in battle. He returned from the campaign with two hundred foreskins of the Philistines and Ṭālūt married him to his daughter Michal the very same day.

Now that Dāwūd was the son-in-law of the king, Ṭālūt saw himself completely shadowed by the presence of this sun in his palace. Dāwūd loved him sincerely and showed him nothing but respect and affection but the more Dāwūd's loved him, the greater Ṭālūt's enmity and hatred born of envy grew. Ṭālūt had a son, Jonathan, who became Dāwūd's friend. Jonathan loved Dāwūd as he loved his own soul. If he had not seen Dāwūd for more than one whole day, he could not sleep at night. Dāwūd also loved Jonathan.

Ṭālūt continued to be king of Isrā'īl but he suffered most from his own iniquity and the evil spirit of envy that had taken possession of him and poisoned his whole life. He sensed that he was not as well-loved as Dāwūd among his people. He knew not the Law and the Tawrāt as Dāwūd did nor had he won any great military victories for himself. He had a low opinion of himself and prayed to the Lord to send him an opportunity for gaining fame and glory on the battlefield.

One day, the prophet Shamwīl sent for Ṭālūt and said to him, "It has been revealed to me that the Lord wishes you to go out and fight the Midianites who have remained unbelievers to this day and are now inciting trouble at the boarders. You shall fight them to the death and leave not a soul alive nor take any booty of their goods and their flocks. You shall be the instrument of Allah's Wrath upon them." Ṭālūt rejoiced when he heard these words from the prophet for it seemed to him the perfect opportunity to prove his own worth both to himself and to his people. He prepared for war and set out on the campaign. With the help of Allah, he triumphed over the Midianites and routed them. Shamwīl had commanded him to destroy their land utterly, leaving no one stone unturned, to smash all their idols and to leave no one alive, no man, woman or child so as to prepare the land for settlement by the believers. But when he had taken the land, Shayṭān conquered Ṭālūt's mind. He said to himself, "Shall I then return from this battle empty handed? How will I make people believe that we have won a great victory and how will I appear in their eyes? They will count only the number of our men slain in battle and they will assume that we lost the war. Surely this time the prophet was mistaken. I will take back the king of Midian as my prisoner along with his flocks and treasures. Then people will realize that I have won a great victory even without the help of Dāwūd."

So, Ṭālūt returned with the king of Midian as his prisoner and took with him all his flocks and valuables. The Israelites welcomed back their triumphant king and began to show him more respect. Ṭālūt convinced himself that soon he would make them forget Dāwūd and that he would soon become the favorite. One day, the prophet Shamwīl came before him, full of anger.

"Oh Ṭālūt," he said to the king, "did not the Lord appoint you king of Isrā'īl while you were a man of common rank?"

"So it was," answered Ṭālūt.

"And when they clamored for a miracle to prove your claim, did the Lord not send down the Ark into your courtyard?"

"Yes, he did."

"And when you were left with only 4,000 steadfast men to fight Jālūt and his army of 80,000, did not the Lord send you Dāwūd who, alone, was able to slay Jālūt with a stone, by the Grace of Him Almighty? And are there not many other favors the Lord has bestowed upon you, so many that they cannot be numbered? Answer me, Ṭālūt. Why have you disobeyed the Lord though I made plain to you His Will and Command?"

"But I have obeyed," said Ṭālūt. "I went out and made war on the Midianites and the Lord granted me success."

"And why have you let the king of Midian live? Why have you brought him with you with all his treasure and his flocks even though I forbade you to do so?"

Ṭālūt said, "I have brought them here to offer them to the Lord as sacrifice."

"No," cried Shamwīl, "that is not true. You brought them with you so that you might convince your people of your might and your success. You did this to win favor in their eyes, however, by so doing you have lost everything. You have lost favor in the sight of the Lord.

The Lord reveals to me that He has taken the kingship from your house. Your descendants will not rule over Isrā'īl. He has stripped your house of this honor forever".

Ṭālūt's brow darkened and he knew not what to answer. Shamwīl got up to leave. Ṭālūt wished to ask the prophet to pray for his forgiveness for in his heart he knew that he had done wrong but he found not the words. So Shamwīl left and Ṭālūt never saw him again.

Shamwīl called for Dāwūd and Dāwūd accompanied him all the way back to Ramah. No one knows of what they spoke on that journey. An escorting soldier heard Shamwīl ask Dāwūd how old he was. Dāwūd answered, "I am now thirty years of age." When they reached the village of Nayut, Shamwīl's birthplace, Shamwīl became ill. He took his bed and he did not rise again. Before Ṭālūt reached the village, the prophet Shamwīl died. He was buried in his house at Ramah. Everyone mourned for him.

On the way home, Ṭālūt rested at Hebron (Khalīl) and visited the tombs of the Patriarchs there. When he went aside to relieve himself, he overheard a conversation between two common foot soldiers.

One said, "Now that Shamwīl has gone, I wonder who will be prophet after him."

"Only Allah knows that," said the other.

"Yes, that is true, but let me tell you one thing. It seems plain to me that there is no man more excellent in all the kingdom than Dāwūd. He is learned and wise. Such qualities as are in him aren't found in any other man in these times, certainly not with Ṭālūt, our king. He is king and may have power in worldly matters but a prophet can come only from among the ranks of the learned the Rabbis or priests."

"That is just your wishful thinking," said the other man. "Allah can make a prophet of whom He wills. How many prophets have come who were not learned at all, unlettered and simple, but possessed of the Holy Spirit?"

All the way home from Hebron, Ṭālūt was unable to forget the words he had overheard. They were like salt upon his wounds. They troubled him so much that he forgot all the prophet had said to him, that the loss of his kingship was a thing decreed by the Divine. He simply couldn't believe it. He began to suffer delusions and saw enemies everywhere who were seeking to overthrow his throne. Now Ṭālūt sought ways to do away with Dāwūd and he moved his principal city out of Yehūdā and went to Gibeah, near Jericho. Dāwūd as a member of the royal household went with Ṭālūt and people often complained to him of Ṭālūt's misrule of their land. But Dāwūd always answered in the king's defence and made excuses for him. There were men who understood Ṭālūt's heart and tried to warn Dāwūd of his intentions "Oh Dāwūd," they would say, "don't trust Ṭālūt, for he is victim of his own delusions. He may strike out at you at any time." In time, he spoke openly to his sons of ways to remove Dāwūd from their midst and so Jonathan came to know of the danger and warned his friend Dāwūd.

Dawud عليه السلام Flees from Talut

One night, Jonathan spoke for a long time to his father trying to, convince him of Dāwūd's innocence and sincerity, until finally, he awakened Ṭālūt's conscience. Consequently, Ṭālūt repented. But the spirit of Ṭālūt remained uneasy. After he retired into his private apartment, he sat up alone for a long time, his spear in his hand and his dark, bitter thoughts enveloped him again. Dāwūd approached him with his harp to play for him and to lighten his mood as he was accustomed to doing. As Dāwūd came in and smiled at Ṭālūt, the evil spirit possessed him and he hurled his spear at Dāwūd and would have pinned him to the wall, had not Dāwūd evaded the spear by a turning rapidly to one side. Dāwūd was saddened by this and asked the king what fault he found in him. Had he not always been as loyal to him as a son?

Ṭālūt made excuses and retired. Dāwūd understood that the time had come for him to flee, for his life was in danger. He saw that Ṭālūt no longer had any control over what he did and his envious spirit controlled him totally. Dāwūd returned to his wife, Michal, and told her of his fears. He had her fill a goatskin with wine and place it in his bed where he slept. Then she helped him escape through the window. Dāwūd hid himself in the garden and waited. Before long he heard angry voices from his room. It was Ṭālūt. He had come to kill him. Finding only the goat hair bag, he was scolding his daughter for having let Dāwūd escape.

Michal said, "He threatened me."

Her father replied, "So how did that goatskin get into his bed? Dāwūd never drank wine and now my spear draws only red wine instead of Dāwūd's blood!"

Dāwūd could no longer doubt that his life was in danger. When all was quiet he left his hiding place and fetched four of his own arrows. Then he went to Ṭālūt's rooms in the dead hour of night and entered unnoticed.

He placed an arrow at each of the corners of Ṭālūt's bed as a sign that he could have killed the king but had refrained from doing so. The next morning, Ṭālūt awoke and Dāwūd was gone. He beheld the four arrows and understood. The devil left him for a moment and he felt true remorse. He called for his son, Jonathan, for he knew of their friendship and he swore holy oaths that he would not harm Dāwūd. He only wished for his return. His heart was sore with longing for him. Jonathan went out to find Dāwūd among the rocks where he had hidden himself. They embraced and wept for a long time. Jonathan reported to him all he had seen and heard but knowing the condition of his father's spirit he counseled Dāwūd not to return but to go into exile. Dāwūd accepted this and left for Hebron and Ramah. Yet, he continued to love Ṭālūt and he grieved for him.

It came to pass as Jonathan had foreseen. After forgiveness, Ṭālūt began to persecute Dāwūd anew and his change of mood became unpredictable. So Dāwūd remained in hiding and only his friend Jonathan knew where to find him.

At the new moon of each month there was a customary feast at the palace at which all the heads of Isrā'īl were obliged to attend lest they be ranked among the dissenters. Again, Ṭālūt had decided to pardon Dāwūd and Jonathan was sent to tell him he was expected at the banquet. Dāwūd was hiding at the rock of Ezel and waited.

On the second night of the feast, Ṭālūt asked, "Where is Dāwūd? Why is his seat empty, if he be free of guilt?" He intended to expose Dāwūd as a rebellious traitor before all the assembled heads of Isrā'īl.

Jonathan knew his intention however, and answered, "He would have come and earnestly begged your pardon but there is an important sacrifice he must attend with his tribe at Bethlehem."

Then, Jonathan went to tell Dāwūd that the time of parting had come and that from now on he must seek safety in exile. They parted tearfully for they loved each other more than two brothers.

Dāwūd turned towards Nob to find the priest, Ahimelech, to whom was entrusted the sword of Jālūt. The priests, seeing he had come alone, knew of his difficulties and asked no questions of Dāwūd but gave him their help. Before he left them Dāwūd asked them for the sword of Jālūt. They gave it to him, blessing Dāwūd whom they knew to be of the righteous.

Ṭālūt came to know of Dāwūd's visit to the priests and summoned Ahimelech and all the priests of Nob to his court. He accused them of having assisted a traitor and for that he had them all put to death. In that way he rid himself of the priests and wise men by whom he felt outdone in wisdom and whom his envy could not tolerate.

In those days, Ṭālūt also gave Michal, Dāwūd's wife, to a man named Paltiel, the son of Laish of Gallim. Now Dāwūd was no longer the son-in-law of the king and Ṭālūt felt himself free from obligation towards him. But Dāwūd continued to pray that the Lord might lead Ṭālūt on the way of righteousness.

Dāwūd gathered around him a small band of faithful followers and they roamed the land by the southern borders of the kingdom, fleeing from one hiding place to the next, for Ṭālūt's men went after them. They lived in caves and fought in many small border skirmishes to secure the peace in Isrā'īl. During one such campaign, a man named Nabal from Carmel insulted Dāwūd and the Lord punished him. His widow was a pious and beautiful woman and Dāwūd took her for a wife. He also married Ahinoam of Jezreel and he begot sons and daughters. For seven years Dāwūd continued his life of roaming and fighting both openly and in secret and Ṭālūt's men could not catch up with him. Once he was hiding in the caves of the wilderness of Ziph to the southeast of the Dead Sea. Dāwūd was told by his men that Ṭālūt had come and that they had a good chance of surprising him and gaining the upper hand. But Dāwūd ordered them to remain safely hidden and not to attack. Ṭālūt and his men searched the area for some days but finding no one, they gave up the search. One night, Ṭālūt was sitting outside his tent on a great rock, musing to himself with a heavy heart. He was so absorbed in his thoughts that Dāwūd slipped up to him unnoticed and cut off the skirt of his robe. Only when he rose to go to his tent Ṭālūt became aware of what had happened and he understood that only the man who had planted arrows at the four corners of his bed and refrained from murdering him could have done this to him.

He called out into the darkness and opened his heart to Dāwūd, saying, "Oh Dāwūd, you have taught me a lesson. I have done you only harm. I drove you into exile and gave your wife to another man. I have persecuted you all the days of your life and made you a hunted fugitive and yet you have spared my life on two occasions. Why is it you do not repay me in kind?"

Dāwūd answered him from the darkness, "Oh Ṭālūt, it is because I have not given up hope in you. There is an evil spirit which possesses your heart from time to time and I believe it will depart from you one day for good. You are anointed to the Lord Almighty. Our story shall become a lesson of wisdom for all the generations of Isrā'īl yet to come. If I were to slay you now it would mean the outbreak of a great civil war and bloodshed in Isrā'īl. There would be no blessing in that."

Ṭālūt then begged Dāwūd to return with him and to rule by his side and to help him against the dark forces that possessed his heart. But Dāwūd knew this was not to be and said no more. He remained in the darkness and prayed. Then he slipped away like a shadow and Ṭālūt remained behind with his heart heavy.

When he returned to Gibeah, he wept day and night for his sinfulness and all he had done to Dāwūd passed before his mind's eye as if on a screen. He lamented and wept for himself and knew not what to do in order to seek the Lord's forgiveness. As he had put all the priests and learned of the land to death, he had nobody to consult with and none to advise him how do repent and atone for his sins. Ṭālūt grew more desperate. One day, he went to the graveyard and invoked the souls of the priests and Rabbis whom he had slaughtered to send him a sign. It seemed to him that they all spoke from their graves in one voice. They seemed to say, "Oh Ṭālūt, is it not enough that you put us to death? Do you wish to continue persecuting us even into the grave?" Ṭālūt returned to his apartments feeling the reproach of the dead souls a heavy burden upon his conscience.

One night, as he sat weeping, one of his guards came to him and such was the state of his melancholy that Ṭālūt found relief in opening his heart even to the plain man who was his servant.

"Oh my officer," he said, "I have slain all my wise men and the learned of Isrā'īl. Who is there now to give me advice? How can I find forgiveness for my sins? What must I do?"

The soldier said to the king, "One day, a cruel king came to a village and ordered all the cocks to be slaughtered and cooked. Then as he lay down to sleep he said, 'I wish to be woken by the cock crowing.' You, oh my king, are like this man. You have killed all the men and women of learning in this land and now you would ask their advice!"

Ṭālūt nodded and sighed and wept even more bitterly than before. The soldier saw that his king was sincere this time and he made him promise not to punish him if he would help him. Ṭālūt assured him and the man confessed to having disobeyed Ṭālūt's order when he had spared one old woman who was a seer. To her, he could now lead the king. The king begged him to take him there and so they went to the house of the woman at Endor. He implored her to help him and to repay his evil with good. Finally, she gave him counsel. She told him to go to the grave of the prophet Shamwīl and to ask of him what he must do. Ṭālūt at once went to Ramah and threw himself upon the prophet's grave. He asked his question and waited for an answer to come out of the grave but as he listened he heard a voice within his own breast and he knew it was the prophet speaking to him in his heart. This is what he heard, "Oh Ṭālūt, I cannot tell you if your repentance is acceptable or not but this is what you must do. Go out and fight in the Jihad that is to come and go there not as a king and general who follows the battle from afar but as a common foot-soldier. Then you will attain your goal!"

Ṭālūt returned to Gibeah. There, he had news of an attack of the Philistines and he prepared for war. He went out with his sons, among them Jonathan, to fight as common men and they were surrounded by the enemy on the hill of Gilboa and fell there as martyrs, having fought bravely to the end. Dāwūd heard the news and mourned for both Ṭālūt and his son Jonathan. He believed that Ṭālūt's death as a martyr had cleansed him of all his sins and that it was a sign of Allah's forgiveness. What of Jonathan however, why did he have to die? Dāwūd thought he had found an answer to console himself in his grief. Jonathan was too pure a soul to be soiled by worldly affairs and so Allah had taken him from the world before he had to suffer the trial of kingship. Dāwūd remembered also the Prophet Shamwīl's words that the kingship should not remain in the house of Ṭālūt after his death. But they made Ishbosheth, the son of Ṭālūt, king to succeed his father. Dāwūd retired to Hebron for two years for he wished not to create disunity among the tribes of Isrā'īl. But the house of Yehūdā followed Dāwūd and his people loved him.

Luqman عَلَيْهِ السَّلَام

Luqmān is mentioned in the Holy Qur'an as a wise man, endowed with knowledge from the Almighty:

وَلَقَدْ ءَاتَيْنَا لُقْمَٰنَ ٱلْحِكْمَةَ أَنِ ٱشْكُرْ لِلَّهِ ۚ وَمَن يَشْكُرْ فَإِنَّمَا يَشْكُرُ لِنَفْسِهِۦ ۖ وَمَن كَفَرَ فَإِنَّ ٱللَّهَ غَنِىٌّ حَمِيدٌ

"Indeed We gave Luqmān wisdom. Give thanks to God. Whosoever gives thanks gives thanks only for his own soul's good and whosoever is ungrateful-surely God is All-sufficient, All-laudable."[57]

It is not certain whether Luqmān was sent as a prophet or whether he held the station of sainthood but his wisdom has been acclaimed through the ages.

One day, Luqmān appeared in Isrā'īl and his men came to Dāwūd at Hebron and told him of the arrival of a very wise and learned man to whom Allah had granted knowledge as to no other man of his time, yet he was black. Dāwūd admonished his men and reminded them that the Lord looks not upon the color of a man's skin but the condition of his heart. Allah gives knowledge to whom He wills. He reproached them for their racial pride and prejudice and had them convey his *salāms* to Luqmān hoping they would meet.

Some sources claim that Luqmān was a descendent of the tribe of 'Ad. His people related that Luqmān used to keep eagles. He raised and fed them all the days of his life. Now the life-span of an eagle is eighty years. Luqmān counted his years by the years of his eagles. When he came to Isrā'īl he had raised four eagles. Therefore, he must

---

[57] Sūrah Luqmān, 31:12.

have been over 320 years of age. During all his days he had seven eagles and when the last bird didn't fly out people knew that Luqmān had died. According to this estimate Luqmān's days must have numbered 560 years.

It is probable that he died in the time of Yunus but only Allah knows.

Luqmān was sent as a teacher to the people of Isrā'īl when they had need of such teaching. He met with Dāwūd and recognized in him the signs of prophethood though this had not yet been disclosed to Dāwūd himself. Dāwūd asked him to stay on in the land of Isrā'īl as his people were again in danger of being corrupted by the ways of the idolaters surrounding them. Luqmān agreed and settled there with his family.

Luqmān had a son and his words of admonishment to him are recorded in the Qur'an

وَإِذْ قَالَ لُقْمَٰنُ لِابْنِهِ وَهُوَ يَعِظُهُۥ يَٰبُنَيَّ لَا تُشْرِكْ بِاللَّهِ ۖ إِنَّ الشِّرْكَ لَظُلْمٌ عَظِيمٌ

"And when Luqmān said to his son, admonishing him, 'Oh my son, do not associate others with God. To associate others with God is a mighty wrong.'"[58]

يَٰبُنَيَّ إِنَّهَا إِن تَكُ مِثْقَالَ حَبَّةٍ مِّنْ خَرْدَلٍ فَتَكُن فِى صَخْرَةٍ أَوْ فِى السَّمَٰوَٰتِ أَوْ فِى الْأَرْضِ يَأْتِ بِهَا اللَّهُ ۚ إِنَّ اللَّهَ لَطِيفٌ خَبِيرٌ يَٰبُنَيَّ أَقِمِ الصَّلَوٰةَ وَأْمُرْ بِالْمَعْرُوفِ وَانْهَ عَنِ الْمُنكَرِ وَاصْبِرْ عَلَىٰ مَا أَصَابَكَ ۖ إِنَّ ذَٰلِكَ مِنْ عَزْمِ الْأُمُورِ وَلَا تُصَعِّرْ خَدَّكَ لِلنَّاسِ وَلَا تَمْشِ فِى الْأَرْضِ مَرَحًا ۖ إِنَّ اللَّهَ لَا يُحِبُّ كُلَّ مُخْتَالٍ فَخُورٍ وَاقْصِدْ فِى مَشْيِكَ وَاغْضُضْ مِن صَوْتِكَ ۚ إِنَّ أَنكَرَ الْأَصْوَٰتِ لَصَوْتُ الْحَمِيرِ

[58] Sūrah Luqmān, 31:13.

'''Oh my son, if it should be but the weight of one grain of mustard-seed and though it be in a rock, or in the heavens, or in the earth, God shall bring it forth; surely God is All-Subtle, All-Aware. Oh my son, perform the prayer and bid unto honor and forbid dishonor. And bear patiently whatever may befall thee. Surely that is true constancy. Turn not thy cheek away from men in scorn and walk not in the earth exultantly; God loves not any man proud and boastful. Be modest in thy walk, and lower thy voice; the most hideous of voices is the voice of the ass.'"[59]

[59] Sūrah Luqmān, 31:16-19.

Dawud عليه السلام as Prophet and King

For seven years Dāwūd had hidden from the persecution of Ṭālūt. He bore his plight with patience for he knew that Ṭālūt was the anointed of the Lord. The Lord had informed Shamwīl that the kingship would be torn from the house of Ṭālūt after his death and so Dāwūd didn't swear allegiance to Ishboheth, the son of Ṭālūt but waited for the Lord to reveal His Command. Ishbosheth was his enemy.

One evening, after Dāwūd and his men had prayed the prayer at sundown Dāwūd took his harp to play for them when Abner the son of Ner, arrived. He had come as a messenger from Ishbosheth asking Dāwūd to come the next day at noon to a certain place and join with them in a campaign against neighboring tribes. Dāwūd promised that he would be there and the messenger left. Dāwūd took up his harp again and sang to his men. His voice was enchanting and his poems and songs were inspired by Divine Love. All the birds and beasts would come out of hiding and listen to Dāwūd. Dāwūd's men said to him, "Let us not go to the meeting place for we fear it is a trap. They will surround us there and overcome us. We fear their deceitfulness." But Dāwūd said he had given his word and he trusted in the Lord to lead him.

After all his men had gone to sleep, Dāwūd remained by himself for a long time, deeply sunk in his reflections. In the darkest hour of night, he suddenly beheld a light in the distance, which drew near. Dāwūd sensed that it was not an earthly light. This light grew until it filled the entire horizon and Dāwūd heard a voice come from the light. It was the angel Gibril (Jibrīl), come to announce to Dāwūd that the Lord had chosen him as His Prophet and to bring him the first verses of the scripture he was to be given, the Zabūr (Psalms).

وَرَبُّكَ أَعْلَمُ بِمَن فِى السَّمَٰوَٰتِ وَالْأَرْضِ ۗ وَلَقَدْ فَضَّلْنَا بَعْضَ النَّبِيِّينَ عَلَىٰ بَعْضٍ ۖ وَءَاتَيْنَا

دَاوُۥدَ زَبُورًا

"And thy Lord knows very well all who are in the heavens and in
the earth and We have preferred some Prophets over other and we
gave to David Psalms."[60]

All night Dāwūd conversed with the angel and Gibril taught him
from the wisdom of the Lord. He left him at dawn and Dāwūd
awakened his men to pray with him the dawn prayer. Then he
disclosed to his men what had been revealed to him during the night.
Great was the joy of his men and they made ready to follow him to
Hebron where he would proclaim his prophethood and kingship to
all people. But first there was the meeting for which he had given
Abner his word. When Dāwūd reached the meeting place, he sat
down and began to play and sing upon his harp. This time the wild
beasts of prey came out of the woods and assembled around Dāwūd
as if they were lapdogs, to listen to him sing. Abner and his men
were indeed planning an ambush. They approached cautiously,
making no sound. But the wild beasts perceived the scent of their
coming and began to growl. Dāwūd's men were warned and reached
for their weapons but Dāwūd called for Abner to step out into the
open.

Abner came out and asked, "What is this is it some show of magic?"

"No," answered Dāwūd, "these animals bear testament to my
appointment as Allah's prophet and king of all Isrā'īl. Come, my
brothers, bear witness, as well, and let us go together to your leader
and inform him of the Will of the Lord."

"And what of the son of Ṭālūt?" asked Abner.

---

[60] Sūratu 'l-Isrā (the Night Journey), 17: 55.

"You may tell him that his kingship has come to an end, as the prophet Shamwīl has already told his father. Come with me and heal the rift in the state of Isrā'īl"

But Abner said, "I have pledged loyalty to my king, the son of Ṭālūt."

"Then I will proceed alone to Hebron and the house of Yehūdā is with me. There will be strife between us until you have accepted the truth from your Lord."

So, Dāwūd was king at first over Yehūdā at Hebron and he preached to them according to what had been revealed to him. He was ordered by his Lord to fight in order to achieve the unity of Isrā'īl. He had made Luqmān the Wise his vizier. One day, they went out to the Mount of Olives and stood gazing at the city of Jebus (later called Jerusalem) before them. Its buildings and streets had fallen into neglect and decay. Dāwūd received a Divine command to rebuild the city once more and to transfer the Holy Ark to it and to make Jerusalem the capital of his kingdom. It later became known as the city of Dāwūd, Al-Quds to the Arabs and is the third most revered place for the Muslims today. It is also reported that Dāwūd beheld a vision as he stood gazing at the city: He saw a great rock suspended in mid-air encircled by many angels above and below. Dāwūd received the inspiration to build a house of worship where that rock was hovering. When the temple was built in this place the rock could be seen plainly suspended and held in place with no visible support, but in later times, when the believers no longer possessed that strength of faith, they filled in the ground around the rock so that it now appears to be a cave with walls of rock and clay. This site is now known as the Dome of the Rock.

But still Ishbosheth ruled over the city of Jebus. He had hoped that Dāwūd's small kingdom would soon collapse but he was mistaken. The house of Dāwūd grew strong and that of Ṭālūt grew weaker. Dāwūd fortified his position by making peace with his neighbors and his people grew to love him more and more for his justice and prophetic wisdom.

One day, a quarrel arose between Abner and Ishbosheth. Abner was accused of taking another man's woman. Abner grew very angry at this and said, "Have I not served you loyally all this time that you should now suspect me because of a woman? Perhaps I was wrong all along for has not the Lord promised to make Dāwūd king of all Isrā'īl?" Abner then sent word to Dāwūd offering his assistance to him. Dāwūd answered, "I accept your help under the condition that you send back to me my wife Michal whom Ṭālūt has taken from me." Abner send word to Ishbosheth who became fearful and so he took Michal away from her husband, Paltiel of Laish, and sent her to Dāwūd at Hebron. Then Abner came before Dāwūd and they spoke together and Abner departed in peace. But on his way, he was pursued and ambushed by Ioab for the blood of his brother and was slain. When the news came to Dāwūd, he wept for Abner and people understood that it had not been the king's will to kill Abner. When Ishbosheth learned that the commander of his army, Abner was dead, he wept also and his courage failed him. As he lay in his tent taking his noonday rest, two of his men came in and slew him. They cut off his head and brought it to Dāwūd. Dāwūd disliked them for their treachery and had them put to death and buried the head of Ishbosheth beside Abner at Hebron.

Now Dāwūd was king over all Isrā'īl. His reign lasted forty years. During all this time, the revelation of the Zabūr continued. It consisted of 150 chapters and it was a book of song and praise of Allah. In it, was revealed that the beginning of wisdom is the fear of the Lord and whoever acts not in accordance with his knowledge, Shayṭān will be his companion. A dervish who sways from his path in order to gain the favor of worldly lords is equal to the dogs and a rich man who gives nothing to the poor is likened to the pig. In the Qur'an, the Zabūr is mentioned several times:

وَلَقَدْ كَتَبْنَا فِى الزَّبُورِ مِن بَعْدِ الذِّكْرِ أَنَّ الْأَرْضَ يَرِثُهَا عِبَادِىَ الصَّلِحُونَ

"For We have written in the Psalms, after the Remembrance, 'The earth shall be the inheritance of My righteous servants.' Surely in this is a message delivered unto a people who serve."[61]

In this passage, 'the earth' refers to the Holy Land stretching from Shām to Sinai. A great many prophets arose in that land and are now buried there. The prophet Ibrahim asked the Lord how it could be that such holy ground could ever be peopled by unholy people as it is written that this land shall be given to the righteous servants of the Lord. "If ever an ungodly people comes to possess that piece of earth," answered the Lord, "they shall not be allowed to live there in peace and I will send upon them calamity and disaster." According to a tradition the most pious people to ever have lived in the Holy Land came to settle in Jerusalem during the time of the Khalifah Umar, After the coming of the last prophet, the right to possession of the Holy Land passed on to the Muslims and only under Muslim rule can the curse of misfortune and disaster be avoided.

It is related that Dāwūd had 99 wives and concubines. Allah gave him such strength that he stayed with every one of them in the course of one night. One day, Dāwūd fell down in his prayer-niche and prayed and wept for a long time.

Then, he raised his head and said, "Oh Lord, you have given excellence and the power of miracles to the prophets who went before me. Ibrahim, You honored by making him Your beloved friend, Khalīl, and You made the fire cool and a safety for him and put down his enemy Nimrūd. You perfected Y'aqūb through his sons and Mūsā attained perfection in that You spoke to him (Kalīmullāh). Hārūn, You made perfect in Knowledge and to Ṣāliḥ You granted Your Divine aid and helped him against his misguided people. Oh

---

[61] Sūratu 'l-Anbīyā (the Prophets), 10:: 105.

Lord, I ask You to give to me blessings by which I will be known and that distinguishes me from my brother-prophets."

The Lord replied, "It is My special favor to you that I have never before created a prophet who is at one time king as well as My Holy servant. As a miracle, I have made for you your gift of song. When you sing, the mountains resound in harmony and all of My creation stops to listen. The wild beasts are tamed by your song and the little birds fly upon your head and hand and have no fear of you. Also, I have made iron to melt in your hand as candle wax and soft as bread dough. Is this not a miracle given to you? And, oh Dāwūd, I have tried each of My prophets with a severe trial. Ibrahim, I tried with fire. When he was surrounded by Nimrūd's flames he complained to no one and accepted My decree. Then I ordered him to sacrifice his son and he obeyed Me and laid him upon the sacrificial altar. Yʿaqūb was tried by grief for his favorite son, Yūsuf ﷺ, and by his blindness. I found him patient with My trial. Mūsā, I tried when he was only a small child and his mother was commanded to place him in a basket of rushes. She was patient and I gave him back to her breast. You, oh Dāwūd, have not yet seen My trials. I have made your life easy for you."

Dāwūd rubbed his forehead in the dust and prayed. "Oh Lord, this is my heart's desire. To be tried by You as you have tried the prophets who have gone before me so that I might attain some of the excellence You have bestowed upon them."

The Lord answered, "Oh Dāwūd, be ready then, for I will try you. I have heard your prayer. Your trial will come upon you without fail on such a day in such a month as I will mention to you. So prepare yourself for it."

The day came and Dāwūd went into his chamber and prayed for a long time in his niche. Then he raised his voice and recited from the Zabūr. As he was singing, Shayṭān entered the room in shape of a golden dove, his wings studded with pearls and precious gems. He flew around the room so that Dāwūd noticed him but he failed to recognize him. He admired the beauty and grace of that little golden bird and forgot the words of the Lord concerning the trial he was to meet on that appointed day. He wished to catch the bird in order to show it to his people so that they too could admire the wondrous bird and praise the Creator who fashions every sort of thing, known, and unknown. But when Dāwūd stretched out his hand to catch the bird, it flew off and settled on a spot just beyond Dāwūd's reach. Dāwūd went after it and followed the bird in its path. The bird, who was Shayṭān, led him into a garden. In that garden, at that very moment, the wife of his commander, Uriah, was taking her bath. Dāwūd's gaze fell upon the beautiful woman as she was bathing. He couldn't take his eyes off her and the harm was done. So great was his desire for the woman who was another man's wife that he called for her husband, Uriah, and sent him off to the front line, where, battle against the Ammonites was being fiercely fought. Uriah fell there as a martyr. Dāwūd then married his widow and she became the mother of Sulaymān.

Some time after these events, two men came into Dāwūd's sanctuary as he was praying there by himself. Dāwūd was afraid of them for he took them for intruders. As it is mentioned in the Qur'an:

وَهَلْ أَتَىٰكَ نَبَؤُا الْخَصْمِ إِذْ تَسَوَّرُوا الْمِحْرَابَ إِذْ دَخَلُوا عَلَىٰ دَاوُدَ فَفَزِعَ مِنْهُمْ ۖ قَالُوا لَا
تَخَفْ ۖ خَصْمَانِ بَغَىٰ بَعْضُنَا عَلَىٰ بَعْضٍ فَاحْكُم بَيْنَنَا بِالْحَقِّ وَلَا تُشْطِطْ وَاهْدِنَا إِلَىٰ
سَوَاءِ الصِّرَٰطِ إِنَّ هَٰذَا أَخِى لَهُ تِسْعٌ وَتِسْعُونَ نَعْجَةً وَلِىَ نَعْجَةٌ وَٰحِدَةٌ فَقَالَ أَكْفِلْنِيهَا
وَعَزَّنِى فِى الْخِطَابِ قَالَ لَقَدْ ظَلَمَكَ بِسُؤَالِ نَعْجَتِكَ إِلَىٰ نِعَاجِهِ ۖ وَإِنَّ كَثِيرًا مِّنَ
الْخُلَطَاءِ لَيَبْغِى بَعْضُهُمْ عَلَىٰ بَعْضٍ إِلَّا الَّذِينَ ءَامَنُوا وَعَمِلُوا الصَّٰلِحَٰتِ وَقَلِيلٌ مَّا هُمْ ۗ
وَظَنَّ دَاوُدُ أَنَّمَا فَتَنَّٰهُ فَاسْتَغْفَرَ رَبَّهُ وَخَرَّ رَاكِعًا وَأَنَابَ

"Has the tiding of the dispute come to thee?
When they scaled the Sanctuary when they entered upon David and he took fright at them and they said,
'Fear not, two disputants we are. One of us has injured the other. So judge between us justly and transgress not and guide us to the right path'.
'Behold, this my brother has ninety-nine ewes and I have one ewe. So he said, 'Give her into my charge,' and he overcame me in the argument. Said he, 'Assuredly he has wronged thee in asking for thy ewe in addition to his sheep.
And indeed, many intermixers do injury one against the other, save those who believe and do deeds of righteousness. And how few they are!'"[62]

Now the men who came into his presence were in reality angels, though Dāwūd knew them not. They revealed themselves to him and said, "Oh Dāwūd, that man with the 99 sheep is yourself for has not the Lord given to you 99 wives of your own? Why then did you desire to take the only wife of your loyal servant, Uriah, for yourself and you sent him to his death so you could do it more easily. The Lord has seen all you have done and know that you were being tested." Then Dāwūd remembered all the Lord had said to him and fell down senseless upon his prayer mat and lifted not his head for forty days. He wept so long that grass began to grow where his tears had fallen and the tears' streaks caused scars upon his blessed face. All the birds and beasts who were his friends wept with him and the whole creation mourned. The angels went to their Lord and interceded on behalf of Dāwūd. The Lord said to them, "It is alright for I am the Lord, the All-Forgiving, the All-Merciful. The gate of

---

[62] Sūrah Ṣād, 38:21-24.

repentance is open for all who sincerely intend to sin no more." Dāwūd cried to the Lord in his prostration,

قَالَ لَقَدْ ظَلَمَكَ بِسُؤَالِ نَعْجَتِكَ إِلَىٰ نِعَاجِهِ ۖ وَإِنَّ كَثِيرًا مِّنَ الْخُلَطَاءِ لَيَبْغِي بَعْضُهُمْ عَلَىٰ
بَعْضٍ إِلَّا الَّذِينَ آمَنُوا وَعَمِلُوا الصَّالِحَاتِ وَقَلِيلٌ مَّا هُمْ ۗ وَظَنَّ دَاوُودُ أَنَّمَا فَتَنَّاهُ فَاسْتَغْفَرَ
رَبَّهُ وَخَرَّ رَاكِعًا وَأَنَابَ فَغَفَرْنَا لَهُ ذَٰلِكَ ۖ وَإِنَّ لَهُ عِندَنَا لَزُلْفَىٰ وَحُسْنَ مَآبٍ يَا دَاوُودُ إِنَّا
جَعَلْنَاكَ خَلِيفَةً فِي الْأَرْضِ فَاحْكُم بَيْنَ النَّاسِ بِالْحَقِّ وَلَا تَتَّبِعِ الْهَوَىٰ فَيُضِلَّكَ عَن سَبِيلِ
اللَّهِ ۚ إِنَّ الَّذِينَ يَضِلُّونَ عَن سَبِيلِ اللَّهِ لَهُمْ عَذَابٌ شَدِيدٌ بِمَا نَسُوا يَوْمَ الْحِسَابِ

"Oh Lord, forgive me my sin for I repent unto you."
"And David thought that We had only tried him. Therefore he sought forgiveness of his Lord and he fell down, bowing and he repented.
Accordingly We forgave him that and he has a near place In Our Presence and a fair resort. 'David, behold, We have appointed thee a viceroy in the earth. Therefore judge between men justly and follow not caprice, lest it lead you astray from the way of God. Surely those who go astray from the way of God- there awaits them a terrible chastisement for that they have forgotten the Day of Reckoning.'"([63]

"Oh Lord," cried Dāwūd, "You are mighty and just and have the power to punish and to forgive. What shall I do on the Day of Judgment when I am faced with my servant Uriah and he speaks out against me?" Again Dāwūd fell down in prostration and wept for a long time. At last an angel of the Lord appeared before him and said, "The Lord says, 'On the Day of Judgment I will take Uriah aside and ask him to forgive you and to give to you his wife and make her

[63] Sūrah Ṣād, 38:24 -26.

lawful to you. For that, I shall open the gates of Paradise for him and he shall dwell there in bliss.' "

It is related from Ibn ʿAbbās:

"When the two angels had gone from Dāwūd, he fell down and lifted not his head from the ground for forty days. He neither ate nor slept but begged only forgiveness from the Lord. He prayed, 'Oh Lord, You have created me and You have made Iblīs to be my enemy, and You have bestowed on me Your favor. How shall I face You on the Day of Judgment? I can't bear even the heat of the sun. How then shall I bear the fire of fires? Oh my Lord, I can't bear the sound of Your Divine voice. How then shall I bear the roaring of hell-fire? Oh my God, You know what is manifest and what is hidden. Forgive me, my Lord."

Dāwūd is also reported to have cried to the Lord, "Oh my God, You are the Possessor of all majesty and power, You do no injustice to anyone. Tell me now what I must do."

The Lord answered Dāwūd and said, "Go to Uriah's grave. Ask his pardon and forgiveness for what you have done to him and ask also his permission for you to live with his wife lawfully. I shall make him hear you and you shall hear his answer."

Dāwūd then went to the grave of Uriah and called to him, "Oh Uriah, do you hear me?"

Uriah answered from his grave, 'Who is it who disturbs my peace and interrupts my enjoyments?"

"It is I, Dāwūd, a sinner."

"Oh prophet of Allah, why do you come to me?"

Dāwūd explained to him what he had done and how he had been the cause of his death. He asked for Uriah's forgiveness for having sent him to the frontline to fight ahead of the Holy Ark so that he might find death more certainly. Uriah answered, "I forgive you, oh prophet of Allah for by suffering this death I have been raised to the ranks of the holy martyrs."

Dāwūd returned and prayed again to the Lord. But the Lord said to him. "Oh Dāwūd, do you not know that I am a king more perfect in justice than any? Go again to Uriah and say to him, 'I have taken your wife, Uriah. Therefore, I had you killed. I ask you to make her lawful to me." Dāwūd returned to Uriah's grave and called to him.

"Uriah!" He cried.

Uriah answered him from his grave, "Who are you?"

"I am Dāwūd."

"Why have you come again. Have I not already forgiven you?"

Dāwūd confessed, "Oh Uriah, I desired to take your wife and that is why I sent you into battle to have you slain."

Uriah answered, "Oh Dāwūd, is that proper conduct for a prophet of Allah? Verily, until the Day of Judgment I shall bear witness against you in the presence of our Lord Allah Almighty!"

Dāwūd fell upon his face and covered his head with dust and remained there weeping for a very long time.

At last, a call from the Lord reached him and the Lord spoke, "Oh Dāwūd, raise your head up and dry your tears for I have heard your prayers and forgiven you."

Dāwūd said, "Oh my God, Uriah will not forgive me for the evil I have done to him!"

The Lord said, "Oh Dāwūd, I will say to Uriah on the Day of Judgment, 'If you don't forgive Dāwūd the crime committed against you, I shall load it upon you, Uriah. Then he will readily forgive you."

Dāwūd said, "Oh Lord, now I know that You have truly anointed me."

After Dāwūd repented, he cried day and night for thirty years. At the time he took Uriah's wife he was seventy years old. After these events he divided up his time. One day he would concern himself with governing his state and ruling his kingdom. The next day, he would spend among his wives and families, on the subsequent day he would go out into the fields and forests and weep under the open sky and on the fourth day he would retreat into his sanctuary and retire from the world. There were 4000 *miḥrāb*s (prayer niches) and 4000 anchorites and they all would weep and pray with Dāwūd. On the days Dāwūd went out into the fields, all of nature wept with him and the beasts shed tears. Whenever Dāwūd ate or drank he wept and his tears ran in streams to the ground and the earth drank them.

It is reported that one day as Dāwūd was preaching to his people of the power and might of the Lord and of how He was to be feared, 400 persons among his listeners surrendered their souls and died during his sermon.

Allah Almighty had taught Dāwūd the skill of making coats of mail with his bare hands. He made one such shirt a day and sold it for 6000 dirhams. Two thousand dirhams he spent on the needs of his families and for what he required, personally and four thousand dirhams he gave to the poor among the Banī-Israil.

Dawud's عليه السلام Conversation with the Lord

"Oh Lord, what is the reward for one who goes to visit the sick?"

"The angels of heaven ask for his forgiveness."

"Oh Lord, what is the reward for one who washes the dead?"

"I shall make him as pure as a new-born baby."

"Oh Lord, what is Your reward for one who wraps a dead person in his shroud?"

"I shall clothe him in the silk and brocade of the garments of Paradise."

"Oh Lord, how do You reward a person who prays over the dead?"

"The angels give him their *salāms* and pray for his soul."

"Oh Lord, what of a person who goes to console another in his grief?"

"I will clothe him in the garment of piety and faith."

"Oh Lord, what of a person who weeps from his fear of You?"

"I will make him secure from the terrors of hell."

"Oh Lord, if a person suffers calamity and shows patience in the face of disaster, what shall be his final reward?"

"I shall elevate him to high stations."

"Oh Lord, what of a person who goes out in the dark of night to pray in the mosque?"

"On the Last Day, I shall give him a light by which he shall find his way, safely."

"Oh Lord, if a person is angered against another and it is within his power to seek revenge and yet he forgoes it, what shall be his reward?"

"I will fill his heart with faith and mercy and give him certainty."

"Oh Lord, if a person suffers injustice and forgives his tormentor in spite of his cruelty, what shall be his reward?"

"On the Last Day, I will give him honor and serenity."

"Oh Lord, what of a person who clears the road and makes it smooth for those who travel on it?"

"I will release as many of his friends and relations from the torments of hell as the number of stones and thorns he picked up from the way, for his sake."

"Oh Lord, how do You reward a person who calls an unbeliever to faith?"

"I will have mercy on him and show him familiarity."

"Oh Lord, what is Your reward for a person who does good to his father and mother?"

"I shall protect that person from the punishment of hell and he will be satisfied by his station in Paradise."

"Oh Lord, what is the punishment of one who disobeys his father and mother?"

"His punishment will be hell-fire."

"Oh Lord, what of one who is separated from his family and the bonds of kinship and makes repairs and returns to them?"

"I will make his life long and prosperous."

"Oh Lord, how do You reward one who remembers You much with his heart and his tongue?"

"On the Day of Judgment he will find Me and be brought close to Me."

"Oh Lord, if a person commits a sin and repents with all his heart?"

"His sin is then forgiven."

"Oh Lord, if a person sins and does not repent, what is his punishment?"

"However much he calls on Me, I do not answer him and I show him no mercy, nor will he attain what he desires."

"Oh Lord, if a person lives on usury, how is he punished?"

"On the Day of Judgment, he will be made to eat of the fruit of the Zaqqūm tree (A tree in hell).

"Oh Lord, if a person lets his eye rove and looks at what is forbidden to him and does not avert his gaze even when he realizes this, what will his punishment be?"

"Even if he is a saint, I will cause his eye to weep."

"Oh Lord, if a person leaves his property in another's trust and departs on a journey and then, upon his return he receives back his property undamaged and undiminished, what is the reward of the person who took on the trust?"

"He will be made safe from My wrath."

"Oh Lord, if a person takes care not to transgress and keeps the company of the pious and god-fearing, what will be his reward?"

"He will be made safe from My punishment on the Day of Reckoning and I shall raise him up in the company of My Messenger and saints."

"Oh Lord, if a person fasts and suffers greatly from thirst during the heat of the day what will be his reward?"

"On the Day of Judgment he will know no thirst."

"Oh Lord, if a person, during his lifetime, repeats the words, '*Lā-ilāha ill-Llāh*', what will he find?"

"I will reward him with such bounty as his eye cannot encompass."

"Oh Lord, which of Your servants do You call miserly?"

"Oh Dāwūd, it is the man who does not greet (give Salams) to people."

"And which of Your servants is most beloved to You?"

"It is he who is humble for My sake."

"Oh Lord, how do You reward one who believes in Your Unity and associates not partners unto You?"

"I will save him from hell-fire."

"Oh Lord, which of Your servants is truly weak?"

"It is he who doesn't ask of Me and of My endless bounties."

"And which of Your servants will You surely punish?"

"The servant who is not pleased by My Decree."

"Oh Lord, which of Your servants is clever?"

"The servant who decides a matter according to My truth not his own opinion."

"And which of your servants can be called wise?"

"A person, who, however great his knowledge, always seeks to know and to learn more."

Then Dāwūd said, "Oh Lord, forgive me my sins, for the sake of Your Prophets, Ibrahim and Ishāq ﷺ and Y'aqūb, and make my prayer acceptable to You and show me mercy"

The Lord spoke, "Oh Dāwūd, I created Ādam ﷺ with My Hand and I blew into him a soul from My breath of life. I made the angels bow down before him in Paradise and I clothed him in the raiment of faith and set upon his head the crown of dignity. When he complained to Me of his loneliness I created Eve (Ḥawā) for him to be his wife and companion. After all that, he was faithless and disobedient to Me so I drove him out of Paradise. Oh Dāwūd, behold the truth. If you listen to Me and obey, I shall listen to you also when you desire a thing and when you are in need, I shall give you safety and when you repent, I shall grant you forgiveness."

From Ka'b-ul-Ahbār ؓ:

> The Lord said to Dāwūd, "Oh Dāwūd, give good tidings to the sinners and warn the righteous to fear Me." Dāwūd asked, "What are the good tidings for the sinners and what is the warning to the righteous?" The Lord answered, "Tell the sinners to repent and not to give up hope in Me and tell the righteous not to take pride in their righteousness. Oh Dāwūd, I have barred the unrighteous from remembrance of My Holy Name and I do not let them come to My house of worship for whoever remembers Me, I remember him. But when the unjust remember Me, I curse them and My mercy is not sent upon them. I accept him who obeys Me and I love him who loves Me. Whoever wishes to know Me and makes it his intention to come to Me will find Me. If he desires to find Me, let him leave behind the urgings of his lower soul. A person who worships for the sake of attaining the bliss of Paradise has wronged his own soul for his worship was not for My sake alone. I love him who loves Me and I have chosen him who chooses Me. Oh Dāwūd, I have created the clay of which

were made the prophets, Ibrahim and Mūsā and Muhammad Muṣṭafā and I created from My Light their hearts which were filled with longing. If your longing for Me is true then make it your quest and cut yourself off from everything other than Me and desire nothing else but My Love for it is a spiritual treasure. When love for Me fills your heart, all else will leave it for love of Me and love of worldliness are never found together in one heart. My remembrance (*dhikr*) is for those who remember Me and My Paradise is for those who obey Me. To remember Me much is reserved for the lovers of God and I, Myself, am for those who love Me. And whoever loves one who loves Me, he too is close to Me."

It is related by Abū Ṭālib al-Makkī:

The Lord spoke to Dāwūd, "Why do you desire Paradise and forget Me?" "Who are Your lovers?" asked Dāwūd. "My lovers," answered the Lord, "are those whose hearts have become purified from all contamination and have been burnt out for love of Me. With My hand of power I give them whatever they desire. I have created the hearts of My lovers for My own pleasure and I have cut them off from all but Myself alone."

Ibn ʿAbbās relates:

Once Dāwūd asked of the Lord, "Who is safe from Your mighty hand, oh Lord?" Allah Almighty answered, "He who assumes humility in the face of My Majesty and who leaves off his evil desires for My sake. He who feeds the hungry and clothes the needy for My sake, who welcomes the stranger and makes him his guest and he who gives protection and safety to those who have suffered cruelty and injustice, for My sake."

One day, Dāwūd entered the house of worship, his head held high and his arms swinging freely. The Lord addressed him and said, "Oh Dāwūd, where are you going with that proud, swinging gait?" From this time on Dāwūd always went out leaning upon a staff, from fear of the Almighty Lord.

Dāwūd said, "Oh Lord, every king has a treasure house, what then is the store of Your treasures?"

Allah answered him, "My treasure house is higher than the lofty Throne and wider than the Divine Court. It is more lavishly decorated than all the heavenly mansions with their immeasurable opulence."

Dāwūd said, "Where can this endless store of Your treasures be found, oh my Lord?"

The Lord answered, "My treasure house is in the breast of the broken-hearted."

The Lord said to Dāwūd, "Oh Dāwūd, be the enemy of your lower soul (*nafs*), and become My friend. If you give your love to Me, I will send you My Love. Oh Dāwūd, rejoice in the mention of My Holy Name and be content with Me. Oh Dāwūd, if a person were to live only for four hours, this is how he should spend his time: One hour in worship and supplication, one hour in fighting his nafs and seeking to conquer his lower inclinations, one hour he should spend visiting his friends and one hour in spending from his lawful earnings."

Dāwūd asked the Lord to show him the Mizan, the scales of balance on the Day of Judgment. Allah gave him the vision of the Mizan and Dāwūd fell down senseless and fainted.

When he came to senses he wept and asked the Lord, "Oh my God who would be able to fill the scales of that balance with his good deeds?

"Oh Dāwūd, "answered the Lord, "if I am pleased with My servant, I cause the scale of his good deed, to descend, even if they contain no more than a date-stone."

Dāwūd then asked to see the Bridge of Sirat. When he was shown the vision, again he fainted.

When he recovered his senses he asked, "Who might be capable of passing over that bridge in safety?"

The Lord answered him, "Oh Dāwūd, if a person just once in his life says with full conviction *'Muḥammadur-Rasulullāh*—Muhammad is the Prophet of Allah', he will pass over the Bridge of Sirat with lightning speed."

There lived a learned man in Isrā'īl, at the time, who possessed eighty chests full of books. The Lord said to Dāwūd, "Go tell that scholar that all his books and even if he had thrice as many, will not profit him if he is deficient in three things. If he has no love for his Muslim brothers then he is not one of them. Secondly, Shayṭān should not be a partner in his knowledge for Shayṭān is no friend of the Muslim and lastly, he should not seek to harm the Muslims, for this is not an Islamic deed."

Dawud's عليه السلام Death and Successor

Allah Almighty had decreed that the kingship over Isrā'īl should remain in the house of Dāwūd and He promised Dāwūd that He would give him a son to succeed him. Now Dāwūd had nineteen sons, one of them being Sulaymān. Dāwūd feared that there might be disagreement about the succession to the throne after his death and prayed to the Lord for guidance. Jibrīl was sent and said to Dāwūd, "Tell all your sons to write their names in sand and ask each to plant his staff beside his name. Let this be done in a closed room which is kept locked. You and everyone with you will know who is to be your successor by a sure sign; one of the staffs will have sprouted by the morning. So let your heart be calm and do as the Lord commands you." Dāwūd called his sons and had them do as the Lord had said. In the morning, they went to look and found that the staff of Sulaymān had grown as high as the ceiling, sprouting forth green leaves and branches. So it was known beyond doubt that Sulaymān was to be king after Dāwūd.

According to another narration the angel Jibrīl came to Dāwūd when Sulaymān was twenty years of age with a golden page in his hand, which, he handed to Dāwūd and said, "Salam's from the Lord Almighty to you, Dāwūd. You shall read all the questions on this golden sheet to your assembled sons and he who answers them all shall be your successor." Dāwūd read them to his sons and only Sulaymān knew how to answer them. Thus it was known that he would become Dāwūd's successor.

The Lord said to Dāwūd about his son Sulaymān, "Of all the ninety portions of wisdom present on Earth, I shall give seventy to your son,

Sulaymān and twenty to all the other kings who are to follow him." Then Dāwūd said to his son Sulaymān, "Oh my son, I leave you three pieces of advice: Don't rely on what you haven't yet attained. Be pleased with whatever the Lord gives to you and be patient with your loss when the Lord takes from you."

One day, when Dāwūd returned to his mosque, he found an unknown man sitting at the gates.

"Who are you?" he asked him.

"I am he from whose hand none can escape," that person said.

Dāwūd knew from his reply that he must be the Angel of Death. Now Dāwūd had a special high place upon which he was accustomed to pray and he prayed there. Then he said to the angel, "Give me leave to descend from here." The angel did not wait however, and he took his soul on the top of his minbar. His attendants carried him down and Sulaymān washed his father's body. Forty thousand people came to Dāwūd's funeral and they buried him in his own city, Jerusalem.

The Prophet Muhammad ﷺ said, "Dāwūd lived for one hundred years and left this world on a Saturday."

Peace be upon him and upon all the prophets, Amin.

sulayman عليه السلام

It is related by Wahab ibn Munabbih that when the Angel of Death retrieved the soul of King Dāwūd, Jibrīl came to Sulaymān, his son, to offer his condolences. He said to him, "The Lord has made you your father's successor and king of all Isrā'īl." Sulaymān understood then that his father had died. He went to Dāwūd's place of prayer and found his body there. He placed the king's turban upon his head, took the staff of Mūsā in one hand and the banner of Yūsuf عليه السلام in the other and stood in front of the Holy Ark.

Angel Jibrīl came to him and said, "The Lord Almighty sends you Salams and asks you what you value the most, this kingship or knowledge?"

Sulaymān fell down and prostrated before the Lord, and said, "Oh my Lord, I would much rather have knowledge from You than kingship!"

The Lord loves those who show humility before Him and was pleased with Sulaymān.

"As you have preferred knowledge," spoke the Lord, "I will give you knowledge as well as the kingship. I give you a sound mind and blameless character. I will remove from you vain pride and give the world into your hands. Travel its width and marvel at the wonders which I have created therein."

Again, Sulaymān prostrated before the Lord and did not lift his head until it was evening.

The Lord said to Jibrīl, "Go to the heavens and bring the Ring of Might and give it to Sulaymān." Jibrīl flew straight to heaven and got the ring. A sweet fragrance issued from it and it shone as brilliantly as a star. It was set in a square and there were certain words written in each of its corners: *'lā ilāha illa-Llāh, Muḥammadun-Rasūlullāh'* in the first corner; *'lā ilāha illa-Llāh,* everything perishes but His Faces, His is the verdict and to Him you shall return' in the second corner, 'His is the Sovereignty and Majesty, His the Might and the Power' in the third and 'Blessed be Allah, the Supreme Creator' in the fourth corner.

This ring was Ādam's ring which he wore when he dwelt in Paradise. When he fell from his station, the ring slipped off his finger during his fall to Earth and was lost to him. It fell near one of the pillars of the Throne. The Lord spoke to it and said, "Oh Ring of Might, as Ādam ﷺ has been heedless of his pact with Me, We will give you to one of his descendants who will keep his word." The ring remained in the heavens until the day Jibrīl was ordered to give it to Sulaymān. This day was Friday and it was the Day of Ashura, the tenth of Muharram. Sulaymān slipped the ring upon his finger and Jibrīl revealed to him the Basmalah. The winds and the Jinn were made subservient to him, as it is written:

وَلِسُلَيْمَٰنَ الرِّيحَ عَاصِفَةً تَجْرِى بِأَمْرِهِۦٓ إِلَى الْأَرْضِ الَّتِى بَٰرَكْنَا فِيهَا ۚ وَكُنَّا بِكُلِّ شَىْءٍ

عَٰلِمِينَ وَمِنَ الشَّيَٰطِينِ مَن يَغُوصُونَ لَهُۥ وَيَعْمَلُونَ عَمَلًا دُونَ ذَٰلِكَ ۖ وَكُنَّا لَهُمْ حَٰفِظِينَ

"And to Solomon, the wind, strongly blowing that ran at his command unto the land that We had blessed and We had knowledge of everything. And of the Shayṭāns Some dived for him and did other work besides and We were watching over them."[64]

Allah Almighty also taught Sulaymān the tongue of the birds:

---

[64] Sūratu 'l-Anbīyā (the Prophets), 10:81-82.

وَوَرِثَ سُلَيْمَٰنُ دَاوُۥدَ ۖ وَقَالَ يَٰٓأَيُّهَا ٱلنَّاسُ عُلِّمْنَا مَنطِقَ ٱلطَّيْرِ وَأُوتِينَا مِن كُلِّ شَىْءٍ ۖ إِنَّ هَٰذَا لَهُوَ ٱلْفَضْلُ ٱلْمُبِينُ

And Sulaymān was Dāwūd's heir and he said, "Men, we have been taught the speech of the birds and we have been given of everything. Surely, this is indeed the manifest bounty."[65]

One morning a quail raised its voice and Sulaymān said to his followers, "Do you not hear what it is saying? It says, 'Oh heedless ones, remember your Lord!' " When the nightingale sang, Sulaymān interpreted its song, "The nightingale says, 'I have tasted of this world but half a date.' " Then the peacock screeched and Sulaymān translated its speech, "It says, 'However much you ask to be spared, in the end you will die!'"' he hoopoe bird called, and Sulaymān understood its words, "It was saying, 'Whoever takes no pity on Allah's creation shall find no pity himself."

The parrot cried, "Whoever works good deeds will receive goodness in return." Then the owl spoke and said, "If only these people had never been created." The dove said, "Praised be the Lord Almighty!" The raven cawed, "He who remained silent was saved from foolishness" The eagle said, "Whatever I may wish for, death will put an end to it all." King Sulaymān understood their speech and translated its meaning for his people.

Sulaymān's mother was Bathsheba. He was born in Jerusalem. He lived only for 53 or 55 years, some sources say sixty. He was of fair complexion and quite tall, had a thick beard and hair on his body. He preferred to dress in white. According to the custom of the times, he married many women, among them Firʿawn's daughter and many other princesses. He was also extremely fond of fine horses and kept a great many in his stables. One afternoon, he was watching his

[65] Sūratu 'n-Naml (The Ant), 27:16.

horses being led in parade. He was so enraptured by their beauty that the time of the afternoon prayer slipped by and it was evening before Sulaymān looked up. He felt great remorse at having let himself be distracted from his worship for love of the world and ordered all his beautiful horses to be killed.

وَوَهَبنا لِداوُدَ سُلَيمٰنَ ۚ نِعمَ العَبدُ ۖ إِنَّهُ أَوّابٌ إِذ عُرِضَ عَلَيهِ بِالعَشِيِّ الصّٰفِنٰتُ الجِيادُ

فَقالَ إِنّى أَحبَبتُ حُبَّ الخَيرِ عَن ذِكرِ رَبّى حَتّىٰ تَوارَت بِالحِجابِ رُدّوها عَلَىَّ ۖ

فَطَفِقَ مَسحًا بِالسّوقِ وَالأَعناقِ

"And We gave unto Dāwūd, Sulaymān, how excellent a servant he was! He was penitent. When in the evening were presented to him the standing steeds, he said, 'Lo, I have loved the love of good things better than the remembrance of my Lord, until the sun was hidden behind the veil. Return them to me!' And he began to stroke their shanks and necks."[66]

Sayyidinā ʿAlī related that Allah ordered the angel of the sun to bring the sun up again so that Sulaymān could complete his prayer before sunset and the sun was brought up again after it had already gone down.

When his prophethood was revealed to him, the angel Jibrīl came and said to Sulaymān, "Oh prophet of Allah! You are now a prophet as well as king. These people are entrusted to your care in worldly as well as spiritual matters. You must take great care in looking after them. Neglect not one of your subjects. For example, I will tell you now that not very far from here, there lives a poor widow with her two small children. Go to her hut and see to her needs." Sulaymān went from his palace to the woman's hut by the shortest route. He found the woman and her children living in great poverty. There was

---

[66] Sūrah Ṣād, 38:30-33.

nothing in the hut but an old mat woven of palm fronds and a sackcloth bag stuffed with palm fiber to make a pillow. That, along with one or two earthenware vessels was all they possessed. Sulaymān met the woman and saw that she was dressed in rags and that her hands were cut and bleeding. He greeted her. Then he inquired about her state of affairs.

"Is this all you possess?" he asked.

"Yes," replied the woman, "this is all we own in the world."

"What has happened to your husband?" asked the king.

"My husband died in battle as a martyr, may God have mercy on him," she answered.

"Have you no relatives then; brothers, cousins or in-laws to look after you?"

"I have no one but Allah," she said.

Then Sulaymān asked about her hands and learnt that at night she bedded her children on her hands and arms so that they should not be hurt by the roughness of the mat.

Sulaymān said, "You are yet youthful. It is only right and proper that you should be wed to a worthy man who will look after you and your daughters, according to Allah Almighty's command. Then you will have some protection."

"I ask whatever I need from the Lord, alone," the woman replied. "I am afraid of remarrying, for who knows how a stepfather will treat them. It is enough that their father left them orphaned."

Sulaymān returned to his palace and prayed to the Lord.

قَالَ رَبِّ اغْفِرْ لِي وَهَبْ لِي مُلْكًا لَّا يَنبَغِي لِأَحَدٍ مِّن بَعْدِي ۖ إِنَّكَ أَنتَ الْوَهَّابُ

"He said, 'My Lord, forgive me and give me a kingdom such as may not befall anyone after me. Surely Thou art All-giving.[67]

"I am poor myself," prayed Sulaymān, "how shall I look after the needs of the poor?"

The angel Jibrīl came to him and said, "Allah has given you power and a kingdom."

That night, by the Grace of Allah, Sulaymān was given power over the worlds above and below. He commanded the Jinn to obey him. It is written:

فَسَخَّرنا لَهُ الرِّيحَ تَجرى بِأَمرِهِ رُخاءً حَيثُ أَصابَ ۝ وَالشَّيٰطينَ كُلَّ بَنّاءٍ وَغَوّاصٍ ۝ وَءاخَرينَ مُقَرَّنينَ فِى الأَصفادِ ۝ هٰذا عَطاؤُنا فَامنُن أَو أَمسِك بِغَيرِ حِسابٍ ۝ وَإِنَّ لَهُ عِندَنا لَزُلفىٰ وَحُسنَ مَـٔابٍ

So We subjected to him the wind that ran at his commandment softly, wherever he might light on and the Shayṭāns, every builder and diver and others also, coupled in fetters: "This is Our gift Which bestow or withhold without reckoning." And he had a near place in Our presence and a fair resort.[68]

Sulaymān commanded the Jinn to dig and burrow for gold and precious stones and by the morning he had a great treasure before him. He took none for himself but loaded it all onto a mule caravan and sent it by route to the house of the poor widow, while he himself took the short road which he knew. Sulaymān reached the hut before the bearers of the treasure and found it crowded full of people at morning. A curtain had been hung up in the room, partitioning off a section for the women and behind it sat the poor woman, while her children played outside. Sulaymān asked and was told that after the

---

[67] Sūrah Ṣād, 38: 35.

[68] Sūrah Ṣād, 38:36-40.

king's visit the woman had finally consented to marry. There was a certain man who had long been asking for her hand in marriage. They had come together to contract the marriage that very day. Sulaymān sat down in the assembly and was silent. The children came in, looking for their mother and not finding her among the men, lifted a corner of the curtain and ran to their mother.

They saw that she was wearing a beautiful new dress and asked her, "Oh mother, from where did you get that beautiful new dress? Why are you all dressed up? Why have so many people come to see us today?"

Their mother embraced them and said, "Oh my beloved children, our lives are going to change today. You will also have nice, new clothes to put on and our life of misery and poverty will be over. We shall live decently like everybody else. Your new father will look after us."

As young as they were, the girls instantly understood that their mother was planning to get married and they tore themselves loose and ran out. Outside they fell into each other's arms and began to weep and cry in a most forlorn manner. "In the whole world we had only our dear mother and now she is being taken from us and given to someone else. She will now sleep in another bed and we have only each other. What is to become of us?" And they cried so hard and sobbed so much that it rent the hearts of all who heard them. Their mother also wept and Sulaymān was moved to tears and the whole gathering suddenly looked unhappy. Then, behind her curtain, their mother quietly took off her nice new dress and said to the man who hoped to marry her, "Take back your nice presents. There will be no wedding today, for I cannot bear to see those children crying. I can't be responsible for their misery. The All-merciful Lord who has kept us alive will give us our provision as He has done so far. I will not be parted from my children." With that, the matter was settled and everyone left the hut except Sulaymān. The woman said to him, "Now you have seen, it is impossible for me to break my children's hearts for the sake of a piece of bread". Just then, the mule train arrived and Sulaymān said, "See here, good woman, what the Lord has sent you." All the bags of gold and jewels were brought in and dumped in a corner of the hut. Sulaymān said to her, "All this gold and the priceless jewels are now yours. Use them as you see fit and bring up your daughters as you wish. This is gift from the Lord Almighty, Allah." With that he rose up to go.

Now the construction of the temple had been begun in the time of Dāwūd but he could not complete it. Sulaymān was ordered to accomplish this task. The poor widow vowed that she would donate the treasure towards the construction of the temple after she had taken what she needed and given plentifully to other poor people. This was the wisdom behind the immense treasure that was given to Sulaymān in that night.

It is related that one day, prophet Sulaymān was traveling by the wind and passed over the Kaʿbah which, at that time, was full of pagan idols. It was revealed to him that the prophet of the Last Times would arise in this place and Sulaymān saluted the Kaʿbah but he did not alight there. The Kaʿbah, itself, wept when the prophet Sulaymān flew by and did not visit it.

The Lord asked, "Why are you weeping?"

"Should I not weep?" said the Kaʿbah. "Your prophet, Sulaymān, flew by overhead and didn't stop to pray here or visit me.

"The Lord then spoke, "Dry your tears, for I will send a prophet to you in the Last Times. Untold millions will then come to you and pray towards you from all directions for I will make you the Qibla of the world. I will cleanse you of all idols and the filth of Shayṭān. I will make you the center of holy rites and the whole world will then yearn to see you."

One of the Prophet's companions relates, "The Lord has spoken in the Holy Qur'an,

وَلَقَدْ فَتَنَّا سُلَيْمَٰنَ وَأَلْقَيْنَا عَلَىٰ كُرْسِيِّهِۦ جَسَدًا ثُمَّ أَنَابَ ۝ قَالَ رَبِّ ٱغْفِرْ لِى وَهَبْ لِى
مُلْكًا لَّا يَنۢبَغِى لِأَحَدٍ مِّنۢ بَعْدِىٓ ۖ إِنَّكَ أَنتَ ٱلْوَهَّابُ

Certainly We tried Solomon, and We cast upon his throne a mere body. Then he repented. He said. "My Lord, forgive me?"[69]

The trial of Sulaymān was this: One day, a son was born to the king. The Jinn who were subjugated by Sulaymān and made to work for him, said among themselves, "If this child lives and succeeds his father to the throne, we will never be free of this bondage and forced labor. It is best we kill the baby or at least drive him mad." The wind brought news of this talk to the prophet and Sulaymān ordered the wind to enfold the child in his breath and carry him up to the clouds and hide him there. The wind obeyed and hid him there but one day the child fell off the cloud and was killed. He fell right upon his father's throne. Sulaymān then realized his fault; his trust in Allah had been deficient when he believed he could hide the child in a cloud. He wept and prayed for forgiveness and for three days did not appear in his court. The Lord reproached him for this also saying, "You have neglected the affairs of My servants in your excessive grief over the death of your baby son."

Another version of this story has also been related.

One day Sulaymān's son fell seriously ill. Having no other son, Sulaymān became sick with grief.

Two persons appeared before him and one of them said to the king, "This man has trampled through my fields and destroyed my grain."

Sulaymān asked the accused man, "Why did you walk through your neighbor's field and make his crop wither?"

---

[69] Sūrah Ṣād, 38:34-35.

The man replied, "I had no choice but to step on it, for he had sown his grain in the middle of the road."

Sulaymān then said to the first man, "Why did you sow in the middle of the road? Don't you know that travelers have the right of way on a public road?"

The man answered Sulaymān, "Why did you sire a son? Did you not know that he was on the road to death as soon as he was born? All people are on the road to death."

With that both men disappeared and Sulaymān knew they had been angels sent to teach him a lesson. He fell down and prayed for forgiveness.

Though Sulaymān was king over all Isrā'īl, he practiced a trade to earn his livelihood. He wove baskets and sold them in the market for two dinars each. He fed the poor and sat and ate with them because he said that the poor man sits with the poor. He wore plain while robes and was modest in his bearing.

Sulayman عليه السلام Loses His Ring

Sulaymān married many women, among them some foreign princesses. One of these was the daughter of the lord of Sidon whom he had defeated in battle. This princess grieved very much for her father and asked Sulaymān to have a statue fashioned in her father's image to remember him. Sulaymān loved this wife and gave the task to the artisans among the jinn. They made a statue, and because it was the work of Jinn the image resembled the dead man so perfectly it was nearly impossible to tell that it was made of stone. Everyone admired the work and secretly the princess began to worship it as some people worship their ancestors.

King Sulaymān had a wise vizier by the name of Āṣif. One day, this vizier called for a general meeting to be held. Āṣif stood up in front of those assembled and gave an address. He recounted many events from the lives of the prophets from the time of Ādam عليه السلام onwards and described in great detail their deeds and the excellence of their characters. He finally made mention of their present prophet-king Sulaymān, who, was also present at the gathering. He said, "When he was very young, Sulaymān attained a very elevated state of illumination." However, Āṣif made no mention of Sulaymān's later life. Afterwards, Sulaymān asked him why he had spoken thus about him as if he considered him to have now fallen from his station. Āṣif replied, "Truly, your condition then was better than it is now. For it has become known to me that for forty days idols have been worshipped under your roof." Sulaymān was ignorant of this fact and the Lord addressed him and reproached him for his negligence. "Oh Sulaymān," spoke the Lord, "who gave you permission to obtain wives from among the idolaters and bring them into your house? Be prepared for disaster to come upon your head!"

One of Sulaymān's wives was named Āminah. Whenever Sulaymān went to perform his ablution he would take off his ring with the holy seal and, saying *"Bismi'l-Lāhi 'r-Raḥmāni 'r-Raḥīm,"* would hand it to his wife who held it for him until he had completed his ablutions. One day, one of the lords of the Jinn saw his chance and decided to take the ring from Sulaymān by some means. It was the very day Allah had reproached Sulaymān for harboring an idol-worshipping wife in his house. That day, Sulaymān forgot to say the Basmalah before he took off his ring. This was enough for the Jinn whose name was Sakhir to enter. He assumed Sulaymān's form (the Jinn have been granted that power by the Grace of Allah Almighty) and went up to Aminah who was holding the ring and asked her for it. Thinking it was Sulaymān before her she gave him the ring without a moment's hesitation. The Jinn, Sakhir, went straight to Sulaymān's throne and occupied his place there. When the true Sulaymān came out from performing his ablutions and asked his wife Aminah for his ring, she cried, "I have given the ring to Sulaymān. Who are you, impostor?" She called at once for the palace guard who threw Sulaymān out of his palace, leaving the false pretender to impersonate him for forty days.

During that time, Sakhir the Jinn did his best to corrupt and undo all the good that Sulaymān had done. He signed orders and issued decrees, making lawful what is forbidden. He taught the practice of the black arts and spread all manner of evil.

Sulaymān wandered the world alone as a beggar. He was hungry and humiliated. At last, he reached the seashore and met some fishermen.

He said to them, "I am Sulaymān, your prophet-king."

The fishermen took a stick and beat him, "How dare you claim to be Sulaymān, the great and wise? You are a liar!"

Sulaymān was at a complete loss of what to do and he wept long and hard. The angels in heaven wept with him. At long last he suggested to the fisherman that they should let him help them with their work and for forty days Sulaymān went out fishing with them. He received two fish each day for his labor, one of which he would eat himself and the other he would give away in charity.

The Jinn on Sulaymān's throne ruled for forty days. By then, Sulaymān's vizier, Āṣif, realized that something was very wrong for the king was perpetrating all sorts of evil. Āṣif knew also of the enmity of the Jinn, Sakhir. He guessed the truth, exposed the impostor and ordered him to be removed from the throne. The Jinn moved with lightning speed and flew away before they could capture him. He dropped the ring into the sea, from the heights of the ramparts. It sank in the sea and by the supreme wisdom of Allah Almighty, a fish swam along and swallowed it. That day, this fish went into the fishermen's nets. When Sulaymān was given his daily portion of two fish, he found his very own ring in the belly of the fish kept for his own consumption! He slipped it on and in great joy and gratitude returned to his palace and resumed his rule.

Building the Temple at Jerusalem

Dāwūd had already intended to build the holy temple at Jerusalem but his son Sulaymān was destined to complete it. Since the time of Mūsā, the direction of Jerusalem had been the *qiblah*[70] for the angels had shown him special lights emanating from that direction. Every attempt Dāwūd made to construct a temple failed and every building he erected there crumbled.

Dāwūd complained of this to Allah Almighty, and Allah answered him, "He who has spilt the blood of My servants is not destined to build My temple."

Dāwūd rejoined, "Oh Lord, I fought only in the Jihad as You commanded me, and the blood I spilt was the blood of unbelievers."

"Yes," said the Lord, "they were unbelievers, and it was holy war but weren't they My servants nonetheless?"

Dāwūd understood and was told that his son, Sulaymān, would build the temple of the Lord.

After Dāwūd had passed away, Sulaymān received the order to begin with the construction. Sulaymān pressed into service the hosts of Jinn at his command and a great number of architects and workmen from all parts of the world. The Jinn were sent to fetch the marble and alabaster out of which the walls were to be built. Another group was sent to mine gold and silver and other precious materials from the depths of the earth. Yet others dived down into the sea to fetch up pearls and corals and there were others still who brought

---

[70] Arabic: *qiblah,* direction and focus of prayer.

amber and musk and costly incense. They worked day and night at the task and when the temple was completed, it shone like the Pole Star. Never has there been such a magnificent temple of worship on earth. There was a great feast to celebrate its completion.

Ibn ʿAbbās has related that an angel was appointed to oversee the Jinn at their work. He held a whip in his hand and flogged the Jinn who were disobedient or lazy.

Sulaymān asked three things of the Lord and the Lord granted him his wishes: Firstly, he asked for wisdom; secondly, he asked for a kingdom such as would never be given to another king on earth and lastly, he asked that whoever prays two *rakaʿat*s in the holy mosque at Jerusalem might be forgiven for his sins.

Sulayman عليه السلام and Bilqis the Queen of Sheba

When the temple was completed, Sulaymān went to perform a pilgrimage at Mecca to glorify the Lord. He sacrificed 5,000 camels and 5,000 oxen and 20,000 sheep. Then he mounted his flying carpet, which, the Jinn had woven for him and flew towards Yemen. He was accompanied by his flock of birds, among them the hoopoe bird. At Sana, the capital of Yemen where Sulaymān had stopped to rest and to pray, Sulaymān's hoopoe bird met another hoopoe whose name was Aifel. They kept each other company and the hoopoe, Aifel described at great length to Sulaymān's hoopoe bird the wonders of the kingdom of Sana. They flew off together so that Aifel might show him what he had described. So it happened that King Sulaymān departed on his carpet and returned to Jerusalem without his hoopoe bird. Sulaymān noticed that the hoopoe bird was not with him and asked for him. At last, the bird came flying home and rubbed its head and its wings in the dust at the king's feet, begging Sulaymān's pardon. Sulaymān grabbed the bird and shook it but the hoopoe said, "Oh my king, there will surely come a day when you too will have to stand before the Presence of your Lord awaiting judgment." Upon these words, Sulaymān forgave him.

وَتَفَقَّدَ الطَّيرَ فَقالَ ما لِىَ لا أَرى الهُدهُدَ أَم كانَ مِنَ الغائِبينَ لَأُعَذِّبَنَّهُ عَذابًا شَديدًا

أَو لَأَاذبَحَنَّهُ أَو لَيَأتِيَنّى بِسُلطٰنٍ مُبينٍ فَمَكَثَ غَيرَ بَعيدٍ فَقالَ أَحَطتُ بِما لَم تُحِط بِهِ

وَجِئتُكَ مِن سَبَإٍ بِنَبَإٍ يَقينٍ إِنّى وَجَدتُ امرَأَةً تَملِكُهُم وَأوتِيَت مِن كُلِّ شَيءٍ وَلَها

عَرشٌ عَظِيمٌ وَجَدتُّهَا وَقَومَهَا يَسجُدُونَ لِلشَّمسِ مِن دُونِ اللَّهِ وَزَيَّنَ لَهُمُ الشَّيطَٰنُ
أَعمَٰلَهُم فَصَدَّهُم عَنِ السَّبِيلِ فَهُم لَا يَهتَدُونَ أَلَّا يَسجُدُوا لِلَّهِ الَّذِى يُخرِجُ الخَبءَ فِى
السَّمَٰوَٰتِ وَالأَرضِ وَيَعلَمُ مَا تُخفُونَ وَمَا تُعلِنُونَ اللَّهُ لَا إِلَٰهَ إِلَّا هُوَ رَبُّ العَرشِ العَظِيمِ

"And he reviewed the birds. Then he said,
"How is it with me, that I do not see the hoopoe? Or is he among the absent? Assuredly I will chastise him with a terrible chastisement or I will slaughter him or he bring me a clear authority."
But he tarried not long and said, "I have comprehended that which thou hast not comprehended and I have come from Sheba to thee with a sure tiding. I found a woman ruling over them and she has been given of everything and she possesses a mighty throne.
I found her and her people prostrating to the sun apart from Allah. Shayṭān has decked out fair their deeds to them and he has barred them from the way and therefore they are not guided so that they prostrate not themselves to Allah, who brings forth what is hidden in the heavens and earth and He knows what you conceal and what you publish.
Allah: there is no god but He, the Lord of the Mighty Throne."[71]

The hoopoe bird told his king all he had seen in the kingdom of Sana and how the queen, Bilqīs and her subjects adored the sun instead of Allah Almighty. "We shall see if you have spoken the truth," said Sulaymān, "and if you have lied, I will punish you harshly." Sulaymān was asked how he would punish the hoopoe and Sulaymān replied, "I would place him among a flock of foreign birds other than his own kind so that he could not understand them nor should they understand him. That punishment would be more

[71] Sūratu 'n-Naml (The Ant), 27: 20-26.

grievous to him than death." But, Sulaymān wisely forgave the hoopoe bird.

Some time passed and the king had not called or asked for the hoopoe bird. The hoopoe grew very sad for having been deprived of the king's company. He confided his grief to his friend, the turtledove. The dove told his friend not to worry. He would take care of the matter. Then he flew off to the king's private gardens, where, Sulaymān was conversing with his vizier, Āṣif.

When the dove had finished speaking, Sulaymān said, "We shall see if he has spoken the truth. I will write a letter to the queen of Sheba, calling her to Islam and ending their idol worship."

"And who will deliver that letter?" Āṣif enquired, for the inhabitants of that country were known for their ferocity.

Sulaymān called for the hoopoe. "You know the way into that country," he said, "so, go take this letter and deliver it and we shall see what is their reply."

قَالَ سَنَنظُرُ أَصَدَقْتَ أَمْ كُنتَ مِنَ الْكَاذِبِينَ اذْهَب بِّكِتَابِي هَٰذَا فَأَلْقِهْ إِلَيْهِمْ ثُمَّ تَوَلَّ عَنْهُمْ فَانظُرْ مَاذَا يَرْجِعُونَ

"Said he, 'Now we will see whether thou hast spoken truly or whether thou art among those that lie. Take this letter of mine and cast it unto them. Then turn back from them and see what they shall return."[72]

The hoopoe bird flew off with the letter and on its way it had to pass by 300 archers who aimed at it but all of them missed their mark and the hoopoe flew by unscathed. It never feared for was the letter not begun "In the Name of Allah, the All-Compassionate, All-Merciful (*Bismi'l-Lāhi 'r-Raḥmāni 'r-Raḥīm*)?" The hoopoe flew past all the

[72] Sūratu 'n-Naml (The Ant), 27: 27-28.

queen's marksmen and landed on top of her palace. Now it happened to be a holiday and the queen was alone in her private apartments, resting. The hoopoe flew straight in through an open window - or perhaps it was broken - and dropped the letter upon her breast. Then he darted out again and flew homewards. The queen awoke and found the letter which bore Sulaymān's seal.

قَالَتْ يٰأَيُّهَا الْمَلَؤُا أَفْتُونِى فِى أَمْرِى مَا كُنتُ قَاطِعَةً أَمْرًا حَتّٰى تَشْهَدُونِ قَالُوا نَحْنُ أُولُوا

قُوَّةٍ وَأُولُوا بَأْسٍ شَدِيدٍ وَالْأَمْرُ إِلَيْكِ فَانظُرِى مَاذَا تَأْمُرِينَ

She said, "O Council, see, a letter honorable has been cast unto me. It is from Solomon, and it is 'In the Name of God, the Merciful, the Compassionate. Rise not up against me but come to me in surrender.'"
She said, "O Council, pronounce to me concerning my affair.I am not used to deciding an affair until you bear me witness."
They said: "We are lords of might and lords of great prowess, but it is for thee to command; so consider what thou wilt command."[73]

"I have received this letter from Sulaymān," she told her advisors," and it frightens me. It is very strongly worded and forceful. What do you advise?"

"Our soldiers are many and our armies number many thousands of men. If only you order it, we will go out to war against them."

But Bilqīs replied, "O my counselors and ministers, listen to me. If Sulaymān falls upon this land, he will destroy all there is within it and leave not one of us alive."

قَالَتْ إِنَّ الْمُلُوكَ إِذَا دَخَلُوا قَرْيَةً أَفْسَدُوهَا وَجَعَلُوا أَعِزَّةَ أَهْلِهَا أَذِلَّةً ۖ وَكَذٰلِكَ يَفْعَلُونَ

---

[73] Sūratu 'n-Naml (The Ant), 27:32-33.

"She said, 'Kings when they enter a city, disorder it and make the mighty ones of its inhabitants abased, Even so will they do. Now I will send them a present and see what the envoys bring back.'"[74]

Her advisors agreed with her for she was their queen and they could easily see that it would be to their advantage not to antagonize such a mighty king as Sulaymān and to sweeten him with precious gifts. Perhaps, they might even win him over to their beliefs and form of worship, they thought. So Bilqīs had a large caravan prepared. She loaded it with bricks of gold and jewels of untold value. She also sent some gifts intended to try Sulaymān to see if he was really as wise as she had been told. There was a box that contained a pierced pearl of majestic size but the hole was so narrow, it was impossible to pass a cord through it. "Let him pass a string through this pearl. Neither man nor Jinn shall touch it." She also sent another pearl, this one not pierced, and asked Sulaymān to pierce it, but again not by the hand of man or Jinn. Then she sent 500 boys and 500 girls to him, all born in the same year, in the same month, on the same day, and at the same hour. They were all of equal stature and wearing identical clothes. Sulaymān was asked to distinguish which of them were girls and which were boys. "If Sulaymān is really a prophet, then he will know the answer to these riddles and if he is only a king, it will just arouse his anger," said Bilqīs. The hoopoe heard all these words and reported them to Sulaymān.

Sulaymān ordered the Jinn to make bricks of silver and gold and tile a space of twenty square miles with them. Then, he placed his throne on this square and lined up all the Jinn and 'Ifrīts and monsters and dragons along the sides of the golden square and surrounded his throne with his counselors and wise men. The dragons and monsters defiled the silver and gold-tiled space and made it unrecognizable by the time the delegation from Sana arrived. They deposited their

[74] Sūratu 'n-Naml (The Ant), 27:34.

presents in one corner of the great square and came before the king, bowing. Sulaymān looked on them with a smiling mien. Then he asked them, "So where is the pearl in the bottle?"

The envoys were much surprised at his knowledge of what hadn't yet been shown to him. The ambassador brought the precious gifts and stated the conditions. Sulaymān gave orders to the woodworm. The woodworm heard and obeyed. It took a length of silk thread in its mouth and crept the crooked, narrow way through the pearl, bringing the thread out the other end. Then Sulaymān ordered the woodpecker to bore a hole through the other pearl and the bird did this perfectly. After this, Sulaymān ordered for water to be brought and had all the girls and youths wash their hands and faces. He saw that some of them let the water fall on the backs of their hands while others cupped their hands to collect the water. The first group were the boys and the second the girls.

Then Sulaymān said to the envoys:

فَلَمَّا جَاءَ سُلَيْمَٰنَ قَالَ أَتُمِدُّونَنِ بِمَالٍ فَمَا ءَاتَىٰنِۦَ ٱللَّهُ خَيْرٌ مِّمَّا ءَاتَىٰكُم بَلْ أَنتُم بِهَدِيَّتِكُمْ تَفْرَحُونَ ٱرْجِعْ إِلَيْهِمْ فَلَنَأْتِيَنَّهُم بِجُنُودٍ لَّا قِبَلَ لَهُم بِهَا وَلَنُخْرِجَنَّهُم مِّنْهَآ أَذِلَّةً وَهُمْ صَٰغِرُونَ

"What, would you succor me with wealth and what God gave me is better than what He has given you? Nay, but instead you rejoice in your gift! Return thou to them. We shall assuredly come against them with hosts they have not power to resist and we shall expel them from there, abased and utterly humbled."[75]

The envoys returned with the gifts Sulaymān had rejected and told their queen what had occurred. She then said, "He is, indeed, a

[75] Sūratu 'n-Naml (The Ant), 27: 37.

prophet and no ordinary king." Sulaymān had also sent word to Bilqīs, inviting her to come to his court, because he intended to marry her. Her maidens agreed that this was a very good plan, "You will rule over the whole of the land, from the Euphrates to the Nile," they said. They advised her to accept Sulaymān's invitation and to show herself to him for she had no equal. No princess or slave-girl could match her beauty. She was also proud and planned to go only if she was accompanied by her entire army. Sulaymān had written to her inviting to the true religion and had said that the only gift he would accept from her was her conversion to Islam.

[Ibn Kathīr relates that as Bilqīs made preparation to travel to the land of Sulaymān, she sent word to him saying: "I am coming to you with the leaders of my people to see what you will instruct us to do and what you are calling us to of your religion." Then she issued commands that her throne, which was made of gold and inlaid with rubies, chrysolite and pearls, should be placed in the innermost of seven rooms, one within the other, and all the doors should be locked. Then she told her deputy whom she was leaving in charge, "Take care of my people and my throne, and do not let anyone approach it or see it until I come back to you." Then she set off to meet Sulayman with twelve thousand of her commanders from the leaders of Yemen, under each of whose command were many thousands of men. Sulayman sent the Jinn to bring him news of her progress and route every day and night, then when she drew near, he gathered together the Jinns and humans who were under his control.]

Sulaymān asked his attendants "Who of you is able to bring me her throne before she arrives here?"

One of the ʿIfrīts, a giant among the Jinn, spoke up and said, "Surely, I will bring it to you before you are able to rise from your place."

But Sulaymān said, "No, I want it here faster than that."

Then Āṣif, his trusted friend, spoke," I will bring it to you faster than your gaze returns to your eye." And he did so. In the Qur'an the story is told in these words:

قَالَ يَٰٓأَيُّهَا ٱلْمَلَؤُا۟ أَيُّكُمْ يَأْتِينِى بِعَرْشِهَا قَبْلَ أَن يَأْتُونِى مُسْلِمِينَ ۝ قَالَ عِفْرِيتٌ مِّنَ ٱلْجِنِّ أَنَا۠ ءَاتِيكَ بِهِۦ قَبْلَ أَن تَقُومَ مِن مَّقَامِكَ ۖ وَإِنِّى عَلَيْهِ لَقَوِىٌّ أَمِينٌ ۝ قَالَ ٱلَّذِى عِندَهُۥ عِلْمٌ مِّنَ ٱلْكِتَٰبِ أَنَا۠ ءَاتِيكَ بِهِۦ قَبْلَ أَن يَرْتَدَّ إِلَيْكَ طَرْفُكَ ۚ فَلَمَّا رَءَاهُ مُسْتَقِرًّا عِندَهُۥ قَالَ هَٰذَا مِن فَضْلِ رَبِّى لِيَبْلُوَنِىٓ ءَأَشْكُرُ أَمْ أَكْفُرُ ۖ وَمَن شَكَرَ فَإِنَّمَا يَشْكُرُ لِنَفْسِهِۦ ۖ وَمَن كَفَرَ فَإِنَّ رَبِّى غَنِىٌّ كَرِيمٌ

"He said, 'O Council, which one of you will bring me her throne before they come to me in surrender?' An 'Ifrīt of the Jinns said, 'I will bring it to thee, before thou risest from this place. I have the strength for it and I am trustworthy.' Said he who possessed knowledge of the Book, 'I will bring It to thee before even thy glance returns to thee.' Then, when he saw it settled before him, he said, 'This is of my Lord's bounty that He may try me, whether I am thankful or ungrateful.
Whosoever gives thanks gives thanks' only for his own soul's good and whosoever is ungrateful, my Lord is surely All-Sufficient, All-Generous.'"[76]

Sulaymān had been given power over all things on earth. Yet it was his friend, Āṣif, who brought him the throne of Bilqīs in less than the winking of an eye. Some of the commentators maintain that it was brought along an underground passage over a distance of two months but how, they cannot say.

---

[76] Sūratu 'n-Naml (The Ant), 27: 39-40.

[Ibn Kathīr relates about the verse:

Disguise her throne for her that we may see whether she will be guided, or she will be one of those not guided.[77]

that commentators of the Salaf said, "He issued orders that it should be changed, so whatever was red should be made yellow and vice versa, and whatever was green should be made red, so everything was altered."]

The greatest Shaykh, Shaykh ul-Akbar Muḥīyddīn ibn 'Arabī says that it was not the throne of Bilqīs but another one made to resemble hers; a copy of the original. For when Bilqīs arrived at Sulaymān's court, she was asked, 'Is thy throne like this?' and not 'Is this your throne?' And she answered, 'As if it were, It seems the same'. Shaykh Muḥīyddīn ibn 'Arabī says it is clear therefore, that the throne did not move in time for any body needs time to change is location. "The Lord," he says, "in the perfection of His Power, can bring into existence what was non-existent in less than one instant and He can make things disappear as He wills. As it is written:

أَفَعَيِينا بِالخَلقِ الأَوَّلِ ۚ بَل هُم فى لَبسٍ مِن خَلقٍ جَديدٍ

What, were We wearied by the first creation? No indeed, but they are in uncertainty as to the new creation.[78]

It was announced that Bilqīs was approaching the borders of Sulaymān's kingdom with a huge army for her escort. She had locked her throne in her palace and guarded the key to it on her own person.

When Sulaymān was told of her approach he said, "I am expecting her. She is my guest." His counselors said, "O Sulaymān, can she be counted as a guest, coming with such an army that could lay all our lands to waste?"

---

[77] Sūratu 'n-Naml (The Ant), 27: 39:41.

[78] Sūrah Qāf, 50:15.

"Who can tell?" answered Sulaymān. "Perhaps it is an honor for us that she comes with such a large retinue."

He had received a revelation in this matter and nothing could sway him. Bilqīs crossed the border with her army of many tens of thousands. "How shall we feed such a tremendous host?" mused the Banī-Isrā'īl. "Surely they have come to make war on us." And they were afraid.

Sulaymān expected the queen to come to his palace and did not go out to meet her. Her officers and ministers said to her, "He is not paying you proper respect. Why doesn't he come out to receive you? After all, you are the daughter of the sun and we are a mighty army not to be belittled." Bilqīs stood firm by her peaceful intentions and wouldn't listen to those who spoke against Sulaymān.

One day, a man was brought to her by her scouts, an Israelite who had fled to Egypt and who was opposed to Sulaymān, wishing to assume power over Isrā'īl himself. He tried to convince the queen that Sulaymān was a powerful sorcerer who would engulf the whole world if he were left unchecked. He hoped to win Bilqīs over and overthrow Sulaymān with her help. Then he would marry the queen and become ruler over the vast kingdom himself. But the queen replied, "You have offered to show us secret ways into the country of Sulaymān which none but a native can know and you wish to defeat Sulaymān by treason. If you were a true and trustworthy man you would have stayed in your country and fought until a decision was reached. Instead, you fled and now have become a traitor to your king and your own people. A traitor can never be trusted." So, she sent him away in disgrace.

Her commanding officers reproached her for this and said, "O our queen, you have wasted a great opportunity. We could have taken the land without a drop of blood being spilt had you only listened to that man but you have missed your chance. You smote the hand that sought to help us."

She replied, "A traitor may never be trusted. If he can do so to his own people, what will he not do to a stranger?"

They continued to grumble and pointed out again that she was being insulted by Sulaymān because he did not come to receive them. While they were yet exchanging such words, three men came bearing a message from Sulaymān. They told the queen, "Our lord and king Sulaymān sends you his welcome and says he would wish to come out to meet you but as you have come with such an enormous escort, it would only be proper for him to come to you accompanied by an army of equal numbers to do you honor. He is afraid that a very slight event or misunderstanding might trigger off a clash between the armies with unforeseeable consequences. Therefore, Sulaymān has refrained from coming out to meet you and lets you know that he is awaiting you in his palace as his highly honored guest."

When the Jinn and 'Ifrīt had learnt that Sulaymān was contemplating marriage with the queen of Sheba they were disturbed for Bilqīs was part Jinn herself. They feared that a child born of that union would perpetuate their yoke and that they would never be freed from the bondage and forced labor that Sulaymān had imposed on them by the Grace of Allah. So they tried to influence Sulaymān against this match by implying that Bilqīs was not of sound mind. "She is mad," they said. "You haven't seen her yet. Besides she has hairy legs and her foot is like a donkey's." To see if this was true Sulaymān had a special hall prepared through which, Bilqīs had to pass on entering the palace. The floor of this hall was made of glass which appeared to be water. Beneath its glittering surface there seemed to be fish and water plants but it was all a great illusion. When Bilqīs came to the mirror glass, she took it to be water and lifted her skirts and exposed her legs for a moment.

قِيلَ لَهَا ادْخُلِي الصَّرْحَ ۖ فَلَمَّا رَأَتْهُ حَسِبَتْهُ لُجَّةً وَكَشَفَتْ عَن سَاقَيْهَا ۚ قَالَ إِنَّهُ صَرْحٌ
مُّمَرَّدٌ مِّن قَوَارِيرَ ۗ قَالَتْ رَبِّ إِنِّي ظَلَمْتُ نَفْسِي وَأَسْلَمْتُ مَعَ سُلَيْمَانَ لِلَّهِ رَبِّ الْعَالَمِينَ

It was said to her, "Enter the pavilion." But when she saw it, she supposed it was a spreading water and she bared her legs. He said, "It is a pavilion smoothed of crystal."[79]

It became obvious that she had not the foot of a donkey. When Bilqīs realized that it was not water she was crossing, she let her robe fall quickly and took a lesson from this; things often are not what they appear to be. Next, she was saw her throne and Sulaymān asked her:

فَلَمَّا جَاءَتْ قِيلَ أَهَٰكَذَا عَرْشُكِ ۖ قَالَتْ كَأَنَّهُ هُوَ ۚ وَأُوتِينَا الْعِلْمَ مِن قَبْلِهَا وَكُنَّا مُسْلِمِينَ

"Is thy throne like this?" She said, "It seems the same"[80]

From her answer, Sulaymān understood that her mind was intact. She had not yet accepted Islam but the moment she set eyes on the prophet and on his shining countenance, all her impure intentions melted away. She beheld the prophetic light that surrounded him. She saw that he stood for everything that was good and holy and that she had been mistaken all along in worshipping the sun. Now it appeared to her no bigger than a pin head.

قِيلَ لَهَا ادْخُلِي الصَّرْحَ ۖ فَلَمَّا رَأَتْهُ حَسِبَتْهُ لُجَّةً وَكَشَفَتْ عَن سَاقَيْهَا ۚ قَالَ إِنَّهُ صَرْحٌ
مُّمَرَّدٌ مِّن قَوَارِيرَ ۗ قَالَتْ رَبِّ إِنِّي ظَلَمْتُ نَفْسِي وَأَسْلَمْتُ مَعَ سُلَيْمَانَ لِلَّهِ رَبِّ الْعَالَمِينَ

She said, "My Lord, indeed I have wronged myself and I surrender with Solomon to God the Lord of all Beings."[81]

---

[79] Sūratu 'n-Naml (The Ant), 27: 44.
[80] Sūratu 'n-Naml (The Ant), 27: 42.
[81] Sūratu 'n-Naml (The Ant), 27:44.

Sulaymān taught her the true religion of Allah and she accepted and surrendered to the truth. Also, her entire court and counselors believed and deplored the days of their ignorance. They stayed as Sulaymān's guests for some days.

According to one narration, Sulaymān married the queen and they had a son, but other traditions state that he married her to the prince of Hamadan and that they returned together to her country and they were blessed till the end their days.

the story of Bilqis

In the kingdom of Sabā (Sheba) there once lived a king. One day, he went out hunting in the mountains around Sana. He went deep into the forests and all his servants remained behind. With his bow and arrow in hand, the king chanced upon two snakes who were struggling with each other in a clearing. One of them was black, the other white. The black snake had the white one in a stranglehold and would have soon killed it, had not the king been suddenly inspired to shoot his arrow at the black snake so that it died, allowing the white snake to escape.

It was night and the king retired into his private apartments. All the doors and windows were closed and everyone in the palace had gone to bed. There, in his bedchamber, the king unexpectedly came upon a strange person who seemed to be waiting for him. It was inconceivable to the king how that person might have entered. How had he passed by all his watchmen who guarded his rooms? He felt afraid.

The person said, "Don't be afraid of me. I am a Jinn and doors and walls mean nothing to me. I can pass through them and enter at will."

"And what is it you want of me?" asked the king.

"I have come to reward you for your good deed. You saved my life today. Do you recall the black snake you killed in the woods? That was the son of my worst enemy and you helped me a great deal. I was that white snake and I am the son of a great jinn king. Therefore, I have come to reward you. What is it you wish?"

"What can you offer?" asked the king.

"I am in possession of great treasures and I will give you so much that your treasure houses will overflow."

"No," replied the king, "I don't need any more treasures. I am already exceedingly rich. Thank you. What else is there?"

"I possess great medical knowledge and healing powers. If you wish I can impart them to you and you will know what no man knows."

"No," said the king, "I also possess sufficient knowledge of medicine. That is not what I want."

"The third thing I have to offer," said the fairy prince, "is my sister. I have a sister whose beauty is unrivaled by any on earth and if you wish, I will give her to you as your lawful bride."

This proposal pleased the king and he consented. The fairy was ready to draw up the marriage contract on the spot but first he informed the king of a few conditions his sister had set. "She desires no material goods. The only thing she asks of you is that you voice no complaint or objection to whatever she may do, even if it seems impossibly wrong to you. She will explain all her actions to you in her own time but the moment you forget your promise and reproach her angrily for what she has done, the marriage will be null and void. She is then free from obligation towards you and you will never find her again." The king readily agreed to this condition, for he thought, "What on earth can a girl want? She will say, 'Buy me this' or 'Buy me that.' He made little of the deal. The contract was signed and the fairy princess appeared. The moment he laid eyes on her he fell madly in love with her, so great was her beauty and charm. The couple was married and knew great happiness with one another.

After a year was over the fairy queen gave birth to a baby girl. The king had secretly hoped for a son to be born to be his heir but when he went to see his baby daughter he saw that she was a lovely little girl and his heart was glad. He kissed his wife and said, "Perhaps Allah will give us a son the next time," He handed the child back to her mother. The fairy queen took the child by her little leg and hurled her into the great log fire that was burning in the open fireplace of the room. The fire flared up and made a great hissing and roaring sound and the baby disappeared. The king was too stunned to speak at first, so he couldn't ask his wife why she had done such a ghastly thing. When he recovered, he remembered the condition of the contract that forbade him to demand explanations from her for her actions. Since he loved her so very much and could not envisage a life without her, he kept his silence and wept for his baby daughter in secret. One year later, a second child was born to them, this time a boy. The king went in to his wife to congratulate her. He spoke prayers and blessings over the child. His mother reached out for the child, asking that he be given back to her. At that very instant, a great dog with enormous fangs appeared in the doorway and the fairy queen tossed her baby up in the air for the dog to catch. The great hound caught the infant in mid-air between his teeth and loped away with his catch.

This time, the king was even more upset at what his wife had done than the first time but he controlled himself and voiced no objection for fear of losing his beloved fairy forever. He slept only in the privacy of her retreat.

Some time passed and they had no further children. One day, the king had reports that his powerful enemy was preparing an invasion into his territory with a great army ready to destroy his kingdom. The king rose and made ready for battle. He mustered his arms and had water skins filled and provisions prepared for the soldiers. Just as the battle was about to begin, the king received a message from the front line. "Oh our king, we are defeated before the battle has begun. Before us is the enemy and behind us there is neither a drop of water nor a morsel of bread to supply the troops, for your own wife, the queen, has slit open all our water skins with a knife and all the water has run into the ground. She has mixed the flour and rice with sand so it has become inedible. Nothing is left for us. Before us the enemy, behind us is the enemy. We are finished!" This time, the poor king could no longer keep his patience with his wife's bizarre actions. He went to her and began to shout at her, "What else shall we have to endure at your hands? Now we are at the mercy of our enemy through your doing. You have robbed us of all our provisions. How shall our men fight the invaders without supplies? When our daughter was born you flung her into the fire and our son you fed to the dog. Now you would have us all perish at the hand of our enemy. What have we done to you that you treat us so cruelly?" And he spoke many bitter words that he had held back in his heart for so long until he had vented all his anger.

At last, his wife said, "Are you finished?"

"Yes," said the unhappy king. "I am totally finished."

"Then, I will explain the matter to you. Up until now you have been patient and that was very good but, alas, your patience has come to an end and this signifies the parting between me and thee. From now on we must be separated and you won't see me ever again. But I will explain to you the meaning of my actions that have made you doubt me. Firstly, your chief vizier has been bribed by your enemy with a great sum of money and he has poisoned all the water and supplies for your men. Had they been left to consume them, all the men and their officers would have perished and your enemy would have taken your place with no trouble at all. If you want you can confirm this. Have the chief vizier brought in and make him eat some of the leftover foodstuff and drink some of the remaining water. You will see that I speak the truth."

The vizier was called for. As he refused to taste any of the food or water, he was forced. From the consumption of a few drops remaining at the bottom of a jug, the man died in convulsions within seconds. The king saw that his queen had spoken truly.

She continued, "This, I have done for the good of your country. As for our daughter, I gave her to be nursed by one of my fairy attendants at my command." She whistled briefly and the sound brought to sight a gigantic Jinn holding the king's daughter upon her knee. "This is your daughter," said the queen, "and she is to remain with you." Then she whistled a second time and another Jinn appeared with the king's son. The queen said, "I gave him to be educated by my people. This is my son. He will stay with me." Then she whistled a third time and all her relatives from among the Jinn and fairies assembled and roused the enemy by unleashing terrible storms and cyclones against them, so that they fled in disorder, barely escaping with their lives, leaving all their belongings behind. The queen then spoke her parting words to her husband, "Take all this as spoils of war. They are yours, and your daughter is also yours but you shall never see me again." With that, she and her whole entourage disappeared from the king's sight.

The king was left with all the riches gained in battle and he paid his army with them. But after the loss of his life's love he could no longer govern his country for his heart was broken. He donned a pair of iron sandals and took a staff of iron and went off into the woods and mountains, to hopelessly seek his lost wife. He was never seen again and they counted him among those whom the Jinn drove to madness. No trace of him was ever found. As the throne was now empty, they set his daughter upon it and she ruled the kingdom. She was Bilqīs, the queen of Sheba.

Sulayman's عليه السلام Rule

Allah Almighty heard Sulaymān's prayer and granted him a kingdom such as no king has ever ruled, not before and not after his time. Sulaymān had many mosques and study houses built so that his people could be instructed in the law of the Tawrāt and the holy rites. Sulaymān supervised all matters personally and made sure that his orders were carried out correctly. The winds transported him wherever he wished to go and he would appear at unexpected moments in surprising places. Sulaymān concerned himself with every aspect of government from road repairs to exacting justice, from farming to establishing hospitals. He was a model king.

All creatures, Jinn, men, 'Ifrīt, the birds and beasts and the winds from east to west were under his command and subdued by his will. Sulaymān assigned men of knowledge to take the seats of wisdom and to be his ministers at court. The jinn were often strange to behold. Some had a human face and a lion's body. Others had the head of an oxen and the body of snakes. Some had dragon's heads and griffin claws. Whilst others had the face of monkeys and the feet of donkeys. Yet others had the heads of lions with elephant trunks. Some had four feet and fire came from their mouths. They ate their food and drank their water only when it boiled. The head of all the birds was the Simurgh and the lion was the king of the beasts of prey. Sulaymān made the elephant king over all the other animals because of his great size and the snakes were ruled by the dragons. But Sulaymān ruled over them all and they were subservient to him.

Sulaymān commanded the Jinn to weave him a carpet. The warp was to be of gold and the weft of silken thread. Its length and breadth were both three miles and Allah only knows what patterns and magical symbols were woven into it. Sulaymān set up his court upon this carpet. He placed his throne upon it, which was named the 'Star of Jenna' and he surrounded it with two thousand seats of honor for all the holy men and seers he kept in his company. He set up another row of 12,000 seats made of sandalwood and cedar for the Rabbis and teachers. Also, there were 70,000 prayer niches made of silver and gold for the saints and dervishes who were always engaged in devotions and the study of the Holy Tawrāt and the Zabūr. The wind brought to Sulaymān the voices of all of them and the constant recitation of sacred knowledge. The wind carried this carpet wherever King Sulaymān wished to go. It covered a distance of one month in a day, as it is written:

وَلِسُلَيْمَٰنَ الرِّيحَ غُدُوُّهَا شَهْرٌ وَرَوَاحُهَا شَهْرٌ ۖ وَأَسَلْنَا لَهُ عَيْنَ الْقِطْرِ ۖ وَمِنَ الْجِنِّ مَن يَعْمَلُ

بَيْنَ يَدَيْهِ بِإِذْنِ رَبِّهِ ۖ وَمَن يَزِغْ مِنْهُمْ عَنْ أَمْرِنَا نُذِقْهُ مِنْ عَذَابِ السَّعِيرِ

And to Sulaymān the wind its morning course was a month's journey and its evening course was a month's journey.[82]

The throne of Sulaymān stood on seventy pillars and at the base of each pillar there was a lion made of pure gold with eyes of red rubies and crowns of beryl upon their heads. Each lion was mounted upon a dragon and above each of them there was a golden peacock. When a person approached the king on his throne with good intention in his heart, pearls were showered upon him, but if he bore any ill will, the lions would growl and lift their paws ready to attack. Behind each of pillars stood a great and terrifying 'Ifrīt and to Sulaymān's right there stood an angel with a drawn sword ready to smite any of the disobedient Jinn. The birds joined their wings above the throne and formed a canopy of shade above Sulaymān where a gentle breeze always fanned him.

---

[82] Sūrah Sabā (Sheba), 34:12.

Sulaymān had three hundred wives and seven hundred concubines. He consorted with them all. One day, he prayed that he might have a son. He promised that he would train his son to become a warrior. However, of all those women, only one of his mates became pregnant. In time, she gave birth to only half a son, he had only one eye, one nostril and one hand, as if he had been cut in half. His wise counselor and friend, Āṣif, came to him and said, "Each of us has a secret which he has revealed to no one up until this time. Let us all come together, you, my king, the child's mother and I and reveal what is hidden in our hearts. If Allah wills, he will make the child complete." The three of them assembled and Āṣif began, "It may seem as if I attached no importance to appearances, and that is the impression I sought to create but I am profoundly attached to appearances. It is most important that I feel honored and respected. This is what I hide from the world." Then Sulaymān himself spoke, "The Lord has given me an overabundance of everything. Every conceivable treasure I can call mine. Yet I am very fond of gifts and I love to receive presents." Last of all, the woman spoke, "'For me it is not so very important to be the Padishah's wife. I would just as soon be the wife of any ordinary person. The thing that matters most to me is to stay young." After they had each voiced their inner and secret thoughts, they prayed together to the Lord, and through His infinite mercy, the child was made whole.

Sulayman's عليه السلام Justice

One day, when Sulaymān was yet a child, his father, Dāwūd, held court and listened to his subjects' complaints. A very poor woman crying bitterly, came to the door where Sulaymān sat. Sulaymān asked her what caused her to grieve so.

The woman said, "Oh, what shall I tell you. I have two orphaned children and I had two handfuls of wheat, which, I took to the miller to be ground. On the way home, the wind blew strongly and lifted up my bag of flour and blew it towards the sea. Now I have nothing to feed my children. That is why I am crying."

Sulaymān said, "Go inside and make your complaint."

"But there is nobody I can complain against," cried the woman. "It was the wind that blew my flour away."

"Do as I say to you," repeated the child Sulaymān. "Go inside and complain."

The woman went inside, hopeful of being paid some indemnity. She came before Dāwūd, sitting on the throne of justice. She told him her story and said she wished to file a complaint against the wind. Dāwūd said, "What shall we do? The wind is neither man nor Jinn. He is not a creature we can bring to court. But I will give you four measures of flour for the two you have lost." The woman was given her four measures of flour and she left the courtroom most contentedly. On the threshold, she met Sulaymān.

He asked her, "Why did you accept the flour? Did I not tell you to file a complaint against the offender?"

"But it was the wind," said the woman, "and nobody can condemn the wind."

But Sulaymān insisted, "Go back and say, 'I don't want your flour. I wish to launch a complaint against the wind. I accuse him of stealing my flour."

The poor woman went back before the judge and spoke as Sulaymān had advised her. Dāwūd said, "But woman, don't you understand. This is not a case for the courts. Nobody can bring the wind to justice." And he ordered her to be given eight measures of flour. The woman took her eight measures and left, even happier than before. Again she met Sulaymān at the gate. "So you have accepted more flour?" he asked. "Go again. Leave the flour and do as I have told you." Again, the woman returned and repeated her words for a third time and came out with sixteen measures of flour and again Sulaymān sent her back in.

Seeing the woman for the fourth time, the prophet Dāwūd, was puzzled and asked her, "Woman, what is it with you? You accept our flour and go away. Outside you change your mind and come back in demanding your rights. Who is there outside giving you this advice?"

She said, "Oh my king, it is your son Sulaymān. He keeps sending me back in here."

Dāwūd called his son to come in and said to him, smiling at the child, "My son, what do you mean to say by your action. We are dealing neither with man nor beast nor Jinn but with the wind. How shall we bring the wind to justice?"

Sulaymān answered, "Oh my father, if you were but a king, this case would not concern us and I wouldn't be sending this woman back in. You have reimbursed her splendidly for her loss and she has no reason to complain but, you are a prophet and so you must look into this affair at a deeper level. There must be a hidden cause for the wind to carry off the woman's bag of flour."

Dāwūd saw that his son spoke truly and prayed that Allah might enlighten him. As he was completing his supplication, the angel Jibrīl came to him and said, "Your son Sulaymān is right. On the high seas there was a ship that struck a rock and a hole opened in its hull through which water is entered. The passengers gave up hope for their lives. They wailed and cried, and pledged half their worldly belongings in *ṣadaqa* (alms), if only the Lord would save them. Allah Almighty heard their prayer and commanded an angel to quickly plug up the hole in the ship. This angel flew in at lightning speed and grabbed the bag of flour off the poor woman's back and stuffed it in the hole in the ship's hull. A firm dough formed around its edges so that the ship was made watertight once more. This ship has now safely reached your shores. This woman is a righteous person. Moreover, her needs are great. The Lord commands you to have the sums paid to her which were pledged by the passengers saved from shipwreck by His Mercy."

Dāwūd then went out with his retainers to meet the ship as it was coming in. The woman was given all the money that had been pledged and life was made easy for her from then on.

Sulaymān was always present when his father sat in court. He listened with interest to every case. After each session he would go to the palace gardens and, gathering his playmates about him, would reenact scenes from the world of the grown-ups, such as he had witnessed in his father's court. He developed his own ideas of justice in this way.

One day, a woman accused of sodomy with a dog was brought in to be sentenced. She had been accused of this act by her husband's brother and a few other witnesses, but the truth of the matter was that she was a virtuous lady and quite innocent of this crime. Her husband had gone away on a pilgrimage and her brother-in-law had come to her, making indecent offers. She had rejected him. He left in anger and threatened revenge. So he went and bought four false witnesses and proceeded against his sister-in-law. The four witnesses bore false testimony under oath. The punishment for the crime of sodomy was death by stoning and since there seemed to be no doubt, the sentence was passed. The boy, Sulaymān, had a strange feeling about this and when he went to play that afternoon with his friends reenacted that morning's scene at court. His father, Dāwūd, had long accustomed himself to following his son's games from a hidden distance, for he found he could learn from the justice and wisdom of his young son.

Each child had his role. One was the plaintiff, the other the accused, four were the witnesses and Sulaymān himself was the judge. When he had arranged everything so as to resemble a real court, he called in the witnesses one by one and interviewed them separately. He asked the first witness if he had actually seen the woman performing the act with the dog and the first witness replied in the affirmative that he had.

Then Sulaymān asked him, "What was the color of the dog?"

The witness answered, "The dog was black."

Then Sulaymān had the second witness brought in and questioned him out of earshot of the other witnesses. This one said the dog had been red and the next witness claimed it had been a yellow dog, while the fourth maintained it had been a white dog with a torn ear. Sulaymān then sentenced all the four witnesses to be whipped for slandering a blameless person. He judged the man who had made the false accusation and let the woman go free.

As he watched his son and his playmates at their game, King Dāwūd, realized that he hadn't shown as much wisdom in the real court case that morning. It hadn't occurred to him to question the witnesses separately. As it was a case involving capital punishment, he decided to reopen the case and called all the persons concerned before his tribunal once more. Then he questioned each of the witnesses separately as he had seen his son do in his game. They got entangled in contradictions for they hadn't discussed such details among themselves. Each witness claimed a different color of the dog. One said he had been lame another said his tail was clipped etc. So Dāwūd knew that they were lying and that the woman was innocent. He revised the sentence. From that time on, it has become the custom of the courts to hear each witness alone.

Sulaymān's wisdom manifested itself at a tender age, a forerunner of his prophethood which was revealed to him while he was still a youth.

Sulayman عليه السلام and the Birds

One day, all the birds stopped feeding on the worms and gathered around the prophet-king, Sulaymān, to hear his address to them. Among them was the Samra bird, which, was the greatest bird that ever flew. Sulaymān said to them, "Allah's decree is foretold and ordained and nothing can change it." The Samra bird, however, disagreed with this. "Careful foresight can override destiny." He said. Sulaymān challenged him to prove his claim. The Samra bird asked Sulaymān to provide him with an opportunity and Sulaymān said, "There lives a king in the east whose daughter has been promised to the son of the king of the west and they are destined for each other. See if you can prevent it from happening for they are both young children still; the girl is only a baby in her cradle."

The Samra bird flew off to the kingdom of the east and kidnapped the girl-child out of her cradle and brought her to his own nest on an uninhabited island in the midst of a thick, dark forest. There he fed and raised the child until she was about fourteen years old.

The son of the king of the west had, meanwhile, grown into a handsome youth.

One day, he boarded a ship with his men to go on a journey. By the decree of the Almighty, the ship was wrecked at sea by a mighty storm and all perished save the king's son. He grabbed hold of a box and clung to it and at long last, drifted ashore. As it happened, he was washed upon the shores of the island where the Samra bird had its nest. When the prince rose, he looked about and to his great amazement beheld a beautiful young maiden in the tallest tree top. The boy called for her to come down, but the girl signaled to him that she could not climb down. Just as the youth was about to attempt the climb, the sky suddenly darkened and the sun was hidden. The Samra bird returned to its nest. The boy went back inside his box and hid himself, for the Samra bird was a huge and dangerous looking bird.

When the Samra bird came home to his nest he found the girl in tears and asked her why. The girl had learned the language of the Samra bird and answered him, "You are gone all day and this nest is so high I can't look over its rim. I can't even see you coming home and it is very boring for me." The Samra bird wondered what to do about this. The girl pointed at the box down below which looked like a tree-stump from above and in a flash the bird dived down, picked up the box with its claws and brought it up into its nest. Then they ate and drank together. After a while, the Samra bird was off again on his way. As soon as he was gone, the girl opened the lid of the box and found the prince inside it. They laughed and played and spent many happy days together. When they saw the Samra bird returning, the girl would quickly hide the prince in the box and climb on top of it, as if she used it only to look over the rim of the nest. The great Samra bird suspected nothing. Four or five months passed by in this manner.

Sulaymān called the birds to a conference and brought up the subject of divinely fore-ordained destiny again.

He said to the Samra bird, "It was written that, by now those two young people should have married and that the girl should be four months pregnant."

The Samra bird answered, "Now you see that I was right. It is possible to waive the Divine Decree after all, through careful planning."

"Bring the girl to us!" ordered the king. "We shall see."

The bird flew back to his island and told the girl that the great king Sulaymān wished to see her. She said, "But how will you bring me there? If you take me in your claws I will be crushed. Turn around and I will climb into this box. Then you can pick up the box and carry me off in it." The bird did as she requested. The girl climbed into the box while his back was turned and closed its lid. The Samra bird picked up the box and flew with it to the court of Sulaymān. Triumphantly, he spoke, "Now you will see. Here is the girl I have raised on my island, far from all humankind and no one has ever seen, touched or spoken to her." Then they opened the box and found the boy and the girl sitting within, holding hands. The Samra bird then understood that all his carefully laid plans had failed against Divine Decree. He hung his head in shame and flew away, mortified and deeply humiliated. No one knew to where he flew and he was never seen again. His line died out and the Samra bird became extinct. He was the greatest bird that ever lived on Earth.

Among his many wives, King Sulaymān had one wife, a Phoenician princess, who was very delicate and spoiled. One day she said to the king, "I wish you to build me a palace which is made entirely of bird's bones." Sulaymān wished to comply with the wish of his wife for he was in love with her, so he called in the assembly of birds. All the birds came, except the owl. The assembly lasted for three days throughout which the owl was absent. On the fourth day, the owl appeared and Sulaymān asked him why he had not come on time.

"We all waited for you and because of your absence the discussions couldn't be concluded."

"I was very busy," answered the owl.

"And what was your very important business?" asked the king. "

"Firstly," said the owl, "I had to answer the very important question of whether there is more water or dry land on Earth. I was engrossed in that calculation."

"And what did you find?" asked Sulaymān.

"I counted traces of water also as water and so I arrived at the conclusion that there is more water than dry land on Earth." "And the second day, what kept you busy?" asked Sulaymān.

"I was occupied in establishing an estimate of dry wood and fresh wood on Earth. Counting every tree that has dried up, branches and even dry leaves as dry wood, I came to the conclusion that there is more dry wood than green wood on Earth."

"And on the third day, what sort of important deliberations kept you from coming?"

"On the third day I was calculating the balance between men and women living on Earth."

"And?" inquired Sulaymān.

"Counting all those men who listen to the words of women as women, I concluded that there must be more women than men."

Sulaymān then understood what the owl was telling him and he repented of his silly intention.

One day, the birds came to Sulaymān when he was holding court and complained of the owl. "The owl," they said, "leaves us no rest at night. He doesn't sleep during the night time and he won't let us get any sleep either. But we need our good night's sleep."

Sulaymān called for the owl and asked him, "What have you to say? The birds are all complaining that you disturb their sleep at night. Why don't you sleep at night like the rest of them?"

The owl responded, "Oh prophet of Allah, if any but you had asked this question I could understand, but that you of all people, a prophet of the Lord, should ask me this. Don't you know that the servant may not sleep while his Lord is wakeful? This is why I don't sleep at night but engage in the remembrance of my Lord."

This answer pleased the prophet Sulaymān and he continued speaking to the owl. "I have also heard that you never touch a grain of wheat. Is it true, and what is the reason for this?"

The owl replied, "Oh my prophet, your father Ādam ﷺ was expelled from Paradise for eating a grain of wheat. For that mouthful of the forbidden he fell from his high station and had to endure centuries of hardship here on Earth; he and his descendants after him. How then should I want to taste of the grain that was the cause of all his suffering?"

"I have also heard," said Sulaymān, "that you never take a single drop of water. Why is that?"

"Oh Sulaymān, do you not know that the curse of Nūḥ ﷺ brought the rain of perdition down upon the Earth, causing all living things to perish? That is why I don't touch a drop of water now."

"And why is it you always choose to nest in ruins?" asked the king.

"O Prophet of the Lord, ruins are Allah's heritage. No one desires such a place. Therefore, I live in peace in what I have inherited from my Lord."

Sulaymān then asked, "Oh owl, will you accept me as your companion?"

"O Sulaymān, you are only mortal. How should I accept as my companion one who will pass away? I choose as my companion, Him the Almighty, who does not, the Eternal, The Ever-Living."

One day, the hoopoe bird came and invited King Sulaymān to a great feast in his house. "O Sulaymān," said the hoopoe, "you accept everyone's invitation. Please will you deign to accept mine and come to me for breakfast? Bring with you all your men and retinue. They will all be my guests." And he pointed with his wing to a certain place on the seashore where he lived. Sulaymān and all his men arrived there the next morning to take their breakfast but they found nothing there but the deserted coastline. There was no sign of a feast or of any preparation and the hoopoe bird himself was absent as well. Sulaymān and his men sat down to wait for a while and before long they saw the hoopoe bird approaching, descending from high in the clouds. When he was close enough they could see that in his beak he held a cricket. He tore off its head and threw it into the sea, calling to Sulaymān, "Oh my king, your breakfast is ready. Please come and eat. Whoever comes too late for the meat may still drink of the broth." That was the hoopoe bird's breakfast invitation.

Sulayman عليه السلام and the Gift of the Ant

One day, the king of the ants heard of Sulaymān's great might and majesty and decided to go and pay him homage. He chose a suitable gift to present to the king; a big cricket leg which was a great delicacy to his people. He set out on his way, dragging with him that cricket leg, many times his own size and made for Sulaymān's kingdom which was many miles away from his own. The winds brought Sulaymān news of the ant's intention and told him of the impossible task he had set for himself. Sulaymān commanded the wind to lift up the ant gently and bring him into his presence. The wind picked up the ant king with his cricket leg and brought him before King Sulaymān. The ant paid his respects to Sulaymān and greeted him with deference. Then, he presented his gift to the king.

Sulaymān bent down to look at the tiny thing the ant had brought, and asked, "What is this, my friend?"

The ant replied, "Oh Prophet of Allah, it is a nice, fat cricket leg for you, a great delicacy among my people."

Sulaymān smiled and said, "Perhaps for the ants this may be, but for us humans, what value could it have?"

The ant spoke, "Never regard as too small or inferior what the Lord has sent you, for if He blesses that gift, it may increase and multiply in such a way that all your men couldn't finish it up. This cricket leg is the very best we have to offer. It is soft and juicy, yet crisp and delicious. Every part of it has a special and different flavor. Try it out and you will see!"

To please the ant, Sulaymān laughingly ordered his chief cook to prepare the kitchen for a feast and when all was ready he had him place the cricket leg in the greatest pot. When it was cooked, he served it and by the grace of Allah, it was enough to feed the entire household, the courtiers, the whole army, and there was still plenty left over. Never had they tasted anything so delicious.

This story teaches us two things: The ant with sincerity of heart set out to present his gift to Sulaymān and intended to cross a vast distance with such a heavy burden that would make this undertaking seem an impossible task. With Divine aid however, he achieved his purpose and fulfilled his intention. Secondly, if the Lord wishes, He can make what seems to us small and insignificant become much more than we could possibly imagine, through the blessings He imparts. To us, it may seem impossible at times to reach our goal and to attain goodness even if we try ever so hard. It is in Allah's power to transport us to where we wish to be, by His Will and not through our own achievements. Allah in His unfathomable mercy doesn't leave us to the merits of our own works. If it be His Will, he can magnify our poor efforts a thousand times and help us to reach unimaginable stations. It is written in the Qur'an:

مَثَلُ الَّذِينَ يُنفِقُونَ أَمْوٰلَهُمْ فِى سَبِيلِ اللَّهِ كَمَثَلِ حَبَّةٍ أَنۢبَتَتْ سَبْعَ سَنَابِلَ فِى كُلِّ سُنۢبُلَةٍ

مِّائَةُ حَبَّةٍ قلے وَاللَّهُ يُضٰعِفُ لِمَن يَشَاءُ قلے وَاللَّهُ وٰسِعٌ عَلِيمٌ

So God multiplies unto whom He will; God is All-Embracing, All-Knowing.[83]

[83] Sūratu 'l-Baqara (The Cow), 2: 261.

sulayman's عليه السلام death

Every day, in Sulaymān's garden a new tree or plant would grow. It was his habit to ask all those plants their names and purpose. This way he learned of their uses and benefits for mankind. He passed this knowledge on to his people.

One day, he saw a new tree sprout and asked it, "Who are you? What uses were you created for?"

The seedling answered, "I am the carob tree. I shall be used for the destruction of the Temple. Make a staff out of me and lean on me."

Sulaymān knew, then that his end was nigh and cried and prayed to the Lord, "Oh Lord, at least make me not a witness to the time when my Iife's work will be destroyed and burned to the ground. And let not the Jinn know of my death, lest they stop their work before the Temple is completed." The Lord heard and granted his wish and released Sulaymān's soul before the destruction of the Temple.

After Sulaymān had spent his years teaching his people and ensuring their adherence to the Law, he left this task to the Rabbis and scholars whom he had trained. He retired for long periods to pray and worship. He left his palace and moved into a little room adjacent the Temple. From there, he would oversee the construction works. As he leaned upon his staff, Sulaymān became a familiar sight to all who worked there. Sometimes he would not come out of his room for weeks at a time so absorbed in his devotions was he. Once, he was gone for such a long time, Iblīs wondered where he might be. He peered through the window but dared not go in for the king wished not to be disturbed. Once, a Jinn had set his mind on teasing the king and flew round and round his head. He was completely burnt to ashes in less than an instant for his actions. So now, even Iblīs dared not enter without permission. Iblīs only saw the figure of Sulaymān, upright and majestic, leaning upon his staff and saw that the plates of food were empty.

One day, the chiefs of the Jinn came to Iblīs, their king, and complained of Sulaymān.

"He is making us work too hard," they said. "All day we may not rest."

"Does he make you work the nights as well?" asked Iblīs.

"No," they answered, "at night we are allowed to rest."

"Be grateful then that you needn't work all night," Iblīs replied.

The wind brought these words to Sulaymān and Sulaymān, commanded them to work at night as well from now on. They came again to Iblīs and complained even more bitterly.

"Now he makes us work day and night."

Iblīs asked, "Are you made to bear loads one way or both?"

"No, we only are loaded one way."

The wind brought these words to the king and this time he ordered them to be laden with burdens both coming and going. Again, they complained to their lord Iblīs. Shayṭān told them then, "Be patient a little while longer. The time is approaching when he will no longer be able to oversee this kind of forced labor."

Before Sulaymān went into his final seclusion, he called his eldest son to him and gave him a long and earnest sermon. "Oh my son, "he advised him, "fear the Lord and don't stray from the path of righteousness. Show mercy on your subjects and lead people along the straight path." He spoke as a king speaks when he is handing over his reign to his successor. Then he dismissed him with these words, "And don't come into this mosque again without having been summoned." Sulaymān retired and the prince went off believing his father had transferred power to him.

A whole year passed and no one had seen or spoken to King Sulaymān. He stayed in his room, leaning on his staff and the plates of food were always empty. Actually, he had died but remained standing upright so that the Jinn would not know of his death and would continue their labor to complete the temple. Days, weeks, months went by. All this while a little woodworm had found its way into Sulaymān's staff, and was gnawing away at it, eating it up from inside, little by little. After a whole year had passed, the staff finally collapsed into powder, and the body of Sulaymān fell to the ground.

When the Jinn learned of Sulaymān's death they said, "We knew of his death all along." But, that was a lie, for had they known they would never have continued their forced labor. They would have dropped everything and run off but they wouldn't admit that. This is proof, however, that the Jinn do not know the unseen. It is hidden from them as it is hidden from men (except for what the Lord reveals). Had the Jinn knowledge of the unseen, they would have known that their taskmaster had died and would have laid down their tools. Thus, the Temple was completed on the very day Sulaymān's death was discovered, Praised be to Almighty God.

About this the Qur'an says:

فَلَمَّا قَضَيْنَا عَلَيْهِ الْمَوْتَ مَا دَلَّهُمْ عَلَى مَوْتِهِ إِلَّا دَآبَّةُ الْأَرْضِ تَأْكُلُ
مِنسَأَتَهُ فَلَمَّا خَرَّ تَبَيَّنَتِ الْجِنُّ أَن لَّوْ كَانُوا يَعْلَمُونَ الْغَيْبَ مَا لَبِثُوا فِي
الْعَذَابِ الْمُهِينِ

Then, when We decreed (Solomon's) death, nothing showed them his death except a little worm of the earth, which kept (slowly) gnawing away at his staff: so when he fell down, the Jinns saw plainly that if they had known the unseen, they would not have tarried in the humiliating Penalty (of their Task)[84]*]*.

The Jinn liked to boast of their achievements and claimed they had built a number of castles and fortresses in the land of Sabā in Southern Arabia. Inscriptions have been found in many of these castles, reading, 'We worked for seven years and have built Salhun, Salwa, Marwa, Bayan and Kalsun castles. And we dug seven moats around these castles for the collection of rainwater.' But the Lord only knows who actually inscribed these lines in rock.

King Sulaymān in all his majesty and perfection of worldly power still found no protection from the ultimate fate of all mortals. He lived on Earth no longer than sixty years. Allah Almighty has not made known to us his gravesite. According to some traditions, the fairies set the body of the king upon his throne and carried both to an island in the seventh sea. Upon this island, there is mountain in which there is a cave and they placed him therein. There he remains seated to this very day. Other accounts say he was buried in the city of Dāwūd, Jerusalem. Allah knows best.

We must remember Sulaymān as a mighty king; a king who was given power not only over this world but also over some of the invisible, higher worlds. His power was not the ordinary power of an earthly sovereign. He was a prophet as well as a king and his knowledge extended far into the unseen. He reigned over Jinn, men and beasts and his name is praised and unforgotten, even to our very day.

May Allah have endless mercy upon his blessed soul.

Āmīn.

---

[84] Sūrah Sabā, (Sheba), 34:14.

GLossARy

'abd (pl. 'Ibād): lit. slave, servant.

'Abd Allāh: Lit., "servant of God"

Abū Bakr aṣ-Ṣiddīq ⬚: one the
    closest Companions to the
    Prophet ⬚, his father-in-law,
    who shared the Hijrah with
    him. After the Prophet's
    death, he was elected as the
    first caliph (successor) to the
    Prophet ⬚. He is known as
    one of the most saintly of the
    Prophet's Companions.

Abū Yazīd/Bayāzīd Bisṭāmī: A
    great ninth century *walī* and
    master in the Naqshbandi
    Golden Chain.

adab: good manners, proper
    etiquette.

adhān: call to prayer.

al: Arabic definite article, "the"

'alamīn: world; universes.

alḥamdūlillāh: Praise God.

'Alī ibn Abī Ṭālib ⬚: the cousin of
    the Prophet ⬚, married to his
    daughter Fāṭimah and fourth
    caliph of the Prophet ⬚.

alif: first letter of Arabic alphabet
    ا.

'Alīm, al-: the Knower, a divine
    attribute

Allāh: proper name for God in
    Arabic.

Allāhu Akbar: God is Greater.

'amal: good deed (pl. *'amāl*).

amīr (pl., *umarā*): chief, leader,
    head of a nation or people.

anā: first person singular pronoun

'aql: intellect, reason; from the
    root *'aqila*, lit., "to fetter."

'Arafah: a plain near Mecca
    where pilgrims gather for
    the principal rite of Hajj.

'arif: knower, gnostic; one who
    has reached spiritual
    knowledge of his Lord.

'ārifūn' bi 'l-Lāh: knowers of God

Ar-Raḥīm: The Mercy-Giving,
    Merciful, Munificent, one of
    Allah's ninety-nine Holy
    Names

Ar-Raḥmān: The Most Merciful,
    Compassionate, Beneficent,
    the most often repeated of
    Allah's Holy Names.

'arsh, al-: Divine Throne

aṣl: root, origin, basis.

astaghfirullāh: lit. "I seek Allah's
    forgiveness."

awliyāullāh: saints of Allah (sing.
    walī).

āyah/āyāt (pl. Ayāt): a verse of the
    Holy Qur'an.

Āyat al-Kursī: the Verse of the Throne, a well-known verse from the Qur'an (2:255).

Badī' al-: The Innovator; a Divine Name.

Banī Ādam: Children of Ādam; humanity.

Bayt al-Maqdis: the Sacred Mosque in Jerusalem, built at the site where Solomon's Temple was later erected.

BBayt al-Ma'mūr: much-frequented house; this refers to the Ka'bah of the heavens, which is the prototype of the Ka'bah on earth and is circumambulated by the angels.

baya': pledge; in the context of this book, the pledge of initiation of a disciple (*murid*) to a shaykh.

bismi'l-Lāhi 'r-Raḥmāni 'r-Raḥīm: "In the name of the All-Merciful, the Compassionate"; this is the introductory verse to all the chapters of the Qur'an except the ninth.

Dajjāl: the False Messiah (Antichrist) whom the Prophet ﷺ foretold as coming at the end-time of this world, who will deceive mankind with pretensions of being divine.

dalālah: evidence

dhāt: self / selfhood

dhawq (pl. adhwāq): tasting; technical term referring to the experiential aspect of gnosis.

dhikr: remembrance, mention of God through His Holy Names or phrases of glorification.

ḍīyā: light.

Diwān al-Awlīyā—the gathering of saints with the Prophet ﷺ in the spiritual realm. This takes place every night.

du'a: supplication.

dunyā: world; worldly life.

'eid: festival; the two major festivals of Islam are 'Eid al-Fitr, marking the completion of Ramadan, and 'Eid al-Adha, the Festival of Sacrifice during the time of Hajj.

farḍ: obligatory worship.

Fātiḥah: Sūratu 'l-Fātiḥah; the opening surah of the Qur'an.

Ghafūr, al-: The Forgiver; a Divine Name.

ghawth: lit. "Helper"; the highest ranking saint the in hierarchy of saints.

ghaybu' l-muṭlaq, al-: the absolute unknown, known only to God.

ghusl: full shower/bath obligated by a state of ritual impurity prior to worship.

Grandshaykh: generally, a *walī* of great stature. In this text, where spelled with a capital G, "Grandshaykh" refers to Mawlana ʿAbd Allāh ad-Daghestani (d. 1973), Mawlana Shaykh Nazim's master.

hā': letter ه

ḥadīth nabawī (pl., ahadith): prophetic hadith whose meaning and linguistic expression are those of the Prophet Muḥammad ﷺ.

ḥadith qudsī: divine saying whose meaning directly reflects the meaning God intended but whose linguistic expression is not Divine Speech as in the Qur'an, it thus differs from a hadith *nabawī* (*see* above).

ḥaḍr: present

ḥaywān: animal.

ḥajj: the sacred pilgrimage of Islam obligatory on every mature Muslim once in his/her life.

ḥalāl: permitted, lawful according to the Islamic Shariʿah.

ḥaqīqah, al-: reality of existence; ultimate truth.

ḥaqq: truth

Ḥaqq, al-: the Divine Reality, one of the 99 Divine Names.

ḥarām: forbidden, unlawful.

hāshā: God forbid!

ḥarf (pl. *ḥurūf*): letter; Arabic root "edge."

hijrah: emigration.

ḥikmah: wisdom

ḥujjah: proof

hūwa: the pronoun "he," made up of the letters *hā'* and *wāw* in Arabic.

ʿibādu 'l-Lāh: servants of God

iḥsān: doing good, "It is to worship God as though you see Him; for if you are not seeing Him, He sees you."

ikhlāṣ, al-: sincere devotion

ilāh (pl. *āliha):* idols or god(s)

ilāhīyya: divinity

ilhām—Divine inspiration sent to *awlīyāullah.*

ʿilm: knowledge, science.

ʿilmu 'l-awrāq: knowledge of papers

ʿilmu 'l-adhwāq: knowledge of taste

ʿilmu 'l-ḥurūf: science of letters

ʿilmu 'l-kalām: scholastic theology.

ʿilmun ladunnī: "Divinely-inspired" knowledge

imān: faith, belief.

imām: leader of congregational prayer; an advanced scholar followed by a large community.

insān: humanity; pupil of the eye.

insānu 'l-kāmil, al-: the Perfect Man; the Prophet Muhammad ﷺ.

irādatullāh: the Will of God.

irshād: spiritual guidance

ism: name

isma-Llāh: name of God

isrā': night journey; used here in reference to the night journey of the Prophet Muḥammad ﷺ.

jalāl: majesty

jamāl: beauty

jamaʿa: group, congregation.

jihād: to struggle in God's Path.

Jinn: a species of living beings, created out of fire, invisible to most humans. Jinn can be Muslims or non-Muslims.

Jumuʿah: Friday congregational prayer, held in a large mosque.

Kaʿbah: the first House of God, located in Mecca, Saudi Arabia to which pilgrimage is made and which is faced in the five daily prayers.

kāfir: unbeliever.

Kalāmullāh al-Qadīm : lit. Allah's Ancient Words, viz. the Holy Qur'an.

kalimat at-tawḥīd: lā ilāha illa-Llāh: "There is no god but Allah (the God)."

khalīfah: deputy

Khāliq, al-: the Creator, one of the 99 Divine Names.

khalq: creation

khuluq: conduct, manners.

lā: no; not; not existent; the particle of negation.

lā ilāha illa-Llāh Muḥammadun rasūlullāh: there is no deity except Allah, Muhammad is the Messenger of Allah.

lām: Arabic letter ل

al-Lawḥ al Maḥfūẓ: the Preserved Tablets.

laylat al-isrā' wa 'l-miʿrāj: the Night Journey and Ascension of the Prophet Muḥammad ﷺ to Jerusalem and to the seven heavens.

Madīnātu 'l-Munawwarah: the Illuminated city; city of Prophet Muḥammad ﷺ. Referred to as Madina.

mahr: dowry given by the groom to the bride.

malakūt: divine kingdom.

Malik, al-: the Sovereign, a Divine Name.

maqām: spiritual station; tomb of a prophet, messenger or saint.

maʿrifah: gnosis.

māshāAllāh: it is as Allah Wills.

Mawlānā: lit. "our master" or "our patron," referring to an esteemed person.

maẓhar: place of disclosure.

mīzān: the Scale which weighs the actions of human beings on Judgment Day.

mīm: Arabic letter م

mi'rāj: the ascension of the Prophet Muḥammad ﷺ from Jerusalem to the seven heavens.

Muḥammadun rasūlu 'l-Lāh: Muḥammad is the Messenger of God.

mulk, al-: the World of dominion

Mu'min, al-: Guardian of Faith, one of the 99 Names of God.

mu'min: a believer.

munājāt: invocation to God in very intímate form.

murīd: disciple, student, follower.

murshid: spiritual guide, *pir*.

mushāhadah: direct witnessing

mushrik (pl. *mushrikūn):* idolater, polytheist.

muwwaḥid (pl. *muwaḥḥidūn)*: those affiriming God's Oneness.

nabī: a prophet of God

nafs: lower self, ego.

nūr: light

Nūḥ: the prophet Nūḥ ﷺ.

Nūr, an-: The Source of Light, a Divine Name.

Qādir, al-: the Powerful, a Divine Name.

qalam, al-: the Pen.

qiblah: direction, specifically, the direction faced by Muslims during prayer and other worship towards the Sacred House in Mecca.

Quddūs, al-: the Holy One, a Divine Name.

qurb: nearness

quṭb (pl. *aqṭāb*): axis or pole. Among the poles are:

Quṭb al-bilād: Pole of the Lands

Quṭb al-irshād: Pole of Guidance

Quṭbu 'l-aqṭāb: Pole of Poles

Quṭbu 'l-a'ẓam: Highest Pole

Quṭbu 't-tasarruf: Pole of Affairs

al-quṭbīyyatu 'l-kubrā: the highest station of poleship

Rabb, ar-: the Lord

Raḥīm, ar-: the Most Compassionate, a Divine Name.

Raḥmān, ar-: the All-Merciful, a Divine Name.

raḥmah: mercy.

Raḥmah: wife of *Sayyidinā* Ayyūb ﷺ.

raka'at: one full set of prescribed motions in prayer. Each prayer consists of a one or more *raka'ats*.

Ramaḍān: the ninth month of the Islamic lunar calendar, the month of fasting.

rasūl: a messenger of God

Rasūlullāh: the Prophet of God, Muhammad ﷺ.

Ra'ūf, ar-: the Most Kind, a Divine Name.

Razzāq, ar-: the Provider

rawḥānīyyah: spirituality, spiritual essence of something.

rizq: provision, sustenance.

rūḥ: spirit. Ar-Rūḥ is the name of a great angel.

rukūʿ: bowing posture of the prayer.

ṣaḥīḥ: authentic; term certifying validity of a hadith of the Prophet ﷺ.

ṣāim: fasting person (pl. *ṣāimūn*)

salām: peace.

Salām, as-: the Peaceful, a Divine Name.

as-salāmu ʿalaykum: peace be upon you (Islamic greeting)

ṣalāt: Islam's ritual prayer.

Ṣalāt an-Najāt: prayer of salvation, done in the wee hours of the night.

Ṣamad, aṣ-: Self-Sufficient, upon whom creatures depend.

Saḥābah (sing., sahabi): the Companions of the Prophet, the first Muslims.

sajda (pl. *sujūd*): prostration.

ṣalāt: prayer, one of the five obligatory pillars of Islam. Also to invoke blessing on the Prophet ﷺ.

ṣalawāt (sing. *salāt*): invoking blessings and peace upon the Prophet ﷺ.

ṣawm, ṣiyām: fasting.

sayyid: leader; also, a descendant of Prophet Muhammad ﷺ.

Sayyidinā/ sayyidunā: our master (fem. *sayyidatunā:* our mistress).

shahādah: lit. testimony; the testimony of Islamic faith: *Lā ilāha illa 'l-Lāh wa Muḥammadun rasūlu 'l-Lāh* or "There is no god but Allah, the One God, and Muḥammad is the Messenger of God."

Shah Naqshband: Grandshaykh Muhammad Bahauddin Shah-Naqshband, a great eighth century *walī*, the founder of the Naqshbandi *Ṭarīqah*.

shaykh: lit. "old man," a religious guide, teacher; master of spiritual discipline.

shifā': cure.

shirk: polytheism, idolatry, ascribing partners to God

ṣiffāt: attributes; term referring to Divine Attributes.

Silsilat adh-dhahabīyya: "golden chain" of spiritual authority in Islam *sohbet* (Arabic *suḥba):* association: the assembly or discourse of a shaykh.

subḥanallāh: glory be to God.

Sulaymān: prophet and king Solomon.

sulṭān/sulṭānah: ruler, monarch.

Sulṭān al-Awlīyā: lit., "the king of the *awlīyā*,"; the highest-ranking saint.

sunnah: the practice of the Prophet ﷺ; that is, what he did, said, recommended or approved of in his Companions.

Sūrah*:* a chapter of the Qur'an; picture, image.

Sūratu 'l- Ikhlāṣ*:* the Chapter of Sincerity, 114.

ṭabīb: doctor.

tābiʿīn: the Successors, generation after the Prophet's Companions.

tafsīr: to explain, expound, explicate, or interpret; technical term for commentary or exegesis of the Holy Qur'ān.

tajallī (pl. tajallīyāt): theophanies, God's self-disclosures, Divine Self-manifestation.

takbīr: lit. "Allāhu Akbar," God is Great.

tarawīḥ: the special nightly prayers of Ramadan.

ṭarīqat/ṭarīqah: literally, way, road or path. An Islamic order or path of discipline and devotion under a guide or shaykh; Islamic Sufism.

tasbīḥ: recitation glorifying or praising God.

tawāḍaʿ: humbleness.

tawāf: the rite of circumambulating the Kaʿbah while glorifying God during Hajj and ʿUmrah.

tawḥīd: unity; universal or primordial Islam, submission to God, as the sole Master of destiny and ultimate Reality.

ʿubūdīyyah: state of worshipfulness. Servanthood

ʿulamā (sing. *ʿAlīm*): scholars.

ʿulūmu 'l-awwalīna wa 'l-ākhirīn: knowledge of the "Firsts" and the "Lasts" refers to the knowledge that God poured into the heart of Muḥammad ﷺ during his ascension to the Divine Presence.

ʿulūm al-Islāmī: Islamic religious sciences.

ummah: faith community, nation.

ʿUmar ibn al-Khaṭṭāb ؓ: an eminent Companion of the Prophet ﷺ and second caliph of Islam.

'umrah: the minor pilgrimage to Mecca, performed at any time of the year.

'Uthmān ibn 'Affān ﷺ: an eminent Companion of the Prophet ﷺ and his son-in-law, who became third caliph of Islam. Renowned for compiling the Qur'an.

walad: a child

waladī: my child

walāyah: proximity or closeness; sainthood.

walī (pl. *awliyā'*): saint, or "he who assists,"; guardian; protector.

wasīlah: a means; a special station granted to the Prophet Muḥammad ﷺ as intermediary to God in the granting the petitioner's supplications.

wāw: Arabic letter و

wujūd, al-: existence; "to find," "the act of finding," as well as "being found".

Y'aqūb: the prophet Ya'qūb ﷺ.

yamīn: the right hand, used to mean "oath."

yawm al-'ahdi wa'l-mīthāq: day of oath and covenant, a heavenly event before this life, when the souls of mankind were present before God where He took from each soul the promise to accept His Sovereignty as Lord.

yawm al-qiyāmah: Day of Judgment.

Yūsūf: the prophet Yūsuf ﷺ.

zīyārah: visitation to the tomb of a prophet or saint.

LaVergne, TN USA
19 January 2010
170467LV00001B/1/P

9 781930 409620